# 400 Questions & Answers about the Doctrine & Covenants

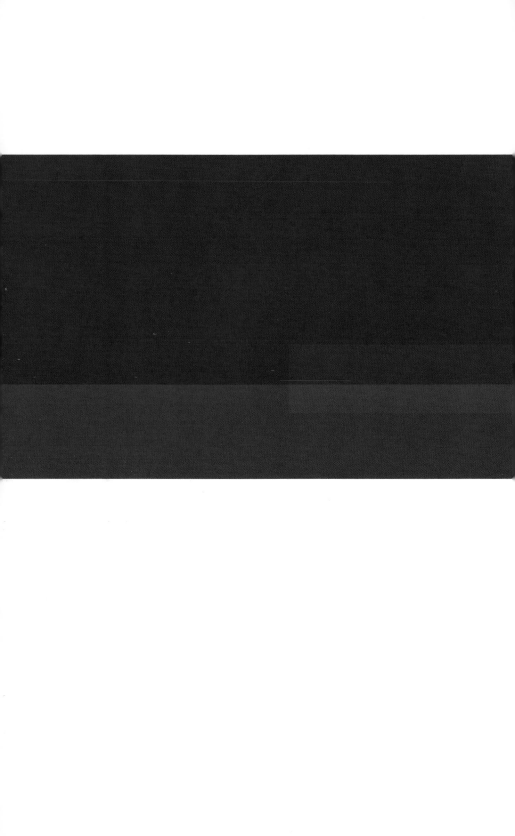

# 400 Questions & Answers

ABOUT THE

# Doctrine & Covenants

SUSAN EASTON BLACK

Covenant

Covenant Communications Inc

Cover image *Praise to the Man* © Jon McNaughton. For more information, visit www.mcnaughtonart.com.


Published by Covenant Communications, Inc.
American Fork, Utah



Printed in Hong Kong
First Printing: October 2012

20 19 18 17 16 15 14 13 12 11 10 9 8 7 6 5 4 3 2 1

ISBN 978-1-62108-198-2

# Introduction

I have listened to many piano solos performed in my local ward. One stands out from the rest, for it was particularly poor. The pianist struggled to find the melody and seldom struck the appropriate key. During the performance, I leaned over and whispered to Reed Nibley, a renowned pianist and professor at Brigham Young University, "How can you bear it?" He queried, "Are you talking about the piano solo?" I assured him that I was and that the pianist should practice before accepting another invitation to perform at Church. "I think the solo is wonderful," Reed said. Noting my surprise, he advised, "You have got to develop ears for Church and ears for the university."

His comment needed to be said, for I had begun to be critical of not just the pianist but of others in my ward. Reed's advice caused me to look inward and examine my own inadequacies in order to discover that change was necessary. The answer came loud and clear—I needed to change not only my thinking, but my behavior. In the spirit of change, I vowed to no longer present the impossible question to the gospel doctrine teacher or to be the person to whom everyone turned for the right answer. I decided to count to ten before commenting and see if I could learn from and enjoy comments made by others. I was surprised to find that before long I had reasons enough to compliment teachers, class participants, and even pianists.

I didn't say good-bye to critical thinking; I just put such thinking in its appropriate place. For me, the quest to know truth and details surrounding truth will always be of personal importance, but I now know that there is never a reason to flaunt such learning. Instead of asking the impossible question or making an esoteric comment, I now write the question and comment in a journal. Of particular interest to me are the questions I have written that relate to revelations contained in the Doctrine and Covenants, for this scripture begins with a preface given by the Lord Himself and follows with revelations received by Joseph Smith and other holy prophets. Through hours of study and library research, most of my compiled questions have now been answered. These answers have led to my strong conviction of the truthfulness of the revelations and teachings contained in the Doctrine and Covenants.

Knowing the eternal truths of the Doctrine and Covenants has been a great blessing in my life. While the world appears satisfied to toss on the waves of uncertainty, I am not! The revelations received by Joseph Smith and other holy prophets have been a beacon leading me to unequivocally profess that Joseph Smith was the Prophet whom the Lord raised up to bring forth the word of God. Revelations, translations, covenants, and eternal truths were the continuum of his life's labors, for he held the keys of this last dispensation, and will forever hold them, both in time and eternity. It is my hope that *400 Questions about the Doctrine & Covenants* will inspire readers to glean their own insights about the Restoration of the gospel of Jesus Christ.

# 1

# Historical Background of the Doctrine and Covenants

**When did Joseph Smith begin to arrange and copy revelations for the purpose of creating a book manuscript?**

As early as July 1830 Joseph arranged and copied the revelations he had received since the beginning of the Restoration. Between 1830 and 1831 the process of arranging and copying went forward at an uneven pace with the assistance of Oliver Cowdery and John Whitmer. By the fall of 1831 about sixty revelations were prepared and ready to be printed in book format. Elder Orson

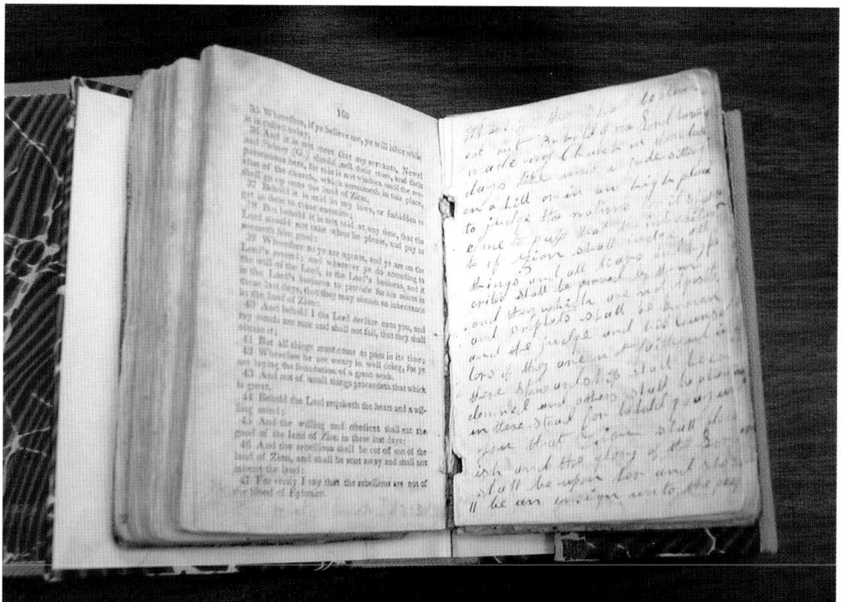

A copy of the first printing of the Book of Commandments.

Pratt and others were given access to these revelations. Pratt recalled, "And so highly were they esteemed by us, that we committed some to memory; and a few we copied for the purpose of reference in our absence on missions; and also to read them to the saints for their edification."[1] The manuscript copies created by Pratt and others provided limited circulation of the revelations. Their copies contained errors, such as misspelled words and incomplete phrases.

**Why was the November 1831 conference held at Hiram, Ohio, so vital to the publication of Joseph Smith's revelations?**

Joseph "called for a conference of high priests" to meet in Hiram, Ohio, "the forepart of November 1831 in several conference sessions." During one session, those attending voted in favor of publishing Joseph's revelations in a book titled "Book of Commandments" or "Covenants and Commandments of the Lord . . ." with ten thousand copies to be printed by W. W. Phelps.[2]

**Who was entrusted with the printer's manuscript copy of the revelations and assigned to carry that copy to W. W. Phelps in Independence, Missouri?**

In mid-November 1831, Oliver Cowdery and John Whitmer were called by revelation to carry the printer's copy of the manuscript to editor W. W. Phelps in Independence. Cowdery and Whitmer left Kirtland, Ohio, about November 20, 1831, and arrived in Independence on January 5, 1832, to present the manuscript to Phelps.

Oliver Cowdery.

**In what ways had W. W. Phelps prepared himself to print a book containing revelations from God?**

William W. Phelps

William W. Phelps had been a longtime printer and newspaper editor by the time Cowdery and Whitmer arrived in Independence with the revelatory manuscript. Phelps had served as an editor of three newspapers in New York, including the *Ontario Phoenix.* After his baptism, Phelps was called to print Church literature (see D&C 55:4). As Church printer, Phelps served as editor of *The Evening and the Morning Star,* an LDS newspaper in Independence "devoted to unfolding the meaning of the revelations of God from the earliest times to the present, but more especially those revelations which God has given in the present dispensation."[3] In the *Star,* beginning in June 1832, Phelps published several revelations that Cowdery and Whitmer had presented to him before such revelations were printed in book format.

**Did the Literary Firm supervise W. W. Phelps in publishing the Book of Commandments?**

The Literary Firm was organized as a publishing venue for the Church. W. W. Phelps was one of three members of a review committee appointed by the Literary Firm to edit Revelation Book #1 and supervise the selections for publication. These selections included publication of the Book of Commandments, the Joseph Smith Translation of the Bible, a Church hymnal, children's literature, an almanac, and *The Evening and the Morning Star.*[4] Although the firm did not participate in the day-to-day printing operation of the Book of Commandments or other Church publications, it did play an important role in providing needed moneys for financing these publications. On April 30, 1832, due to limited financial resources and possibly a shortage of paper, the firm decided to publish as a first run three thousand copies of the Book of Commandments instead of the ten thousand copies agreed upon at the November 1831 conference at Hiram, Ohio. Proceeds from the sale of the Book of Commandments were to be used to compensate members of the Literary Firm—Joseph Smith, Oliver Cowdery, Sidney Rigdon, John Whitmer, and Martin Harris—for the "diligence of our brethren . . . in bringing to light by grace of God these sacred things."[5]

**Were the revelations printed and bound together in a book format titled the Book of Commandments?**

None of the revelations were bound in a book format, although necessary preparations had been made. William W. Phelps had deposited a copy of the title page with the United States District Court for Missouri. On February 13, 1833, when the copyright of the Book of Commandments had been secured, some of the revelations containing introductory headnotes and proofs had been sent to Joseph Smith for his approval, yet no books were published. When the press in Independence, Missouri, was destroyed, the Book of Commandments was scrapped and, thus, never published. The first bound copy of the revelations was the Doctrine and Covenants rather than the proposed Book of Commandments.

**How close were the revelations to being bound in book format in Independence?**

In May 1833 it was announced in *The Evening and the Morning Star* that the Book of Commandments would be "published in the course of the present year, at from 25, to 50 cents a copy. We regret that in consequence of circumstances not within our control, this book will not be offered to our brethren as soon as was anticipated. We beg their forbearance, and solicit an interest in their prayers, promising to use our exertions with all our means to accomplish the work."[6]

W. W. Phelps and his staff were close to binding the book by early July when a 2 July 1833 letter from Sidney Rigdon to W. W. Phelps was received. Rigdon advised Phelps to ship the work to N. K. Whitney & Co. in Kirtland. Unfortunately, shipping was delayed. By mid-July five large forms, each containing thirty-two pages—hence a total of 160 pages in all—had been printed with the title page: "A Book of Commandments for the Government of the Church of Christ, Organized According to Law, on the 6th of April, 1830. Zion: Published by W. W. Phelps & Co. 1833." Due to destruction of the printing office, the text of the printed sheets ended at what is today the midpoint of the 36th verse in section 64 of the Doctrine and Covenants.

Mary and Caroline Rollins carried leaves from the unbound Book of Commandments away from the mobs intent on destroying them.

**When did mobs attack the W. W. Phelps printing establishment and destroy most of the printed sheets of the revelatory manuscript?**

On July 20, 1833, a mob broke into the establishment of W. W. Phelps and destroyed his printing office and most of the printed sheets. A few sheets were rescued by sisters Mary and Caroline Rollins. Nine days after the press was destroyed, Phelps wrote to Church leaders in Kirtland reaffirming his faith in the power of God: "Although the enemy has accomplished his design in demolishing the Printing establishment they cannot demolis[h] the design of our God, for his decree will stand & his purposes must be accomplished."[7]

### Why the title change from Book of Commandments to the Doctrine and Covenants?

The exact reason for the title change is unknown. *Doctrines* are the basic saving truths of the gospel of Jesus Christ. *Covenants* signify agreements between God and man (see Ps. 89:3; Heb. 6:13–20). Thus, the title *Doctrine and Covenants* suggests that the contents of the book contain saving truths of the gospel of Jesus Christ and agreements between God and man that enable man to return to the presence of God.

Joseph Smith.

### What is the purpose of the Doctrine and Covenants?

The main purpose of all standard works is to testify that Jesus is the Christ. Christ is the author of the standard works. Through His holy prophets, He reveals much of eternity in these works. It was Brigham Young who described the Doctrine and Covenants and other testaments of Christ as "a lighthouse in the ocean or a finger-post which points out the road we should travel."[8] Joseph Smith said that the Doctrine and Covenants was the "foundation of the Church in these last days, and a benefit to the world, showing that the keys of the mysteries of the kingdom of our Savior are again entrusted to man" (D&C 70: Section Heading).[9]

### What is the sequence of events that led to the first publication of the Doctrine and Covenants?

After failing to publish the Book of Commandments in Independence, plans were initiated to combine the sixty-five revelations that were printed for the Book of

The Printing Office in Nauvoo.

Commandments with other revelations Joseph had received since November 1831. On April 19, 1834, "Sidney Rigdon was set apart to assist Oliver Cowdery in publishing . . . the Book of Covenants." Oliver Cowdery was then "set apart to assist Elder Rigdon in arranging the Book of Covenants." On September 24, 1834, the high council at Kirtland appointed "a committee to arrange the items of the doctrine of Jesus Christ for the government of the church." Members of that committee—Joseph Smith, Oliver Cowdery, Sidney Rigdon, and Frederick G. Williams—labored for a year arranging and preparing the revelations for publication. One of the great difficulties they faced was obtaining necessary funds to print the Doctrine and Covenants. In hopes of alleviating this difficulty, the Saints were asked to "donate and loan us all the means and money you can that we may be enable[d] to accomplish the work as a great means towards the salvation of Men."[10]

**Besides the revelations Joseph Smith received from God, what other inspired writings were included in the first edition of the Doctrine and Covenants?**

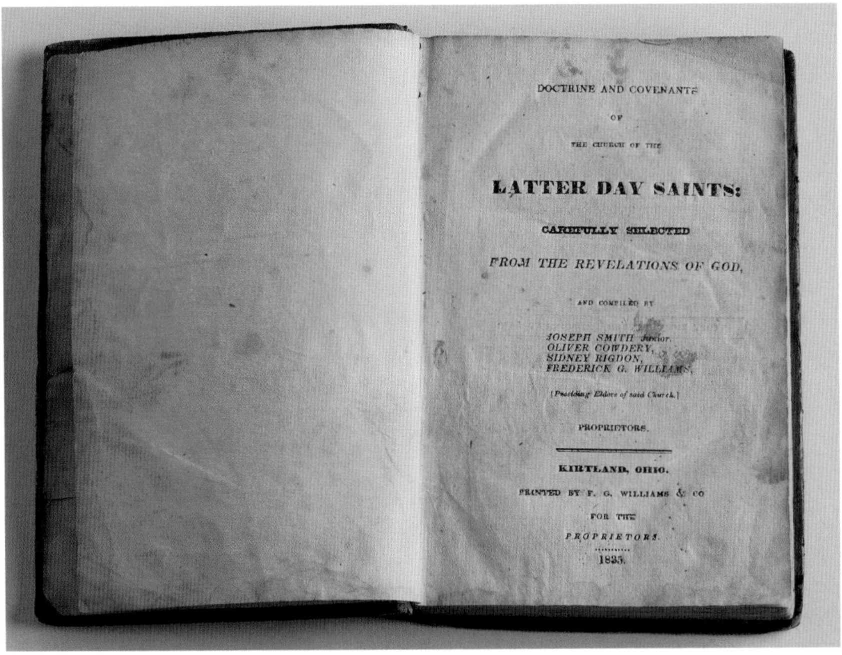

The title page from the 1935 edition of the Doctrine and Covenants.

At a conference held on August 17, 1835, several present "testified of the truth and correctness of the revelations and the 'Lectures on Faith,' because they had read them all or in part." Those attending the conference voted in what appears a solemn assembly with quorums voting followed by members (male and female) voting. The vote was in favor of accepting the revelations as scripture and printing the revelations in book format. Approval was sought and granted to include with the revelations the Lectures on Faith; a preface written by a committee consisting of Joseph Smith, Oliver Cowdery, and Sidney Rigdon; an article on marriage written by Oliver Cowdery; and an article on governments and laws. Minutes of the September 24, 1834, high council meeting in which the Doctrine and Covenants was officially authorized and minutes of the August 17, 1835, conference in which the Doctrine and Covenants was approved were also approved for inclusion in the book.[11]

**When was the first edition of the Doctrine and Covenants bound and ready for purchase?**

The 1835 printed sheets of the Doctrine and Covenants were sent to Cleveland, Ohio, for binding. Bound copies of the Doctrine and Covenants were available for purchase by mid-September 1835 at a cost of one dollar per copy.

**Were the Lectures on Faith regarded as being equal in value to the revelations contained in the 1835 Doctrine and Covenants?**

According to the preface of the 1835 Doctrine and Covenants, "The first part of the book will be found to contain a series of Lectures as delivered before a Theological class [the School of the Prophets] in this place, and in consequence of their embracing the important doctrine of salvation, we have arranged them into the following work." It is important to note that a clear distinction was made between lectures to the School of the Prophets and revelations received by Joseph Smith. The Lectures on Faith title page reads, "On the Doctrine of the Church of the Latter Day Saints." The revelation title page reads, "Part Second Covenants and Commandments." Even though Joseph Smith edited and otherwise prepared the lectures for publication and appears to recognize them as scripture, some contend "they were never presented to nor voted upon by the . . . Church" as being otherwise than theological lectures or lessons." They were never regarded as being equal in value to the revelations contained in that volume.[12]

**When were the Lectures on Faith deleted from the Doctrine and Covenants?**

The Lectures on Faith were printed in every edition of the Doctrine and Covenants until 1921, when they were deleted.

**What was the textual order of the 1835 Doctrine and Covenants?**

The 1835 Doctrine and Covenants began with a preface written by Joseph Smith, Oliver Cowdery, and Sidney Rigdon. The preface was followed by the seven Lectures on Faith comprising pages 6–74, usually attributed to Sidney Rigdon with Joseph's approval. Revelatory sections followed on pages 75–254. Next were pages of minutes followed by an index and a one-page "Notes to the Reader." The 1835 edition included the following sections that appear in the current Doctrine and Covenants: 1, 3–12, 14–76, 78–84, 86, 88–102, 104, 106–107, and 133–134.

**What is the difference between the 1835 Doctrine and Covenants and the 1844 edition of that sacred text?**

Eight more sections were added to the Doctrine and Covenants under the direction of Joseph Smith in the 1844 edition. In the current edition these sections are 103, 105, 112, 119, 124, 127, 128, and 135.

**What happened to the stereotype plates used in printing the 1844 Doctrine and Covenants?**

On April 1, 1846, Brigham Young asked Church trustees—Almon Babbitt, Joseph Heywood, and John Fullmer—to "be sure and have a watchful eye to the stereotype plates of the Book of Mormon and Doctrine and Covenants, that no evil befall them, and that they be forwarded to us with all safety,

Stereotype room from the mid 1800s.

this season."[13] It is not known whether the trustees fulfilled this assignment. The whereabouts of the stereotype plates is a mystery. It is known, however, that they were never used again for printing the Doctrine and Covenants.

**Why were the writings of Oliver Cowdery on marriage that were included in the Doctrine and Covenants from 1835 to 1876 deleted from subsequent editions?**

The first section to be deleted from the Doctrine and Covenants was the section on marriage written by Oliver Cowdery. The reason given for the deletion was that "it had now been superseded by a revelation from God on the subject of marriage" (see D&C 132).[14] Another reason may be that the original document by Cowdery no longer reflected the Church's position on marriage.

**Which member of the Quorum of the Twelve Apostles was assigned to oversee preparation of the 1876 Doctrine and Covenants?**

Preparation of the 1876 Doctrine and Covenants was assigned to a committee chaired by Elder Orson Pratt under the direction of Brigham Young. With President Young's approval, twenty-six revelations received by Joseph Smith were added to the 1876 Doctrine and Covenants. The additional revelations are now numbered as sections 2, 13, 77, 85, 87, 108–111, 113–118, 120–123, 125, 126, 129–132, and 136. The 1876 edition for the first time divided the revelations into verses, arranged revelations in chronological order according to the date they were received, and added footnotes.[15] At the October 10, 1880, general conference, President George Q. Cannon said, "I hold in my hand the Book of Doctrine and Covenants . . . As there have been additions made to it . . . it has been deemed wise to submit these books with their contents to the Conference to see whether the Conference will vote to accept the books and their contents as from God. . . . President Joseph F. Smith said, 'I move that we receive and accept the revelations contained in these books as revelations of God to the Church of Jesus Christ of Latter-day Saints, and to all the world.'"[16] The vote was unanimous.

**What changes were made to the 1921 edition of the Doctrine and Covenants?**

In 1921, Elder George F. Smith—with Anthony W. Ivins, James E. Talmage, Melvin J. Ballard, Joseph Fielding Smith, and other prominent Church leaders—formed a committee to review the Doctrine and Covenants and revise the text where necessary. Elder Talmage reported, "Preliminary steps [have] already been taken toward a 'thorough revision of the Doctrine and Covenants, and we all

James E. Talmage.

know that current editions . . . [contain] many errors by way of omission.' Moreover there are certain improvements by way of Section Headings, amplification of notes, and rearrangement of text in the double column style to be made, if the present tentative plans are carried into execution." Through the work of the committee, "Changes were made in the footnotes, the introductory statements at the beginning of the revelations were expanded, the text was divided into double columns, and the 'Lectures on Faith' were deleted."[17]

**What changes, revisions, or additions were made to the 1981 Doctrine and Covenants?**

The 1981 edition was completed under the direction of President Spencer W. Kimball, with Elder Thomas S. Monson as chair of the Scriptures Publication Committee. Through the work of this committee, sections 137–138 and two official declarations (OD 1 and OD 2) were added to the Doctrine and Covenants. New footnoting, cross-referencing, section headings, maps, a topical guide, and an index were also added.

**Why is the Doctrine and Covenants viewed as the "capstone" of the Church of Jesus Christ of Latter-day Saints?**

President Ezra Taft Benson said, "The Book of Mormon is the 'keystone' of our religion, and the Doctrine and Covenants is the capstone, with continuing latter-day revelation. The Lord has placed His stamp of approval on both the keystone and the capstone."[18] President Benson also said, "Excluding the witnesses to the Book of Mormon, the Doctrine and Covenants is by far the greatest external witness and evidence which we have from the Lord that the Book of Mormon is true."[19] Joseph Fielding Smith added, "This Doctrine and Covenants contains the word of God to those who dwell here now. It is our book. It belongs to the Latter-day Saints. More precious than gold, the Prophet says we should treasure it more than the riches of the whole earth."[20] Church historian John Whitmer penned, "I would do injustice to my own feelings, if I did not here notice, still further the work of the Lord in these last days: the revelations and commandments given to us, are, in my estimation, equally true with the book of Mormon, and equally necessary for salvation, it is necessary to live by every word that proceedeth from the mouth of God; and I know that the Bible, book of Mormon and book of Doctrine and Covenants of the church of Christ of Latter Day Saints, contain the revealed will of heaven."[21]

The capstone being set on the Washington Monument.

**What are the divine promises given for putting into practice the laws, rights, and ordinances presented in the Doctrine and Covenants?**

If the laws, rights, and ordinances set forth in the Doctrine and Covenants are put into practice, the promises are, "We will keep the commandments of the Lord, we shall know the truth and there shall be no weapon formed against us that shall prosper. There shall be no false doctrines, no teaching of men that will deceive us. There are many cults and many false faiths, there are many strange ideas in the world, but if we search these revelations then we will be fortified against errors and we will be made strong."[22]

**Where and when did Joseph Smith receive most of the revelations recorded in the Doctrine and Covenants?**

Most of the revelations recorded in the Doctrine and Covenants were received between

1829 and 1832. During that interim Joseph Smith resided in New York, Pennsylvania, and Ohio. Twenty-five revelations were received in New York, fifteen in Pennsylvania, and sixty-four in Ohio, with several editions and modifications to the revelations from their original form. About 90 percent of the revelations were received in the daylight hours, typically with others present. Scholars contend that these sections and others can be divided into seven categories. The first and largest category is revelation, which is subdivided into revelation given to individuals (D&C 4), groups of elders (D&C 58), the Church (D&C 42), and the world (D&C 12). The remaining categories are as follows: epistles (D&C 127), statements of Church belief and policy (D&C 134), minutes of a high council meeting (D&C 102), prophecies (D&C 87), instructions (D&C 123), and historical accounts (D&C 135).

**In what ways does the Doctrine and Covenants testify to the truthfulness of the Bible?**

The Doctrine and Covenants affirms that God created man in "his own image and in his own likeness" (D&C 20:18). It attests that Adam was the first man (see D&C 84:16) and that he holds "the keys of salvation under the counsel and direction of the Holy One" (D&C 78:16). It tells of Adam and Eve being tempted by Satan, transgressing, and being cast out of the Garden of Eden (see D&C 20:20; 29:36–50). It speaks of Adam presiding at a future council to be held at Adam-ondi-Ahman (see D&C 116).

Other Old Testament events verified by the Doctrine and Covenants include Noah being ordained to the patriarchal priesthood (see D&C 107:52), and numbered among the mighty in the world of spirits (see D&C 138:38). The Doctrine and Covenants tells of Abraham's willingness to offer Isaac as a sacrifice (see D&C 101:4; 132:36), of Enoch and his City of Zion being taken up by the Lord (see D&C 38:4; 45:11–14), and of Melchizedek being honored for his righteousness (see D&C 107:2–4). The Doctrine and Covenants also quotes hundreds of biblical passages, such as:

Matthew 7:24–27
Wise men build on the rock
D&C 50:44; 90:5

Matthew 24:35
Heaven and earth shall pass away
D&C 56:11

John 4:35
Field is white ready to harvest
D&C 4:4; 6:3–4

John 10:16
Other sheep not of this fold
D&C 10:59–60

1 Corinthians 15:29
Baptism for the dead
D&C 128:16–18

Ephesians 4:12
Perfecting of the Saints
D&C 124:143[23]

In addition, a number of revelations in the Doctrine and Covenants tell of Joseph translating the Bible, his interruption and subsequent resumption of translation activities (see D&C 37:1; 45:60–61; 73:3), and of facilities needed for translating (see D&C 41:7; 124:89).

**What revelations received by Joseph Smith are not part of the Doctrine and Covenants?**

The Doctrine and Covenants contains a selection of revelations that Joseph Smith received from God. Most of these revelations are concerning gospel doctrines, principles, and the Church organization. The following is a sampling of revelations received by Joseph Smith that are not included in the Doctrine and Covenants:

1835: Reynolds Cahoon is to set his house in order[24]

Isaac Morley and Edward Partridge are to attend a solemn assembly[25]

If Harvey Whitlock repents, his sins will be forgotten[26]

1838: Brigham Young is to provide for his family[27]

1840: Orson Hyde's mission to Palestine will be shown him in a dream[28]

1842: The Twelve are to edit the *Times and Seasons* according to the Spirit[29]

# 2

# Sections 1–24

## Section 1

**D&C 1: Section Heading—Did Joseph Smith intend for a committee of elders to write the preface to the Book of Commandments?**

Several elders attending the November 1, 1831, conference at Hiram, Ohio, had previously been assigned to form a committee to draft a preface to the Book of Commandments. When the committee reported to the assembled elders at the November conference, they concluded their remarks by asking Joseph Smith to inquire of the Lord as to His acceptance of their work. As the elders united in prayer, Joseph pled with the Lord for an answer. When Joseph's prayer ended, he dictated a preface with Sidney Rigdon acting as scribe. The

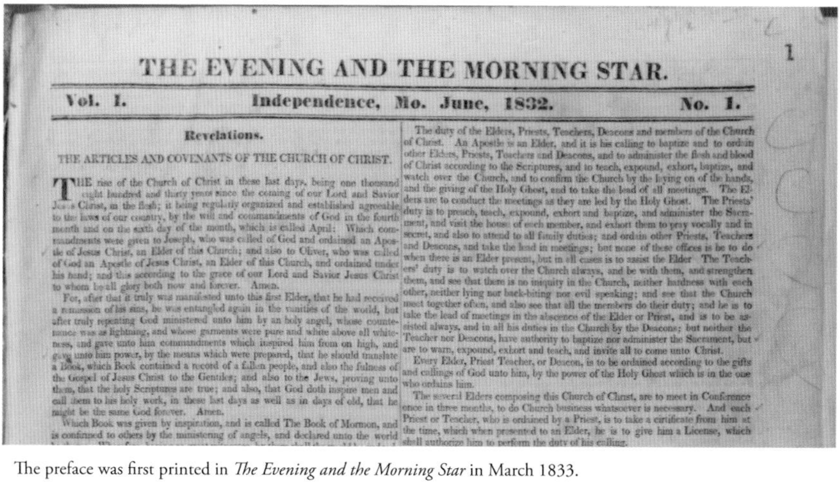

1

THE EVENING AND THE MORNING STAR.

Vol. I. Independence, Mo. June, 1832. No. 1.

Revelations.

THE ARTICLES AND COVENANTS OF THE CHURCH OF CHRIST.

THE rise of the Church of Christ in these last days, being one thousand eight hundred and thirty years since the coming of our Lord and Savior Jesus Christ, in the flesh; it being regularly organized and established agreeable to the laws of our country, by the will and commandments of God in the fourth month and on the sixth day of the month, which is called April: Which commandments were given to Joseph, who was called of God and ordained an Apostle of Jesus Christ, an Elder of this Church; and also to Oliver, who was called of God an Apostle of Jesus Christ, an Elder of this Church, and ordained under his hand; and this according to the grace of our Lord and Savior Jesus Christ to whom be all glory both now and forever. Amen.

For, after that it truly was manifested unto this first Elder, that he had received a remission of his sins, he was entangled again in the vanities of the world, but after truly repenting God ministered unto him by an holy angel, whose countenance was as lightning, and whose garments were pure and white above all whiteness, and gave unto him commandments which inspired him from on high, and gave unto him power, by the means which were prepared, that he should translate a Book, which Book contained a record of a fallen people, and also the fulness of the Gospel of Jesus Christ to the Gentiles; and also to the Jews, proving unto them, that the holy Scriptures are true; and also, that God doth inspire men and call them to his holy work, in these last days as well as in days of old, that he might be the same God forever. Amen.

Which Book was given by inspiration, and is called The Book of Mormon, and is confirmed to others by the ministering of angels, and declared unto the world

The duty of the Elders, Priests, Teachers, Deacons and members of the Church of Christ. An Apostle is an Elder, and it is his calling to baptize and to ordain other Elders, Priests, Teachers and Deacons, and to administer the flesh and blood of Christ according to the Scriptures, and to teach, expound, exhort, baptize, and watch over the Church, and to confirm the Church by the laying on of the hands, and the giving of the Holy Ghost, and to take the lead of all meetings. The Elders are to conduct the meetings as they are led by the Holy Ghost. The Priests' duty is to preach, teach, expound, exhort and baptize, and administer the Sacrament, and visit the house of each member, and exhort them to pray vocally and in secret, and also to attend to all family duties; and ordain other Priests, Teachers and Deacons, and take the lead in meetings; but none of these offices is he to do when there is an Elder present, but in all cases is to assist the Elder. The Teachers' duty is to watch over the Church always, and be with them, and strengthen them, and see that there is no iniquity in the Church, neither hardness with each other, neither lying nor back-biting nor evil speaking; and see that the Church meet together often, and also see that all the members do their duty; and he is to take the lead of meetings in the absence of the Elder or Priest, and is to be assisted always, and in all his duties in the Church by the Deacons; but neither the Teacher nor Deacons, have authority to baptize nor administer the Sacrament, but are to warn, expound, exhort and teach, and invite all to come unto Christ.

Every Elder, Priest Teacher, or Deacon, is to be ordained according to the gifts and callings of God unto him, by the power of the Holy Ghost which is in the one who ordains him.

The several Elders composing this Church of Christ, are to meet in Conference once in three months, to do Church business whatsoever is necessary. And each Priest or Teacher, who is ordained by a Priest, is to take a certificate from him at the time, which when presented to an Elder, he is to give him a License, which shall authorize him to perform the duty of his calling.

The preface was first printed in *The Evening and the Morning Star* in March 1833.

Joseph Smith preface is considered a revelation from God. The revelatory preface "stamped the revelations" Joseph had received with "divine endorsement."[30] The preface was first printed in *The Evening and the Morning Star* in March 1833 in Independence, Missouri. The preface was chapter 1 in the 1833 Book of Commandments and section 1 in the 1835 Doctrine and Covenants. In the preface the Lord summarizes His message to the world and prepares readers for the revelatory content of the Doctrine and Covenants as He declares His voice is "unto all men" (D&C 1:2), the coming of the Lord is nigh (see D&C 1:12), and prophecies in this latter-day scripture will be fulfilled (see D&C 1:37–38).

Joseph Fielding Smith and Jessie Evans Smith.

**D&C 1:1—Why do some argue that the revelations in the Doctrine and Covenants are intended only for members of the LDS Church?**

On this subject Joseph Fielding Smith wrote, "We hear the expression from time to time . . . the revelations in the Doctrine and Covenants are intended solely for members of the Church." He assured all that such was not the case, for the Lord had "counseled otherwise."[31] The introductory salutation "O ye people of my church" should not be so narrowly interpreted as to exclude all nonbelievers, for in the same verse the Lord addresses, "Ye people from afar; and ye that are upon the islands of the sea" (D&C 1:1). Throughout the preface the Lord again addresses His intended audience: "For verily the voice of the Lord is unto all men" (D&C 1:2), a "voice of warning shall be unto all people" (D&C 1:4), "the voice of the Lord is unto the ends of the earth, that all that will hear may hear" (D&C 1:11), and "I the Lord am willing to make these things known unto all flesh" (D&C 1:34). It should be noted that a few revelations from Revelation Book 1 and 2 were not intended for publication in the Doctrine and Covenants.

**D&C 1:1–2—Does "the voice" —whether in the phrase "the voice of him who dwells on high" or "hearken unto the voice"—refer to God?**

In the Doctrine and Covenants, "the voice" is a reference to the Lord God or the word of God, such as "hear my words, which are my voice" (D&C 84:60). Readers of the Doctrine and Covenants are admonished to hear the voice of the Lord and hearken to His divine counsel to flee the carnal state of Babylon and prepare to meet the bridegroom at His Second Coming.[32]

**D&C 1:6—Did members of the Quorum of the Twelve Apostles include their testimony of the truthfulness of the revelations in the Book of Commandments?**

During the afternoon session of the November 1831 conference, elders were asked if they were "willing to bear testimony to all the world of mankind, to every creature upon the face of all the earth and upon the islands of the sea, that the Lord has borne record to our souls, through the Holy Ghost, shed forth upon us, that these commandments were given by inspiration of God, and are profitable for all men, and are verily true" (D&C: Introduction). All elders present were willing to so testify. The names of the elders were Joseph Smith, Oliver Cowdery, David Whitmer, John Whitmer, Peter Whitmer Jr., Sidney Rigdon, William E. M'Lellin, Orson Hyde, Luke Johnson, and Lyman E. Johnson. It was not until 1835, four years after the November 1831 conference, that faithful brethren, including a few who had testified in 1831, were eventually called to the Quorum of the Twelve Apostles. Their names were attached as witnesses of the Lord's commands in the Doctrine and Covenants. Their testimony has been printed in every published copy of the Doctrine and Covenants.

### D&C 1:6—Why was it important to publish the revelations of Joseph Smith?

One reason for the heightened necessity of publishing the revelations was to prepare the inhabitants of the earth for the coming judgments of God. Such phrases as "Prepare ye, prepare ye for that which is to come, for the Lord is nigh" are frequent reminders to readers of the Doctrine and Covenants of the imminent judgments of God (D&C 1:12). Of these judgments Joseph Fielding Smith said, "The cleansing process is going on, but eventually it will come with dreadful suddenness, and none who work iniquity shall escape."[33] Those who think to escape the Lord's judgments will find all too soon sorrow, for "their iniquities shall be spoken upon the housetops, and their secret acts shall be revealed" (D&C 1:3). As for the righteous, they are assured that the work of the Lord will roll forth no matter the extremity. Elder Marion G. Romney admonished, "Learn whom to worship and how to worship and the course to take in order to escape the calamities" (see D&C 5:19–20).[34] To avoid the calamities of pride and doubt, the Lord suggests humility and faith. When humility and faith are implemented, weaknesses become strengths, for the Lord will fight the battles of the righteous, destroy enemies, and bring prosperity to the faithful. Of the Lord's promises for the latter-day work, Joseph Smith declared, "No unhallowed hand can stop the work from progressing; persecutions may rage, mobs may combine, armies may assemble, calumny may defame, but the truth of God will go forth boldly, nobly, and independent, till it has penetrated every continent, visited every clime, swept every country, and sounded in every ear, till the purposes of God shall be accomplished, and the Great Jehovah shall say the work is done."[35]

### D&C 1:8–9—Did the sealing power Joseph received mirror the sealing power given to ancient prophets?

"The power to seal" is defined more broadly than sacred power from God. Anciently, seals were used as identification marks on documents and objects. Some seals were small, like a signet ring, while others were quite large. In Ezekiel 9:4–6, the man wearing

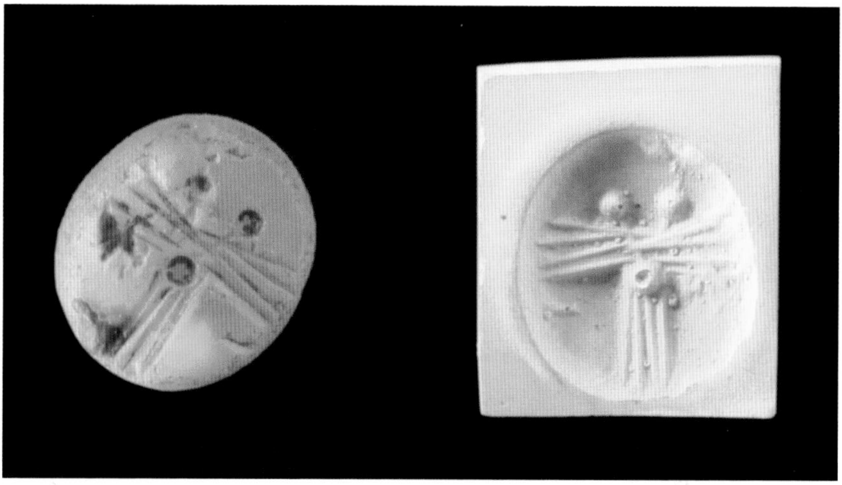

Seal of Ishtar, Neo-Babylonian Empire, 600–400 BCE.

a linen garment was commanded to put a mark on the foreheads of those who refused to participate in the abominations in Jerusalem. In Revelation 7:3–8, an angel was commissioned to seal the servants of God on their foreheads. The marking or the process of sealing was first done to save those marked from the Lord's destruction. According to scholar John Gee, "To seal a document or an object, a person would wrap string or twine around it, place a daub of mud on the knot, and press the seal into the mud. Affixing this sort of seal marked the object as the possession of the person in whose name it was sealed."[36] On April 3, 1836, Joseph received power to bind or seal on earth as in heaven from the ancient prophet Elijah.

## D&C 1:13—What is the meaning of "The Lord's sword is bathed in heaven"?

The word *sword* is a symbol of destruction and judgment wielded without constraint upon the wicked and rebellious. A *sword bathed in heaven* may be symbolic of a sword in a striking position, unsheathed and raised, or it may be a representation of the ancient practice of bathing a sword in oil before battle. Either way, it is ready at a moment's notice to pierce the wicked and those who love creation more than the Creator (see Rom. 1:25). According to scholars Stephen E. Robinson and H. Dean Garrett, "Until now the Lord has allowed good and evil to exist together in the world, but at the last day—the day of his coming in glory—anything or anyone that cannot tolerate his glorious presence will be cut off and removed by the sword, which is about to fall."[37]

**D&C 1:19–24—Why would the Lord choose the "weak things of the world" to carry the important message of Jesus Christ when those of greater ability have proven their capacity to lead and speak with authority?**

The "Lord's ways are not man's ways." He is not constrained to choose those who are too proud or too wise in their own estimation to be taught. He does not rely on the "arm of flesh," for those who are grand and mighty in their own eyes do sin and are out of harmony with God, being unteachable. Although they are numbered among the great and mighty ones of the nations, they cannot carry the word of God, for they fail to acknowledge His hand in all things.[38]

**D&C 1:30—What is the promise given to those who "treasure up the word of the Lord"?**

Those who treasure the word of God have "power to lay the foundation of this church, and to bring it forth out of obscurity and out of darkness, the only true and divine church upon the face of the whole earth" (D&C 1:30). "If you treasure up the word of the Lord, if you study these revelations, not merely those that are in the Doctrine and Covenants, but those that are in all the standard works of the Church," wrote Joseph Fielding Smith, "You put into practice the commandments that are here found, you will not be deceived in these perilous times, but you shall have the spirit of discernment and you will know the truth and shall know falsehood, for you shall have power to know the spirits of men and to understand the Spirit of the Lord."[39] These sacred promises are available to all who hearken to the word of the Lord and obey His commandments. The Lord promises to receive those who come unto Him and bless them with all that the "Father has to give."[40]

**D&C 1:36—How is the word "Idumea," meaning "worldly," associated with an ancient nation south of the Salt Sea?**

Mountains of Edom and the Arabah Plain.

In antiquity, inhabitants of Idumea, or Edom, were known as Idumeans or Edomites, being descendants of Esau. Evil practices of the Edomites were symbolic of materialism and satanic carnality. To travel on the King's Highway through Edom symbolized a pilgrimage through a wicked world, thus the meaning of Idumea being "worldly" or "the world."[41] Ancient prophets and the apostle John warned against the symbolic Idumea as did writers in the book of Isaiah (see 1 Jn. 2:15–17; Isa. 34:5).

# Section 2

**D&C 2: Section Heading—When was section 2 added to the Doctrine and Covenants?**

Section 2 of the Doctrine and Covenants was first published on April 15, 1842, in the *Times and Seasons*, an LDS newspaper published in Nauvoo, Illinois. The section was not included in the Doctrine and Covenants until 1876. Elder Orson Pratt, acting under the direction of Brigham Young, added the section to the Doctrine and Covenants. Section 2, like other early sections in the Doctrine and Covenants, centers on the Book of Mormon and the translation of that sacred record.

**D&C 2: Section Heading—What is the historical background of section 2?**

On Sunday evening, September 21, 1823, in Manchester, New York, young Joseph Smith supplicated the Lord "for forgiveness of all my sins and follies, and also for a manifestation to me, that I might know of my state and standing before him" (JS—H 1:29). While calling on the Lord,

Joseph said, "I discovered a light appearing in my room, which continued to increase until the room was lighter than at noonday, when immediately a personage appeared at my bedside, standing in the air, for his feet did not touch the floor" (JS—H 1:30). The angelic being "called [Joseph] by name, and said unto [him] that he was a messenger sent from the presence of God to me, and that his name was Moroni" (JS—H 1:33). The messenger told Joseph that "God had a work for [him] to do; and that [his] name should be had for good and evil among all nations, kindreds, and tongues, or that it should be both good and evil spoken of among all people" (JS—H 1:33). The conflicting reputation would center on a book written on plates that had the appearance of gold and that were accompanied by interpreters prepared "for the purpose of translating the book" (JS—H 1:35). As the angel conversed with Joseph, "the place where the plates were deposited" was shown him in vision (JS—H 1:42). When the vision closed, "the room was again left dark" and Joseph was left alone with his thoughts (JS—H 1:43). Before dawn, the messenger appeared two more times to converse with the seventeen-year-old youth.

The reconstruction of the small Smith log cabin where Moroni first visited Joseph Smith.

The angelic visit of September 21, 1823, as recorded in Joseph's 1838 history, is the most detailed description of an angelic appearance in holy writ. On that occasion, the angel Moroni told Joseph Smith that Elijah would return to the earth.

**D&C 2: Section Heading—Was it Moroni or Nephi who visited Joseph Smith on the evening of September 21, 1823? Early accounts do not name the angel.**

Joseph Smith was clear when he said that the angelic personage "called me by name, and said unto me that he was a messenger sent from the presence of God to me, and that his name was Moroni" (JS–H 1:33). On April 15, 1842, when Joseph Smith was the editor of the *Times and Seasons*, an article in that newspaper referred to the angel as "Nephi." The Nephi reference was perpetuated in the *Millennial Star*, an LDS newspaper published in England. In an attempt to correct the erroneous assumption of the angel being named "Nephi"—an assumption that may have stemmed from Lucy Mack Smith's unabridged history of Joseph Smith—Elder Orson Pratt wrote: "To John Christensen, Dear Bro.—Yours of the 9th inst. is rec'd. You inquire whether it was the Angel Nephi or Moroni who visited the Prophet on the night of the 21st and the 22nd Sept. 1823? As Moroni holds the keys of the stick or Record of Ephraim we have reason to believe that Moroni was that angel. This discrepancy in the history to which you refer may have occurred through the ignorance or carelessness of the historian or transcriber."[42]

**D&C 2: Section Heading—What is known of the mortal life of the angel Moroni?**

Moroni, son of Mormon, was the last writer of the Book of Mormon. Moroni saw Jesus Christ and was ministered to by three Nephite disciples (see Ether 12:39; Morm. 8:11). Moroni was entrusted with the records of two civilizations—the Nephites and the Jaredites. Following the battle at Cumorah, he wandered alone for many years in the Americas.[43]

**D&C 2:1—What is meant by the phrase "great and dreadful day of the Lord"?**

The prophesied "great and dreadful day" is "the day of the Lord's coming in glory." It is also referred to as the "last day" or the day of His Second Coming. The day will be great for the righteous, both living and dead. It will be dreadful for those who squandered their days of probation and failed to heed the word of the Lord and acknowledge His servants.[44]

*Elijah Destroys the Messengers of Ahaziah.*

### D&C 2:1—How did Elijah use the sealing power?

Elijah, who lived in approximately 800 BC, began his ministry during the reign of Ahab, historically revered as an important political monarch of the Northern Kingdom. However, Ahab did "evil in the sight of the Lord above all that were before him" (1 Kgs. 16:30). Ahab's construction of worship sites to pagan deity "did more to provoke the Lord God of Israel to anger than all the kings of Israel that were before him" (1 Kgs. 16:33).

To combat the evil worship of Ahab, the Lord did not send legions of destroying angels, an army of vengeful hosts, or a devastating plague. He commissioned just one man, Elijah, whose name means "God is Jehovah." His name symbolizes his divinely appointed mission to "confess that Yahweh (Jah) is his God (Eli)."[45] Elijah was endowed by the Lord God with a virtual abundance of priesthood power. With this power he sealed the heavens and prophesied to Ahab that "there shall not be dew nor rain these years, but according to my word" (1 Kgs. 17:1). The unprecedented events that followed include the story of Elijah confronting hundreds of false prophets on Mount Carmel.

### D&C 2:1—Who anticipates that Elijah will return to the earth?

Contemporaries of John the Baptist thought that he was Elijah, while others viewed Jesus Christ as the returned prophet (see John 1:21; Matt. 16:14; Luke 9:8). Observant Jews maintain that Elijah is the "Angel of the Covenant" and the hoped-for guest at Passover as a door is left ajar for his entrance and a cup of wine at a Sabbath dinner awaits to slake his thirst. Moslems contend that when he returns he will be a young man, for they believe that he drank of the water of life and has never grown old. The Catholic Carmelite Monastery at Mount Carmel holds that Elijah still lives in a grotto beneath the monastery and that he will return by emerging from the grotto. Some Greeks believe that he is the patron saint of elevated climes, and look to tall peaks as the probable site of his return. The Talmud states, "[He] often appear[s] to the wise and good rabbis—at a prayer, in the wilderness, or on their journeys—generally in the form of an Arabian merchant."[46]

The Catholic Carmelite Monastery at Mount Carmel.

Elijah did not return to Mount Carmel or to a Jewish Passover. He did not return to the Moslems or the Greeks. Elijah returned first to the Lord Jesus Christ and His disciples on the Mount of Transfiguration (see Matt. 17:3). He returned again, more than eighteen hundred years later, to Joseph Smith and Oliver Cowdery in the temple at Kirtland, Ohio (see D&C 110).

**D&C 2:1–3—Is it a coincidence that the closing words of Malachi are the opening words for Doctrine and Covenants 2?**

In the Old Testament, four hundred years after Elijah had confronted false prophets on Mt. Carmel, Malachi quotes the Lord as saying, "Behold, I will send you Elijah the prophet before the coming of the great and dreadful day of the Lord: And he shall turn the heart of the fathers to the children, and the heart of the children to their fathers, lest I come and smite the earth with a curse" (Mal. 4:5–6). These closing words became the climax of modern editions of the Old Testament. The promise of restoring covenants that God made with ancient Israel, along with priesthood power, gave hope to a people estranged from God. Likewise, Doctrine and Covenants 2 gives hope to those in the latter days that hearts will again turn to the fathers of the house of Israel.

### D&C 2:2—Have Latter-day Saint leaders addressed the promises made to the ancient fathers—Abraham, Isaac, and Jacob?

According to Elder John A. Widtsoe, covenants and promises extend beyond the ancient fathers back to "our preexistent state, in the day of the great council" in which "the Lord proposed a plan, conceived by him. We accepted it. . . . We agreed, right then and there, to be not only saviors for ourselves but measurably, saviors for the whole human family."[47] When Elijah appeared to Joseph Smith and Oliver Cowdery on April 3, 1836, he gave priesthood keys to seal on earth as in heaven. The keys make it possible to extend the promises and covenants made anciently with Abraham to all worthy men and women in holy temples.

### D&C 2:2—What is the effect of the Spirit of Elijah?

The Spirit of Elijah culminates in turning, binding, and sealing our hearts to our fathers—Abraham, Isaac, and Jacob—by making and keeping sacred covenants in a house of the Lord. The spirit of turning to covenants moves Latter-day Saints to find necessary information about their ancestry so that their family, both living and dead, can be sealed eternally and enjoy the same covenants made by the ancient fathers with God. Of the Spirit of Elijah, Joseph Smith declared, "If you have power to seal on earth and in heaven, then we should be wise. The first thing you do, go and seal on earth your sons and daughters unto yourself, and yourself unto your fathers in eternal glory."[48]

### D&C 2:3—Why would the earth have been utterly wasted if Elijah had not returned and given keys and power to seal on earth as in heaven to Joseph Smith and Oliver Cowdery?

The simplest answer is that the great work of God would have come to naught. The bestowal of sealing keys was essential to complete the work of God on earth. Joseph Smith said, "God destroyed the world by a flood" in the days of Noah and the Lord promised to "destroy [the earth] by fire in the last days: but before it should take place, Elijah should first come and turn the hearts of the fathers to the children."[49]

## Section 3

**D&C 3: Section Heading—What were the mechanics of translating and scribing the book of Lehi?**

As soon as Martin Harris arrived in Harmony, Pennsylvania, in early 1828, he commenced writing as Joseph translated the book of Lehi, the first abridged book in a series of books inscribed on the gold plates.[50] The majority of the translation process took place in the east end of an upstairs room of the Joseph Smith farmhouse. According to Martin Harris, "a thick curtain or blanket was suspended" from the ceiling in the room. Once Joseph "concealed [himself] behind the blanket," he looked "through his spectacles, or transparent

Martin Harris, first scribe of the Book of Mormon.

stones" to read the inscriptions. He "would then write down, or repeat, what he saw." When his words were "repeated aloud," each word was "written down by [Martin], who sat on the other side of the suspended blanket."[51] Thus, the mechanics of translating and scribing commenced. Note that other scribes recall the translating and scribing process differently.

**D&C 3: Section Heading—Does the very fact that the Book of Mormon exists testify that Joseph Smith was the translator of ancient plates?**

Through the instrumentality of Joseph Smith, Nephi's intent in writing—"that I may persuade men to come unto the God of Abraham, and the God of Isaac, and the God of Jacob, and be saved"— is now a reality. People all over the world have access to the words of Nephi and other ancient American prophets due to the inspired translation of Joseph Smith (1 Ne. 6:4). The "difficulty of engraving . . . words upon plates" has proven fruitful, and the purposes of the Lord have been fulfilled as the word of God has "come forth unto the Gentiles, by the gift and power of the Lamb" through the instrumentality of Joseph Smith (see Jacob 4:1; 1 Ne. 13:35). The very fact that the Book of Mormon exists is a testament that Joseph was the translator of ancient records.

### D&C 3: Section Heading—What is known of the Urim and Thummim?

The Hebrew origin of *Urim and Thummim* means "lights and perfections." The Urim and Thummim consists of two stones set in metal frames "connected by a rod to a breastplate." In antiquity the Urim and Thummim was used by prophetic leaders such as Abraham to do the will of God (see Ex. 28:30; Lev. 8:8; 1 Sam. 28:6; Ezra 2:63; Abr. 3:1-4; JS–H 1:35). [52] For example, "And when Saul inquired of the Lord, the Lord answered him not, neither by dreams, nor by Urim, nor by prophets" (1 Sam. 28:6).

The Urim and Thummim was given to the brother of Jared when he talked face-to-face with God (see D&C 17:1). When the brother of Jared was commanded to seal up a record of his vision of Christ, he sealed two stones with the record (see Ether 3:21–28). The whereabouts of the Urim and Thummim among the Jaredites after the death of the brother of Jared is unknown. Perhaps the stones were held by the Jaredite kings, much like the Nephite kings retained the small plates, the Liahona, and the sword of Laban. If that were the case, Coriantumr, the last surviving leader of the Jaredites, may have had the stones with him when he was discovered by the people of Zarahemla (see Omni 1:21). Mosiah translated the Jaredite record, which was written on twenty-four gold plates "by the means of those two stones which were fastened into the two rims of a bow"

(Mosiah 28:13). These stones were initially referred to as "interpreters" and later as the Urim and Thummim (Mosiah 8:13). According to D&C 17:1, the Urim and Thummim anciently possessed by the brother of Jared was given to Joseph Smith. After Joseph received the revelation contained in section 3, the stones were taken from him and a severe chastisement was pronounced by the Lord: "When thou [Joseph] deliveredst up that which God had given thee sight and power to translate, thou deliveredst up that which was sacred into the hands of a wicked man [Martin Harris], Who has set at naught the counsels of God, and has broken the most sacred promises which were made before God" (D&C 3:12–13).

**D&C 3:2—What is the meaning of "one eternal round"?**

The phrase "one eternal round" appears twice in the Doctrine and Covenants (see D&C 3:2; 35:1) and three times in the Book of Mormon (see 1 Ne. 10:19; Alma 7:20; 37:12). Although it is well known that God's course is straight and never varies, it is also a circle or an eternal round that ends at the beginning. The reference to Jesus Christ as Alpha and Omega, the beginning and the end, best illustrates this concept (see 3 Ne. 9:18; Rev. 1:8, 11; 21:6; 22:13). These titles reflect the first and last letters of the Greek alphabet and suggest that Jesus began with the creation of the world and ends with the judgment of the world. The titles denote the preeminent position of Jesus Christ in that all creatures are subject to Him and none are saved except through His great sacrifice (see Acts 4:12; 2 Ne. 25:20; Mosiah 3:17; 5:8).[53] When the end and the beginning are the same point, then the course is circular or one eternal round—meaning the work of God is without beginning or end.[54]

**D&C 3:5—Why did Joseph Smith allow Martin Harris to take the 116 pages of written manuscript to Palmyra, New York?**

Within two months of commencing the translation/scribing process of the book of Lehi, Martin Harris expressed reservations and even doubts about the veracity of the work in which he and Joseph were engaged. Hoping to free himself of doubts, Martin asked Joseph if he could see the plates, suggesting that with a witness of their existence he would have reason for the hope within. His request was denied. The denial did not stop Martin from repeatedly inquiring about the matter or asking for "liberty to carry the writings home and show them" to his wife, Lucy, and other family members. Joseph said, "[He] desired of me that I would inquire of the Lord, through the Urim and Thummim, if he might not do so. I did inquire, and the answer was that he must not."[55]

Martin was very disappointed. He did not view his request as unreasonable. Nevertheless, Martin continued to scribe as Joseph dictated during the months of April and May 1828, but he was not placated. He wanted tangible evidence of the existence of gold plates and to know the validity of the words he scribed. His doubts were exacerbated by the protests of his wife, Lucy, who

This house now sits on the site of the Martin Harris farm, the location where the first pages of the Book of Mormon manuscript were lost. The original house is no longer standing.

feared Martin was being taken in by fraud. He again broached the subject of taking the manuscript to show his family members. Joseph inquired of the Lord a second time and the answer was as before. Disappointed and perhaps angry, Martin left Harmony and returned to Palmyra, hoping for a respite from his doubts. Martin told his wife, Lucy, that he had been denied the privilege of showing her the translation. She was angry and insisted that he ask a third time.[56]

Upon returning to Harmony, Martin scribed the remainder of the book of Lehi translation. A benchmark had been reached, perhaps a momentary stopping point, and in Martin's way of thinking, it was the right time to ask Joseph again. With unabashed boldness, Martin asked the third time for permission to take the manuscript to Palmyra. This time "permission was granted." [57]

**D&C 3:8—What are the "fiery darts of the adversary"?**

*Fiery darts of the adversary* (see D&C 3:8; 1 Ne. 15:24) and *fiery darts of the wicked* (see D&C 27:17; Eph. 6:16) refer to arrows dipped in pitch and lit before being shot from an archer's bow. In ancient warfare it was necessary to hold a strong shield for protection from "fiery darts." In a symbolic manner, the righteous ward off Satan's fiery darts or carnal enticements by holding a strong shield or armament of faith.[58]

**D&C 3:10—How does this revelation combine the Lord's law of justice with His law of mercy?**

There are juxtaposed positions in section 3 that reveal the Lord's law of justice and His law of mercy. For example, Martin Harris lost the 116-page manuscript but the Book of Mormon still came forward. Joseph Smith lost the ability to translate but was called again to accomplish the great work of translating the Book of Mormon. The descendants of Lehi were scattered in the Western hemisphere but are being gathered in to stakes of Zion.

**D&C 3:12–13—Who was permitted to see the manuscript pages of the book of Lehi?**

Martin Harris received permission to show the manuscript pages to his wife, Lucy; his brother, Preserved Harris; his father and mother, Nathan and Rhoda Harris; his wife's sister, Polly Harris Cobb; and none else. Martin agreed to the specified conditions. He entered into a written covenant with Joseph "in a most solemn manner that he would not do otherwise than had been directed [and] required of him." On June 14, 1828, about two months after the translation process had begun, he "took the writings, and went his way."[59]

**D&C 3:12–13—How many weeks did Martin Harris have the 116-page manuscript in his possession?**

Martin had the manuscript in his possession for three weeks or until about July 7, 1828. Soon after his arrival in Palmyra, he showed the manuscript to his wife. Upon seeing the manuscript, Lucy was placated to a degree, just as Martin had hoped. Nothing is written about the

During the time Martin Harris had the 116 pages of the manuscript, Emma became seriously ill.

reactions of Martin's extended family—his parents, his brother, and Lucy's sister. In violation of his written covenant with Joseph, Martin showed the manuscript to others. "A very particular friend of his made him a visit, to whom he related all that he knew concerning the record. The man's curiosity was much excited, and, as might be expected, he earnestly desired to see the manuscript. Martin was . . . anxious to gratify his friend," and showed him the manuscript. Having broken his covenant once, it was easier for Martin the second time to do the same. In fact, as days passed, Martin showed the manuscript to others again—or, as Joseph Smith wrote, "Notwithstanding . . . the great restrictions which he had been laid under, and the solemnity of the covenant which he had made with me, he did show them to others."[60]

**D&C 3:14—What was Joseph's reaction to the lost manuscript and his lost privilege to translate?**

When Martin did not return to Harmony, Pennsylvania, Joseph determined to journey to Palmyra to see Martin and recover the manuscript. Mother Smith reported that as soon as Joseph arrived at her farmhouse, he requested that Martin be summoned at once. Anticipating Martin's quick response, victuals were set on the table at 8 A.M. The Smiths "waited till nine, and he came not—till ten, and he was not there—till eleven, still he did not make his appearance." It was not until "half-past twelve" that Martin was seen "walking with a slow and measured tread towards the house, his eyes fixed thoughtfully upon the ground." When he reached the gate in the yard, "he stopped, instead of passing through, and got upon the fence, and sat there some time with his hat drawn over his eyes." When he entered the house, he sat down at the table next to those who were already seated. "He took up his knife and fork as if he were going to use them, but immediately dropped them." Seeing this, Hyrum Smith asked, "Martin, why do you not eat? are you sick?" He pressed "his hands upon his temples" and cried with "a tone of deep anguish, 'Oh, I have lost my soul! I have lost my soul!'" Joseph, who was seated at the table, jumped to his feet and asked, "Martin, have you lost that manuscript? Have you broken your oath, and brought down condemnation upon my head, as well as your own?"

"Yes, it is gone," replied Martin, "and I know not where."

"Oh, my God!" said Joseph, clenching his hands. "All is lost! all is lost! What shall I do? I have sinned—it is I who tempted the wrath of God. I should have been satisfied with the first answer which I received from the Lord; for he told me that it was not safe to let the writing go out of my possession."

Joseph then "wept and groaned, and walked the floor continually."[61]

**D&C 3:17–18—The Doctrine and Covenants reveals the names of several societies or "ites" in ancient America. How many "ites" were there in the Americas?**

Each of the sons of Father Lehi, with the exception of Sam and the addition of Zoram, had a posterity or people who took upon themselves their names. For example, Jacob, a Book of Mormon prophet, records, "Now the people which were not Lamanites were Nephites; nevertheless, they were called Nephites, Jacobites, Josephites, Zoramites, Lamanites, Lemuelites, and Ishmaelites" (Jacob 1:13–14). Note: The "ites" spoken of in these verses were only the ones the Nephites had contact with or were aware of. On the small plates Jacob simplified the political situation in which he lived by referring to the "ites" as only Nephites and Lamanites. This same title distinction, Nephites and Lamanites, was followed by Mormon and Moroni, who wrote abridged accounts of civilizations in ancient America (see Alma 47:35; Morm. 1:8–9).[62] There were no "ites" for two hundred years following the appearance of Jesus Christ in ancient America.

## Section 4

**D&C 4: Section Heading—In what ways did Joseph Smith Sr. show that he believed in the Restoration of the gospel of Jesus Christ?**

Young Joseph Smith was promised by angel Moroni in September 1823 that his father would "believe every word you say to him."[63] Why the surety of the promise? Joseph Smith Sr. was known by name centuries before his birth and had been foreordained to a great work in the latter days (see 2 Ne. 3:15). After hearing his son's remarkable recitation of the visit of angel Moroni, Father Smith declared, "My son, be not disobedient to this heavenly vision!"[64] Where many fathers might have lacked the humility to follow their son, Joseph Smith Sr. never sought prominence over young Joseph. He was supportive of his son's prophetic calling and even willing to suffer persecution to follow his teachings. He was privileged to be one of the Eight Witnesses of the Book of Mormon who saw the plates and the engravings, "all of which has the appearance of ancient work, and of curious workmanship" (The Testimony of Eight Witnesses). On the day of the organization of the Church, Father Smith was baptized. Of his testimony, Father Smith declared, "I have never denied the Lord. . . . The Lord has often visited me in visions and dreams, and has brought me, with my family, through many afflictions, and I this day thank his holy name."[65]

**D&C 4:1—Does "marvelous work" refer solely to the coming forth of the Book of Mormon or does it include other Restoration events?**

A "marvelous work" is an obvious reference to the coming forth of the Book of Mormon, but is not limited to that sacred scripture. The "marvelous work" also includes other events of the Restoration—revelations, priesthood keys, organization of the Church, and fulness of the gospel.

A "marvelous work" is best illustrated by using harvest imagery, such as a "field of wheat, no longer green, but a brilliant gold, which almost seems dazzling white in the summer sunshine. Such a sight signified that the time of the harvest was at hand (see Matt. 9:36–38; Luke 10:1–2; D&C 33:3; 101:64–66)."[66] Similar harvest imagery appears throughout the Doctrine and Covenants. For example, "the world is ripening" (D&C 18:6), "they shall be gathered in" (D&C 29:8), "the rebellious shall be cut off" (D&C 64:35), "bound in bundles" to await the day of burning (D&C 88:94), or sifted "as chaff" (D&C 52:12). The righteous shall "joy in the fruit of your labors" (D&C 6:31) and "shall be laden with sheaves upon your back" (D&C 31:5). Then the promise, "He that is faithful . . . shall be kept and blessed with much fruit" before the harvest is over (D&C 52:34).

**D&C 4:1–4—Why are the expressions, admonitions, and qualifications given to Joseph Smith Sr. restated to others called to the work of God?**

It cannot be a coincidence that the first contemporary of Joseph Smith mentioned by name in the Doctrine and Covenants was his father, Joseph Smith Sr. Likewise, it cannot be circumstantial that many of the expressions, admonitions, and qualifications given to Joseph Smith Sr. were restated to others called to the work of the Lord: Oliver Cowdery (see D&C 6:1–6), Hyrum Smith (see D&C 11:1–6), Joseph Knight Sr. (see D&C 12:1–6), and David Whitmer (see D&C 14:1–6). David O. McKay, in noting the repetitious nature of the qualifications for being called to the work, concluded that those so called had "not the possession of wealth, not social distinction, not political preferment, not military achievement, not nobility of birth; but a desire to serve God with all your 'heart, mind, and strength'—spiritual qualities that contribute to nobility of soul."[67] Mission presidents encourage missionaries to memorize section 4 and to contemplate the qualifications needed to carry the gospel message of Jesus Christ and to recommit their heart, might, mind, and strength to the service of God.

**D&C 4:3—Does the phrase "If you have desires to serve God ye are called" apply just to missionaries or does it apply to those not formally called to missionary service?**

Although the phrase definitely applies to those called and set apart as missionaries, President George Albert Smith said, "It is not necessary for you to be called to go into the mission field in order to proclaim the truth. Begin on the man who lives next door by inspiring confidence in him, by inspiring love in him for you because of your righteousness, and your missionary work has already begun."[68]

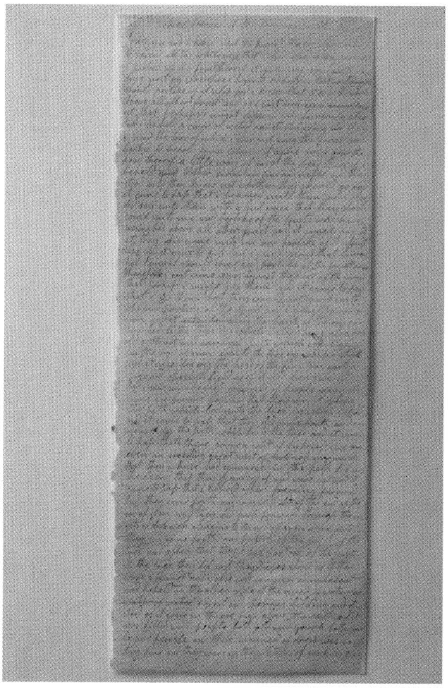

Book of Mormon manuscript.

# Section 5

### D&C 5:1—In what ways did Martin Harris continue to manifest his interest in the Book of Mormon translation?

One example of Martin Harris's continued interest in the translation was told by Lucy Mack Smith: "For nearly two months after Joseph returned to his family, in Pennsylvania, we heard nothing from him, and becoming anxious about him, Mr. Smith and myself [made plans] to make him a visit." News of their impending visit was shared with Martin Harris. Lucy Smith explained the reason for so doing: "We loved the man, although his weakness had cost us much trouble." Upon hearing news of their travel plans, Martin "greatly rejoiced, and determined to go straightway" to again see Joseph. Being called a "wicked man" and suffering much in consequence of the lost manuscript had not curbed his interest or curiosity in Joseph Smith or the translation process. In fact, news of its progress "produced in him a desire" to return to Harmony to learn for himself how the translation was prospering.[69] He joined the Smiths and journeyed to the Whitmer home in Fayette, arriving in June 1829, just as the translation was nearing completion.

### D&C 5:1, 1–14—What is the law of witnesses?

The apostle Paul taught, "In the mouth of two or three witnesses shall every word be established" (2 Cor. 13:1; Matt. 18:15–16; Deut. 19:15; D&C 6:28). President Joseph Fielding Smith wrote, "We are called upon in this life to walk by faith,

Near the back of the Whitmer farm is swampy land that is unsuitable for raising crops. It is traditionally held that this location, or one like it, may have been where the Three Witnesses were shown the gold plates.

not by sight, not by the proclamation of heavenly messengers with the voice of thunder, but by the proclamation of accredited witnesses whom the Lord sends and by whom every word shall be established."[70]

**D&C 5:2—Was it Lucy Mack Smith who wrote of Joseph Smith's reaction to Oliver Cowdery, David Whitmer, and Martin Harris becoming witnesses of the Book of Mormon?**

Lucy Mack Smith recorded that Oliver Cowdery, David Whitmer, and Martin Harris returned to the Whitmer home after becoming witnesses to the Book of Mormon. Also returning to the home was Joseph, who exclaimed, "Father, mother, you do not know how happy I am; the Lord has now caused the plates to be shown to three more besides myself. They have seen an angel, who has testified to them, and they will have to bear witness to the truth of what I have said, for now they know for themselves, that I do not go about to deceive the people, and I feel as if I was relieved of a burden which was almost too heavy for me to bear, and it rejoices my soul, that I am not any longer to be entirely alone in the world."[71]

**D&C 5:2—When was the Testimony of the Three Witnesses included in the publication of the Book of Mormon?**

The Testimony of the Three Witnesses has appeared in each copy of the Book of Mormon since 1830. Their testimony is as follows: "Be it known unto all nations, kindreds, tongues, and people, unto whom this work shall come: That we, through the grace of God the Father, and our Lord Jesus Christ, have seen the plates. . . . And we also know that they have been translated by the gift and power of God, for his voice hath declared it unto us; wherefore we know of a surety that the work is true. . . . the voice of the Lord commanded us that we should bear record of it."[72]

**D&C 5:14—What is the meaning of "out of the wilderness—clear as the moon"?**

The phrase "clear as the moon" first appears in the Song of Solomon (see D&C 6:10; 105:31; 109:73).[73] In that song Shulamite is seen as "fair as the moon, clear as the sun, and terrible as an army with banners," meaning Shulamite was indescribably beautiful, but inaccessible to flatterers or conquerors who were no match for an army under banners. This expressive phrase is applied to The Church of Jesus Christ of Latter-day Saints.

## Section 6

**D&C 6: Section Heading—Who received revelations with Joseph Smith as recorded in the Doctrine and Covenants?**

The wording in the section headings takes on added significance when a distinction is made between the phrases "revelation given through Joseph Smith" and "revelation given to Joseph Smith the Prophet *and* [so and so]," meaning in conjunction with another person. The Doctrine and Covenants records three individuals who were privileged to receive revelations with Joseph Smith: Oliver Cowdery, Sidney Rigdon, and David Whitmer. Of these three men, Oliver was the first to receive revelations with Joseph. Over a seven-year period

(1829–1836), Oliver received at least seven revelations in conjunction with the Prophet (D&C 6, 7, 13, 18, 24, 26, 110) and, of course, other revelations not contained in the Doctrine and Covenants. Of these, two revelations were received through the Urim and Thummim (D&C 6, 7), three by the revelatory process of mind and heart (D&C 18, 24, 26), and two as visions in which ancient prophets restored priesthood keys (D&C 13, 110).

**D&C 6: Section Heading—What did Joseph Smith and Oliver Cowdery learn in the joint revelation received through the Urim and Thummim?**

In section 6, Joseph and Oliver were told that a "marvelous work is about to come forth unto the children of men" and "the field is white already to harvest" (D&C 6:1, 3). They were admonished to "keep my commandments, and seek to bring forth and establish the cause of Zion." By so doing, the promise given was knowledge of the mysteries of God, the gift to translate holy writ, and an opportunity to do much good in this generation (see D&C 6:1, 3, 6). To accomplish the expected good, Oliver learned that the Lord knew his thoughts and the intents of his heart. He was reminded of the night that he cried unto the Lord. "Did I not speak peace to your mind concerning the matter?" asked God. "What greater witness can you have than from God? . . . [Therefore] perform with soberness the work which I have commanded you" (D&C 6:23, 35).

**D&C 6: Section Heading—How many revelations in the Doctrine and Covenants mention Oliver Cowdery?**

Oliver Cowdery.

More than 22 percent of the revelations in the Doctrine and Covenants are linked in one way or another to Oliver Cowdery. Except for Joseph Smith, no other person is mentioned more often in the Doctrine and Covenants than Oliver. Either his name appears or he is specifically addressed in thirty sections. In at least six sections, his name is linked with Joseph Smith as having received a revelation with him (see D&C 6, 7, 13, 18, 24, 110). Three entire sections were received by Joseph specifically for or in behalf of Oliver (see D&C 8, 9, 28). Two sections recount Joseph and Oliver receiving priesthood keys from holy messengers (see D&C 13, 110). Nineteen sections mention Oliver's name in conjunction with a specific assignment. Finally, one section is attributed to Oliver as the author (see D&C 134). Reviewing the place of Oliver Cowdery in the Doctrine and Covenants reveals the sacred role of a man called by God to do a marvelous work among the children of men. That role included being the principal scribe of the Book of Mormon translation, first "preacher" of the restored Church, second elder, apostle, and associate president of the Church.

## D&C 6:1–9—Why are there "revelatory repetitions" in the Doctrine and Covenants?

Joseph received four revelations within a month of Oliver Cowdery's arrival in Harmony, Pennsylvania. These revelations as well as others have repetitive phrases. For example, with slight variation, the wording of D&C 6:1–9 is the same as D&C 11:1–9. In addition, D&C 6:1–6 (intended for Oliver Cowdery) has the same wording as D&C 12:1–6 (intended for Joseph Knight). Similarly, D&C 6:1–5 has the same wording as D&C 14:1–5, a revelation intended for David Whitmer.

One reason for the repetitive nature is the universal application of the word of the Lord: "What I say unto one I say unto all" (D&C 61:18, 36; 82:5; 92:1; 93:49). Scholars Stephen E. Robinson and H. Dean Garrett conclude, "This repetition should not be understood as a divine 'form letter' implying less than personal or individual concern for the recipients. Rather, it emphasizes the importance of the calling made to these servants and to all who have followed them in the Lord's service."[74]

## D&C 6:2—What is the meaning of the phrase "sharper than a two-edged sword"?

The phrase "sharper than a two-edged sword" descriptively illustrates the power of God to penetrate the thoughts and intents of the heart (see D&C 6:2; 11:2; 12:2; 14:2; 33:1; 85:6; Heb. 4:12; Isa. 49:2; Eph. 6:17; Rev. 2:16; 3 Ne. 11:3). The Lord can reach the repentant and rebellious alike (see D&C 85:6). With His power the Lord defends the repentant. With His strength He pierces the rebellious for embracing false ideas and carnal thoughts (see D&C 136:33; Hel. 3:29).

## D&C 6:6—Why is it important to "seek to bring forth and establish the cause of Zion"?

Joseph Smith advised, "We ought to have the building up of Zion as our greatest object."[75] Elder John A. Widtsoe taught, "We are here to build Zion to Almighty God, for the blessing of all the world. In that aim we are unique and different from all other peoples. We must respect that obligation, and not be afraid of it."[76]

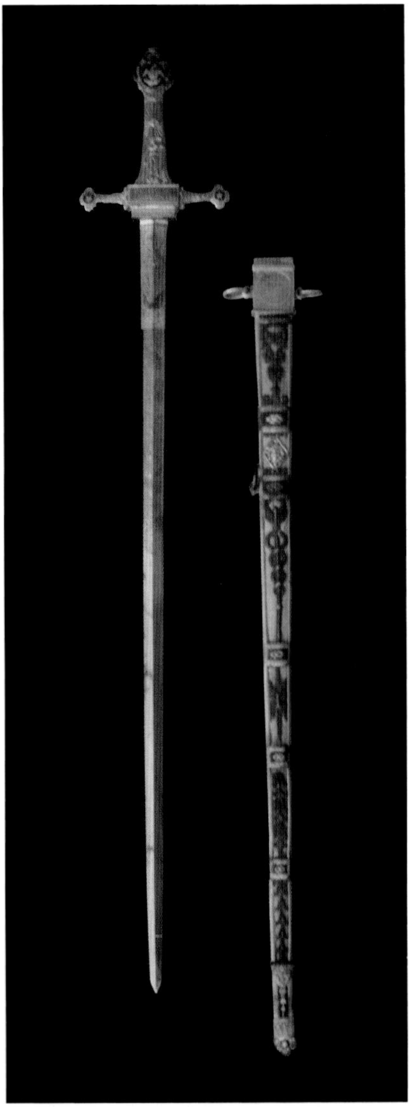

Both sides of a two-edged sword are sharp.

## D&C 6:7—What mysteries were made known to Oliver Cowdery?

Too often mysteries are misconstrued as unnecessary or superfluous knowledge—what some label as "gospel trivia." Such is not the case with godly mysteries as spoken of in the revelations. To solve a mystery is to unlock godly truths. Oliver Cowdery unlocked godly truths through revelation and priesthood administration.

### D&C 6:15–16—Which of Oliver Cowdery's contemporaries were aware of his gift of revelation or revelatory experience by 1829?

Joseph Smith wrote, "After we had received this revelation [section 6,] Oliver Cowdery stated to me that after he had gone to my father's to board, and after the family had communicated to him concerning my having obtained the plates, that one night after he had retired to bed he called upon the Lord to know if these things were so, and the Lord manifested to him that they were true, but he had kept the circumstances entirely secret, and had mentioned it to no one; so that after this revelation was given he knew that the work was true, because no being living knew of the thing alluded to in the revelation, but God and himself."[77] The writings of David Whitmer, however, intimate that he knew something of Oliver's gift: "When Oliver Cowdery went to Pennsylvania, he promised to write me what he should learn about these matters, which he did. He wrote me that Joseph had told him his (Oliver's) secret thoughts, and all he had meditated about going to see him, which no man on earth knew, as he supposed, but himself, and so he stopped to write for Joseph."[78]

### D&C 6:26—Which records of the gospel of Jesus Christ "have been kept back"?

The phrase "contain much of my gospel, which have been kept back" is a reference to missing accounts in the Bible. Scholars Hyrum M. Smith and Janne M. Sjodahl extend the phrase by stating, "A great many records have been kept since the beginning of history, which are now hidden. . . . To man those records are lost, but to God, they are only 'hidden,' and He can bring their contents to light."[79] In the summer of 1830, Joseph began working on an inspired revision of the Bible with the intent of bringing to the forefront the missing accounts. As he "commenced to translate the words of Moses which were given to Moses when he was caught up into a high mountain where he talked with the Lord face to face," a vision of Moses was presented to him.[80] His dictation of what he saw in vision is found in the book of Moses in the Pearl of Great Price.

**D&C 6:27—How long after meeting Joseph Smith did Oliver Cowdery agree to be the principal scribe for the Book of Mormon translation?**

Upon learning of Joseph Smith and the golden plates, Oliver Cowdery wrote, "The subject . . . seems working in my very bones, and I cannot, for a moment, get it out of my mind. . . . If there is a work for me to do in this thing, I am determined to attend to it." Accordingly, after the session of the School of the Prophets in Palmyra, New York, in 1829, Oliver journeyed with Joseph's brother Samuel Smith to Harmony, Pennsylvania, to meet the young Prophet. "On the 5th day of April, 1829, Oliver Cowdery came to my house, until which time I had never seen him," wrote Joseph. "He stated to me that, having been teaching school in the neighborhood where my father resided, and my father being one of those who sent to the school, he went to board for a season at his house, and while there the family related to him the circumstances of my having received the plates." His visit proved providential, for Joseph had "called upon the Lord, three days prior to the arrival of . . . Oliver, to send him a scribe, according to the promise of the angel; and he was informed that the same should be forthcoming in a few days."[81] Joseph wrote, "Two days after the arrival of Mr. Cowdery (being the 7th of April) I commenced to translate the Book of Mormon, and he began to write for me."[82]

**D&C 6:27—How many revelations did Joseph receive while Oliver acted as his scribe?**

The number of revelations recorded or written by Oliver Cowdery may never be known, since many of the earliest copies of the revelations are missing. Oliver was probably the scribe for most of the early revelations received between 1829 and 1831, including sections 6–9, 11–12, 14–18, 20–

24, 26, 28–32, and the early Missouri revelations, including sections 57–62 and 63–70. He also wrote a portion of the minutes of a February 17, 1834, meeting of the first high council in Kirtland (see D&C 102).

**D&C 6:28—What circumstances led to Oliver Cowdery, David Whitmer, and Martin Harris being chosen to be the Three Witnesses of the Book of Mormon?**

In June 1829, within the small confines of the Peter Whitmer Sr. home, the Smiths, the Whitmers, Oliver Cowdery, and Martin Harris read passages from the completed Book of Mormon manuscript and "rejoiced exceedingly."[83] They spoke of the witnesses who were to testify of the truthfulness of the gold plates and wondered aloud who would be chosen. Oliver Cowdery, David Whitmer, and Martin Harris asked Joseph to "inquire of the Lord" if they might be privileged to be the designated witnesses. Joseph wrote, "They became so very solicitous, and urged me so much to inquire that at length I complied, and through the Urim and Thummim"[84] received an answer: "In addition to your testimony, the testimony of three of my servants, whom I shall call and ordain, unto them I will show these things, and they shall go forth with my words that are given through you" (D&C 5:11)

The next morning, worship services—namely "reading, singing, and praying"—took place in the Whitmer home. During the services, Joseph said, "Martin Harris, you have got to humble yourself before your God this day, that you may obtain a forgiveness of your sins. If you do, it is the will of God that you should look upon the plates, in company with Oliver Cowdery and David Whitmer."[85]

**D&C 6:28—Why was Martin Harris not with Oliver Cowdery and David Whitmer when they were shown the plates by an angel?**

Joseph Smith and Oliver Cowdery brought David Whitmer from the field, where he was plowing, and in company with Martin Harris ventured into a nearby "piece of woods" to "try to obtain by fervent and humble prayer, the fulfillment of the promises given"—that of

REV. XIV-6
OLIVER COWDERY
JOSEPH
JUDAH
DAVID WHITMER
MARTIN HARRIS
THE HILL CUMORAH

viewing the plates. After kneeling down, "according to previous arrangements," Joseph prayed vocally. He was followed "by each of the rest in succession," yet they did not receive a "manifestation of the divine favor." Believing it still possible to receive the desired answer, they "again observed the same order of prayer, each calling on, and praying fervently to God in rotation." The result was as before. After the second failure, Martin "proposed that he would withdraw himself from us, believing as he expressed himself that his presence was the cause of our not obtaining what we wished for." Accordingly, he walked away from the others. Joseph, Oliver, and David then "knelt down again, and had not been many minutes engaged in prayer," when an angel appeared and showed them the plates.[86]

There were now two witnesses of the Book of Mormon, but what of the third? Joseph wrote of his desire for Martin to be a witness: "I now left David and Oliver, and went in pursuit of Martin Harris, whom I found at a considerable distance, fervently engaged in prayer. He soon told me, however, that he had not yet prevailed with the Lord, and earnestly requested me to join him in prayer, that he also might realize the same blessings which we had just received. We accordingly joined in prayer, and ultimately obtained our desires, for before we had yet finished, the same vision was opened to our view, at least it was again opened to me, and I once more beheld and heard the same things; whilst at the same moment, Martin Harris cried out, apparently in an ecstasy of joy, 'Tis enough; 'tis enough; mine eyes have beheld; mine eyes have beheld;' and jumping up, he shouted, 'Hosannah,' blessing God, and otherwise rejoiced exceedingly."[87]

### D&C 6:28—In what way does the experience of the Eight Witnesses of the Book of Mormon differ from that of the Three Witnesses?

The Three Witnesses were shown in vision the plates by an angel in Fayette, New York. The Eight Witnesses were shown the plates by Joseph Smith near the Joseph Smith Sr. log home in Manchester, New York. The Eight Witnesses handled the plates and observed "the engravings thereon." Their testimony appears in each copy of the Book of Mormon: "Joseph Smith,

Jun., the translator of this work, has shown unto us the plates of which hath been spoken, which have the appearance of gold; and as many of the leaves as the said Smith has translated we did handle with our hands; and we also saw the engravings thereon, all of which has the appearance of ancient work, and of curious workmanship. And this we bear record with words of soberness."[88]

## Section 7

### D&C 7: Section Heading—What circumstances led Joseph Smith and Oliver Cowdery to inquire about John, the beloved disciple of Jesus Christ?

Joseph Smith wrote, "During the month of April I continued to translate, and he [Oliver Cowdery] to write, with little cessation, during which time we received several revelations. A difference of opinion arising between us about the account of John the Apostle, mentioned in the New Testament, as to whether he died or continued to live, we mutualy [sic] agreed to settle it by the Urim and Thummim."[89] By this means, Joseph and Oliver learned that the resurrected Lord asked, "John, my beloved, what desirest thou?" He replied, "Lord, give unto me power over death, that I may live and bring souls unto thee." His request was granted. John was promised that he would "prophesy before nations, kindreds, tongues and people" and be as "flaming fire and a ministering angel; he shall minister for those who shall be heirs of salvation who dwell on the earth" (D&C 7:1–3, 6).

### D&C 7: Section Heading—Did Joseph Smith see the parchment on which John the Beloved wrote?

Scholar Daniel H. Ludlow said, "There is no indication that the actual parchment containing the writings of John was at any time physically in the hands of the Prophet. . . . It was just as easy for the Spirit of the Lord to communicate the contents of that record to the Prophet, without the actual presence of it, as it would have been to enable him to understand the language in which John wrote it, whether Greek or Aramæan, which languages neither Joseph nor Oliver could have read, except by special divine interposition,

*Saint John the Evangelist's Vision of Jerusalem* (detail) by Alonso Cano.

even if they had had the manuscript before them."[90] Scholars Robinson and Garrett reached a different conclusion: "Through the Urim and Thummim, Joseph translated a parchment document that had been written anciently by the Apostle John himself and which gave a more full account of the episode recorded in John 21:21–23 than is now found in the New Testament. This parchment may have been an original manuscript of John's Gospel, or it may have been another account written by John concerning the same incident." [91] Perhaps the definitive answer lies in the heading of this chapter published in the 1833 Book of Commandments: "Translated from parchment, written and hid up by John the Revelator." However, there is no indication in the heading that the parchment was ever in Joseph's hands.

**D&C 7:6–7—Why were verses 6–7 added after the 1833 printing of the Book of Commandments?**

D&C 7:6–7 first appeared in the 1835 edition of the Doctrine and Covenants. The reason for the inclusion is unknown. It is surmised, however, that as Joseph Smith worked on the translation of the Bible, he had additional insights about the beloved disciple being a "minister for those who shall be heirs of salvation" and determined to add these insights to the revelation.[92] By the June 1831 conference, John the Beloved was still on the Prophet's mind, for he "prophesied that John the Revelator was then among the Ten Tribes of Israel who had been led away by Shalmaneser, King of Assyria, to prepare them for their return from their long dispersion, to again possess the Land of their fathers."[93] Joseph later stated, "It was a mission and an ordinance for [John] to gather the tribes of Israel" (D&C 77:14). In 1836, Heber C. Kimball said that after the First Presidency, the Twelve, and the presiding bishop had received their endowments in the Kirtland Temple, "The beloved disciple John was seen in our midst by the Prophet Joseph, Oliver Cowdery and others."[94]

# Section 8

### D&C 8:2—What is the "spirit of revelation"?

The spirit of revelation or the Spirit of the Lord leads one to do good, walk humbly, and judge righteously. When a person seeks the Spirit of the Lord, the promise given is that the Spirit will "enlighten your mind" and "fill your soul with joy" (D&C 11:13). Of the Spirit of the Lord, Lorenzo Snow said, "From the time we receive the Gospel, go down into the waters of baptism, and have hands laid upon us afterwards for the gift of the Holy Ghost, we have a friend, if we do not drive it from us by doing wrong. That friend is the Holy Spirit, the Holy Ghost, which partakes of the things of God and shows them unto us. This is a grand means that the Lord has provided for us, that we may know the light, and not be groveling continually in the dark" (D&C 88:66–68).[95]

Joseph Smith taught, "A person may profit by noticing the first intimation of [the Spirit of the Lord or] revelation; for instance, when you feel pure intelligence flowing into you, it may give you sudden strokes of ideas, so that by noticing it, you may find it fulfilled the same day or soon; (i.e.) those things that were presented unto your minds by the Spirit of God, will come to pass; and thus by learning the Spirit of God and understanding it, you may grow into the principle of revelation, until you become perfect in Christ Jesus."[96] Elder Dallin H. Oaks taught, "Visions do happen. Voices are heard from beyond the veil. I know this. But these experiences are exceptional. . . . Most of the revelation that comes to leaders and members of the Church comes by the still, small voice or by a feeling rather than by a vision or a voice that speaks specific words we can hear. I testify to the reality of that kind of revelation, which I have come to know as a familiar, even daily, experience to guide me in the work of the Lord."[97]

**D&C 8:2, 6—What were the divine gifts the Lord promised Oliver Cowdery in this revelation?**

Through revelation Oliver Cowdery was told to claim two divine gifts. The first gift was the spirit of revelation whereby the Lord would present to him revelations in his heart and mind "by the Holy Ghost, which shall come upon you and which shall dwell in your heart" (D&C 8:2). The second gift was the gift of Aaron, which had "told [him] many things" (D&C 8:6). Both divine gifts were given in connection with translation and are not succinctly segregated, for Oliver was told heavenly truths in his mind and heart through "Aaron's rod." It has been suggested that this gift gave Oliver the right to be a spokesman for Joseph Smith, just as anciently Aaron was the mouthpiece for his brother Moses. In the printer's manuscript copy of the Book of Commandments, the "gift of Aaron" was referred to as the "rod of Aaron." The concept of a *rod* introduces

*Aaron's Rod that Budded* referred to in Numbers 17:8.

the possibility of a tangible sacred relic or instrument that Oliver could hold in his hand and through which he could receive dialogic revelation, as Joseph did with the seer stone.[98] Anciently, the rod was used by Moses and Aaron to perform signs and wonders (see Ex. 4:20; 17:9; Num. 17:6–10).

## Section 9

**D&C 9:2—Oliver Cowdery was given the gift to translate in one revelation and rebuked in another for not acting upon the gift. What are the historical underpinnings that brought about this situation?**

Because Oliver Cowdery did not continue to translate as he had commenced, he lost the gift to translate. By revelation the Lord had told Oliver to "study it out in his mind," suggesting that the gift to translate or to use a God-given gift is an active process. Oliver did not seek diligently to obtain and magnify this gift. Therefore, the Lord rebuked him: "Behold, you have not understood; you have supposed that I would give it unto you, when you took no thought save it was to ask me" (D&C 9:7). The revelation ends with a plea for Oliver to "stand fast in the work" and obtain the promise of being "lifted up at the last day" (D&C 9:14). Joseph Fielding Smith concluded, "Oliver's failure came because he did not continue as he commenced, and the task being a difficult one, his faith deserted him. . . . There must have been some . . . impatience in having to sit and act as scribe, but when [Oliver] failed to master the gift of translating, he was then willing to accept the will of the Lord."[99]

**D&C 9:8–9—Is the "stupor of thought" or the "burning of the bosom" figurative, metaphoric, or symbolic?**

A "stupor of thought" and the "burning of the bosom" are tangible feelings. Elder Melvin J. Ballard taught that those who experience a "stupor of thought" turn their hearts away from that which is wrong.[100] Elder Boyd K. Packer taught that the "burning of the bosom" is "not purely a physical sensation. It is more like a warm light shining within your being," suggesting that which is right.[101]

## Section 10

**D&C 10: Section Heading—Why is determining the correct date of this revelation so important to understanding the coming forth of the Book of Mormon?**

Knowing the correct date would help determine when Joseph Smith again received the plates after the loss of the 116-page manuscript of the book of Lehi. Editions of the Doctrine and Covenants published before 1921 list May 1829 as the month and year the revelation was received.[102] Historian B. H. Roberts and a committee charged with publishing the 1921 Doc-

Site of the Smith home from 1828–1830.

trine and Covenants concluded the actual date was sometime in the summer of 1828. If their conclusion is correct, there would be greater clarity as to when the plates were returned to Joseph. This would mean that chronologically section 10 would be placed following section 3. If chronological sequencing were the determining factor for sections 1–13, they would appear as follows: section 2 on September 21, 1823; section 3 in July 1828; section 10 in September 1828; sections 4–9 from February to April 1829; section 13 on May 15, 1829; sections 11–12 in late May 1829; and section 1 on November 1, 1831.

**D&C 10:4—Does the admonition "Do not run faster or labor more than you have strength" suggest an excuse for moderate service in the kingdom of God?**

According to Elder Neal A. Maxwell, the scriptural command "Do not run faster or labor more than you have strength" suggests "paced progress, much as God used seven creative periods in preparing man and this earth. There is a difference, therefore, between being 'anxiously engaged' and being over-anxious and thus underengaged."[103]

**D&C 10:8–13—Is there any trace of the lost manuscript today?**

Joseph Smith believed that someone or some persons had stolen the manuscript and that "by stratagem they got them away."[104] Martin Harris was convinced that the culprit was his wife.[105] For years, Lucy Harris adamantly denied any responsibility for the loss, although many believed her responsible for the theft. Without her confession and since others did not admit to the deed, speculation has run rampant as to what happened to the manuscript. Opinions vary and answers are few. The most definitive answer was received by revelation to Joseph in July 1828: "Because you have delivered the writings into [Martin's] hands, behold, wicked men have taken them from you. . . . they have altered the words, they read contrary from that which you translated and caused to be written" (D&C 10:8, 11).

Speculation arises as to how wicked men acquired the manuscript from the Harris home. Lucy Mack Smith stated that Lucy Harris gave the manuscript to a neighbor when Martin was away from home: "[She] seize[d] the manuscript and put it into the hands of one of her neighbors for safer keeping."[106] Palmyra historian Thomas Cook begged to differ. He claimed that Lucy Harris threw the manuscript into a fire and that there was no attempt made to alter any word.[107] In later years, Lucy confessed to being a party to the incendiary demise of the manuscript.[108] Her confession, however, is questioned because it was given long after the Book of Mormon was published.

**D&C 10:41–42—Who took the place of Martin Harris as scribe for the Book of Mormon translation?**

Martin Harris lost more than a manuscript in Palmyra—he lost the trust and confidence of Joseph Smith. Although he had the talent and inclination to scribe, the privilege to write as Joseph dictated was now denied him. Several others took his place as scribes. Among them were Joseph's wife, Emma Smith, and Oliver Cowdery, a Palmyra schoolteacher. Emma said of her opportunity, "I am satisfied that no man could have dictated the writing of the manuscripts unless he was inspired; for, when acting as his scribe [Joseph] would dictate to me hour after hour; and when returning after meals, or after the interruptions, he would at once begin where he had left off, without either seeing the manuscript or having any portion of it read to him. This was a usual thing for him to do. It would have been improbable that a learned man could do this; and, for one so ignorant and unlearned as he was, it was simply impossible."[109]

Schoolteacher Oliver Cowdery spoke of his gratitude for the opportunity to be a scribe for the Book of Mormon translation: "These were days never to be forgotten—to sit under the sound of a voice dictated by the *inspiration* of heaven, awakened the utmost gratitude of this bosom! Day after day I continued, uninterrupted, to write from his mouth, as he translated, with the *Urim* and *Thummim* . . . the history, or record, called 'The book of Mormon.'"[110]

**D&C 10:45–46—When did Joseph Smith explain the process used in translating the Book of Mormon?**

Joseph said, "It was not intended to tell the world all the particulars of the coming forth of the Book of Mormon." Nevertheless, witnesses of the translation described the process variously. On November 13, 1843, Joseph Smith wrote a letter to James Arlington Bennett. In the letter he explained to this man the process used in translating the Book of Mormon: "By the power of God I translated the Book of Mormon from hieroglyphics; the knowledge of which was lost to the world; in which wonderful event I stood alone, an unlearned youth, to combat the worldly wisdom, and multiplied ignorance of eighteen centuries, with a new revelation; which, (if they would receive the everlasting Gospel,) would open the eyes of [the world], and make 'plain the old paths,' wherein if a man walk in all the ordinances of God blameless, he shall inherit eternal life."[111]

**D&C 10:63—What is the meaning of "wrest the scriptures"?**

There are at least two definitions for the word *wrest*. One is to direct to an unnatural or improper use. The other is to deflect or change from a true or normal bearing, significance, or interpretation. To "wrest the scriptures" means to misinterpret or add to the revealed word of God that which was not intended by the Lord. Such interpretation is not pleasing to God. Knowing the displeasure of the Lord over such actions, the apostle Peter cautioned, "No prophecy of the scripture is of any private interpretation" (2 Pet. 1:20).[112]

## Section 11

**D&C 11: Section Heading—What were the historical events that led Joseph Smith to inquire of the Lord about his brother Hyrum?**

This revelation was received soon after Joseph Smith and Oliver Cowdery had the Aaronic Priesthood conferred upon them by John the Baptist. Following that heavenly manifestation, Joseph said, "Our minds being now enlightened, we began to have the Scriptures laid open to our understandings, and the true meaning and intention of their more mysterious passages revealed unto us in a manner which we never could attain to previously, nor ever before had thought of." A few days later Hyrum Smith arrived in Harmony, Pennsylvania, to visit with Joseph. "At his earnest request [Joseph] inquired of the Lord through the Urim and Thummim, and received for him" the revelation contained in section 11.[113] In this revelation Hyrum is told to prepare for future missionary work. This is the first of fourteen separate instances that the name of Hyrum appears in the Doctrine and Covenants (see D&C 11, 23, 112, 115, 124, 135).

**D&C 11:8—Was Hyrum Smith, like Oliver Cowdery, given a spiritual gift from God?**

In order to accomplish the Lord's design for him, Hyrum Smith was promised by the Lord that "[he] shall be the means of doing much good in this generation" (D&C 11:8). According to Joseph Fielding Smith, the "great gift which [Hyrum] possessed was that of a tender, sympathetic heart; a merciful spirit."[114] This gift is best seen in his watchcare over Joseph and other members of the Smith family. In 1841 the Lord said of Hyrum, "Blessed is my servant Hyrum Smith; for I, the Lord, love him because of the integrity of his heart, and because he loveth that which is right before me, saith the Lord" (D&C 124:15).

**D&C 11:19—Can it be assumed that the phrase "cleave unto me with all your heart" refers to binding oneself to the Lord when the verb "to cleave" has more than one meaning?**

The verb *to cleave* means to bind together, such as in the marriage of a man and a woman. *To cleave* also means "to separate or split," such as in a divorce.[115] Since the admonition "to cleave" was intended for Hyrum Smith, it is safe to assume that the intention was for him to bind himself to the Lord. Hyrum fulfilled the intended purpose. He wrote, "I had been abused and thrust into a dungeon, and confined for months on account of my faith, and the 'testimony of Jesus Christ.' However, I thank God that I felt a determination to die, rather than deny the things which my eyes had seen, which my hands had handled, and which I had borne testimony to, wherever my lot had been cast; and I can assure my beloved brethren that I was enabled to bear as strong a testimony, when nothing but death presented itself, as ever I did in my life."[116]

Hyrum Smith.

## Section 12

**D&C 12: Section Heading—What was the relationship between Joseph Knight Sr. and Joseph Smith?**

Near the time the revelation was given to Joseph Smith

Farm of Joseph Knight.

for his brother Hyrum Smith, Joseph Knight Sr. came to Harmony, Pennsylvania, to make the acquaintance of the young Prophet. Joseph wrote, "I wish to make honorable mention—Mr. Joseph Knight, Sen., of Colesville, Broome County, New York, who, having heard of the manner in which we were occupying our time, very kindly and considerately brought us a quantity of provisions, in order that we might not be interrupted in the work of translation [of the Book of Mormon plates] by the want of such necessities of life; and I would just mention here, as in duty bound, that he several times brought us supplies, a distance of at least thirty miles, which enabled us to continue the work when otherwise we must have relinquished it for a season." On one of his visits to the Prophet, Joseph Knight was "very anxious to know his duty as to this work." It was then that Joseph Smith inquired of the Lord in his behalf and received the revelation contained in section 12, in which Knight was told to "bring forth and establish the cause of Zion" (D&C 12:6).[117]

Joseph Knight fulfilled the admonition. "For fifteen years he has been faithful and true, and even-handed and exemplary, and virtuous and kind, never deviating to the right hand or to the left," wrote Joseph Smith. "Behold he is a righteous man . . . and it shall be said of him, by the sons of Zion, while there is one of them remaining, that this man was a faithful man in Israel; therefore his name shall never be forgotten."[118]

**D&C 12:8—By way of revelation Joseph Knight is told that in order to assist with this work he must be filled with love. Why love and not faith, humility, or a pure heart?**

Joseph Smith taught, "Love is one of the chief characteristics of Deity, and ought to be manifested by those who aspire to be the sons of God. A man filled with the love of God, is not content with blessing his family alone, but ranges through the whole world, anxious to bless the whole human race."[119] Brigham Young said that such a man "who testifies by the power of the Holy Ghost will convince and gather many more of the honest and upright than will the merely logical reasoner."[120]

## Section 13

**D&C 13: Section Heading—What did Joseph Smith and Oliver Cowdery say about receiving the Aaronic Priesthood from John the Baptist?**

Of receiving the Aaronic Priesthood from John the Baptist, Joseph wrote, "What joy! what wonder! what amazement! While the world were racked and distracted—while millions were groping as the blind for the wall, and while all men were resting upon uncertainty, as a general mass, our eyes beheld, our ears heard. As in the 'blaze of day;' yes, more—above the glitter of the May sunbeam, which then shed its brilliancy over the face of nature! Then his voice, though mild, pierced to the centre, and his words, 'I am thy fellow-servant,' dispelled every fear. We listened, we gazed, we admired! 'Twas the voice of an angel from glory, 'twas a message from the Most High! and as we heard we rejoiced, while his love enkindled upon our souls, and we were wrapt in the vision of the Almighty! Where was room for doubt? Nowhere; uncertainty had fled, doubt had sunk no more to rise, while fiction and deception had fled forever!"[121]

Of this sacred manifestation, Oliver Cowdery wrote,

The Youthful Prophet, Joseph Smith, Jr., and Oliver Cowdery, Receiving the Aaronic
Priesthood under the hands of John the Baptist, May 15, 1829.


Joseph and Oliver receiving the Aaronic Priesthood.

"On a sudden, as from the midst of eternity, the voice of the Redeemer spake peace to us, while the veil was parted and the angel of God came down clothed with glory, and delivered the anxiously looked for message, and the keys of the gospel of repentance! . . . Then his voice, though mild, pierced to the center, and his words, 'I am thy fellow servant,' dispelled every fear. We listened—we gazed—we admired! 'Twas the voice of an angel from glory—'twas a message from the Most High! I shall not attempt to paint to you the feelings of this heart, nor the majestic beauty and glory which surrounded us on this occasion; but you will believe me when I say, that earth, nor men, with the eloquence of time, cannot begin to clothe language in as interesting and sublime a manner as this holy personage."[122]

## D&C 13:1—Who was baptized first: Joseph Smith or Oliver Cowdery?

On May 15, 1829, John the Baptist, acting under the direction of the ancient apostles Peter, James, and John, conferred the lesser priesthood upon Joseph Smith and Oliver Cowdery. Recalling the event, Joseph wrote, "I baptized [Oliver] first, and afterwards he baptized me, after which I laid my hands upon his head and ordained him to the Aaronic Priesthood, and afterwards he laid his hands on me and ordained me to the same Priesthood—for so we were commanded. . . . No sooner had I baptized Oliver Cowdery, than the Holy Ghost fell upon him, and he stood up and prophesied many things which should shortly come to pass. . . . We were filled with the Holy Ghost, and rejoiced in the God of our salvation."[123]

### D&C 13:1—What does it mean to possess priesthood keys?

Priesthood keys are the right to administer in the Church and kingdom of God. Priesthood leaders hold keys to preside over and direct the work of God on a local and general level. For example, missionaries can baptize investigators only after receiving permission from a presiding priesthood leader who holds the keys, such as a bishop.[124] The keys given to Joseph Smith and Oliver Cowdery by John the Baptist are the same keys once held by Aaron and his descendants.

### D&C 13:1—What is the difference between the Aaronic and Levitical priesthoods?

Even though the Aaronic Priesthood was divided into two distinct categories—Aaronic and Levitical—it was one priesthood. Elder James E. Talmage explained that the Levitical Priesthood was "an appendage to the Priesthood of Aaron, not comprising the highest priestly powers."[125] Anciently, Levites assisted the priests of Aaron (see Num. 3; 4; 8) with keeping a fire burning on the sacred altar (see Lev. 1:13), dressing burnt offerings (see 2 Chron. 29:34), slaughtering pascal lambs (see Ezra 6:20), receiving sacrificial blood (see Ex. 24:6), and sprinkling that blood around the altar. They disposed of meat and other offerings, performed purification ceremonies (see Lev. 12:6–7), and judged cases of leprosy.

### D&C 13:1—What is the "offering unto the Lord" that the sons of Levi will offer in the latter days?

In the latter days Levites will again bear the Aaronic Priesthood and assist the priests of Aaron. One of their assignments will be to offer unto the Lord a sacrifice. Of this sacrifice, Joseph Smith said, "It is generally supposed that sacrifice was entirely done away when the Great sacrifice . . . was offered up, and that there will be no necessity for the ordinance of sacrifice in the future; but those who assert this are certainly not acquainted with the duties, privileges and authority of the Priesthood, or with the Prophets. . . . These sacrifices as well as every ordinance belonging to the Priesthood, will, when the Temple of the Lord shall be built, and the sons of Levi be purified, be fully restored and attended to in all their powers, ramifications, and blessings."[126] Elder Charles W. Penrose added, "Descendants of Levi, holding the Priesthood of Aaron, . . . will make the offerings predicted by the prophets to be presented to the Lord in latter days in Zion and in Jerusalem" (see Mal. 3:2–4; D&C 124:38; 128:24).[127] Joseph Fielding Smith viewed the resumption of blood sacrifice as temporary: "The sacrifice of animals will be done to complete the restoration when the temple spoken of is built; at the beginning of the millennium, or in the restoration, blood sacrifices will be performed long enough to

Levitical sacrifice.

complete the fulness of the restoration in this dispensation. Afterwards sacrifice will be of some other character."[128]

# Section 14

**D&C 14: Section Heading—What circumstances brought Joseph Smith in contact with the Peter Whitmer Sr. family of Fayette, New York?**

On a business trip to Palmyra, New York, in 1828, David Whitmer learned of Joseph Smith and the gold plates through Oliver Cowdery. Apparently Oliver suggested to him that there was foundation for the circulating rumors of gold plates and that it was his intention to investigate the matter. David asked Oliver to inform him of his investigation. Sometime later David received a letter from Oliver convincing him that Joseph possessed gold plates. It was David who brought Joseph and Oliver in a conveyance to his father's home in Fayette, New York.[129]

Joseph wrote of being well received in the Peter Whitmer Sr. home: "It was arranged that we should have our board free of charge, and the assistance of one of his brothers to write for me, and also [David's] assistance when convenient." Joseph resided in the Whitmer home until he completed the translation of the Book of Mormon. During his stay, Joseph recalled, "David, John, and Peter Whitmer, Jun., became our zealous friends and assistants in the work; and being anxious to know their respective duties, and having desired with much earnestness that I should inquire of the Lord concerning them, I did so, through the means of the Urim and Thummim, and obtained for them in succession" revelations comprising sections 14, 15, and 16.[130]

**D&C 14:7—In the revelation addressed to David Whitmer, he was told that eternal life is "the greatest of all the gifts of God." What is the gift of eternal life?**

To be granted the gift of eternal life is to be exalted in the celestial kingdom of God. It is to live as God lives—an exalted son or daughter of the Most High. Although personal worthiness, obedience, and good works are important benchmarks in describing a righteous life, no amount of upright living can merit exaltation. Exaltation is a gift of God through the Atonement and Resurrection of Jesus Christ.[131]

## Section 15

**D&C 15: Section Heading—What were the contributions of John Whitmer to the Restoration?**

John Whitmer was one of the Eight Witnesses to the Book of Mormon. His influence in the early days of the Church was matched by few. Whitmer strengthened the Saints in Colesville, New York; acted as a scribe for the Bible translation; served several missions; wrote a history of the Church; and was a Church leader in Clay County, Missouri (see D&C 47:1). Unfortunately, on March 10, 1838, he was cut off from the Church for mishandling land sales in Missouri. Whitmer's public reaction was penitent and sympathetic to the Saints until the "Salt Sermon," which caused him and other dissenters to be driven from Far West out of fear of violence from

Danites. He later wrote of asking the Lord that "I may be forgiven of my faults, and my sins be blotted out, and in the last day be saved in the kingdom of God, notwithstanding my private situation, which I hope will soon be bettered, and I find favor in the eyes of God, all men and his Saints."[132]

**D&C 15:3—How is the revelation intended for John Whitmer similar to the revelation addressed to Oliver Cowdery in section 6?**

In an earlier revelation addressed to Oliver Cowdery, the Lord said, "There is none else save God that knowest thy thoughts and the intents of thy heart" (D&C 6:16). In the revelation given in June 1829 directed to John Whitmer, he is told essentially the same thing: "I will tell you that which no man knoweth save me and thee alone."[133] John is then promised that he will "rest" with others in the kingdom of God and be exalted in God's presence (see D&C 84:24; JST, Ex. 34:2).

# Section 16

**D&C 16: Section Heading—Can it be assumed that since the revelation directed to Peter Whitmer Jr. is basically the same as the revelation intended for his brother John that the brothers had similar responsibilities to fulfill in the Restoration?**

Like his brother John Whitmer, Peter Whitmer Jr. assisted Joseph Smith in scribing a portion of the Book of Mormon translation. Both brothers were shown the gold plates by Joseph Smith and became witnesses of the Book of Mormon. Both were

John Whitmer.

stalwart missionaries, giving valiant service in their designated fields of labor. On October 25, 1831, Peter said, "My beloved brethren ever since I have had an acquaintance with the writing of God I have [viewed] eternity with perfect confidence," much like a promise later given to his brother John (see D&C 84).[134] The difference between the brothers is that Peter died in the faith. He proclaimed in his "last moments, the certainty of [his] former testimony."[135] In contrast, John Whitmer lost fellowship with the Saints in 1838 and never returned to Church activity.

## Section 17

**D&C 17:1—At the door of Lehi's tent was a ball of curious workmanship known as the Liahona. What is the meaning of "Liahona"?**

According to scholars George Reynolds and Janne M. Sjodahl, the word *Liahona* is "Hebrew with an Egyptian ending. . . . *L* is a Hebrew preposition meaning 'to,' and sometimes used to express the possessive case. *Iah* is a Hebrew abbreviated form of 'Jehovah,' common in Hebrew names. *On* is the Hebrew name of the Egyptian 'City of the Sun' . . . *L-iah-on* means, therefore, literally, 'To God is Light'; or, 'of God is Light.' That is to say, God gives light, as does the Sun. The final *a* reminds us that the Egyptian form of the Hebrew name *On* is *Annu*, and that seems to be the form Lehi used."[136] Reynolds and Sjodahl's interpretation of the word *Liahona* is not accepted by modern Egyptologists.

**D&C 17:1—What ancient Nephite relics were shown to the Three Witnesses of the Book of Mormon by the angel Moroni?**

The Three Witnesses—Oliver Cowdery, David Whitmer, and Martin Harris—were privileged to see precious treasures of the Nephite and Jaredite civilizations. They saw the sword of Laban that had been wielded by rulers of the Nephite nation. They were shown the Liahona, the compass that guided Father Lehi's family to the promised land, and a breastplate that was instrumental in the translation process. They saw the Urim and Thummim, or interpreters, that proved vital to the translation of the Book of Mormon. And, of course, they saw the gold plates from which the Book of Mormon was translated. Each of these ancient relics is mentioned in the Book of Mormon as being of great worth and as passing from one generation to another.

# Section 18

**D&C 18: Section Heading—When was the Melchizedek Priesthood restored to Joseph Smith and Oliver Cowdery?**

The exact date of the Melchizedek Priesthood restoration is unknown. Joseph recorded that he and Oliver were "forced to keep secret the circumstances of having received the Priesthood . . . owing to a spirit of persecution which had already manifested itself" (JS–H 1:74). In 1878, Elders Orson Pratt and Joseph F. Smith visited David Whitmer and asked him, "Can you tell the date of the bestowal of the Apostleship upon Joseph, by Peter, James, and John?" David replied, "I do not know, Joseph never told me."[137]

It is difficult to establish the exact date of the Melchizedek Priesthood restoration. Scholars suggest the restoration occurred between May 15, 1829, and the end of June 1829 "in the wilderness between Harmony, Susquehanna county, and Colesville, Broome county, on the Susquehanna river" (D&C 128:20). Recent evidence narrows the date to between May 15 and 29, 1829. The evidence is as follows: 1) a letter written on June 14, 1829, to Hyrum Smith by Oliver Cowdery contains wording similar to that of section 18, suggesting that the revelation had been earlier recorded by Oliver; and 2) David Whitmer claimed that Joseph and Oliver resided at the Whitmer farmhouse from June 1, 1829, to July 1, 1829. The location of the farmhouse is a three-day journey from the locale where the Melchizedek Priesthood was restored. It is unlikely that Joseph and Oliver would have made that journey during their stay with the Whitmers.[138]

**D&C 18: Section Heading—Are there historical accounts of Joseph Smith and Oliver Cowdery receiving the Melchizedek Priesthood from apostles Peter, James, and John?**

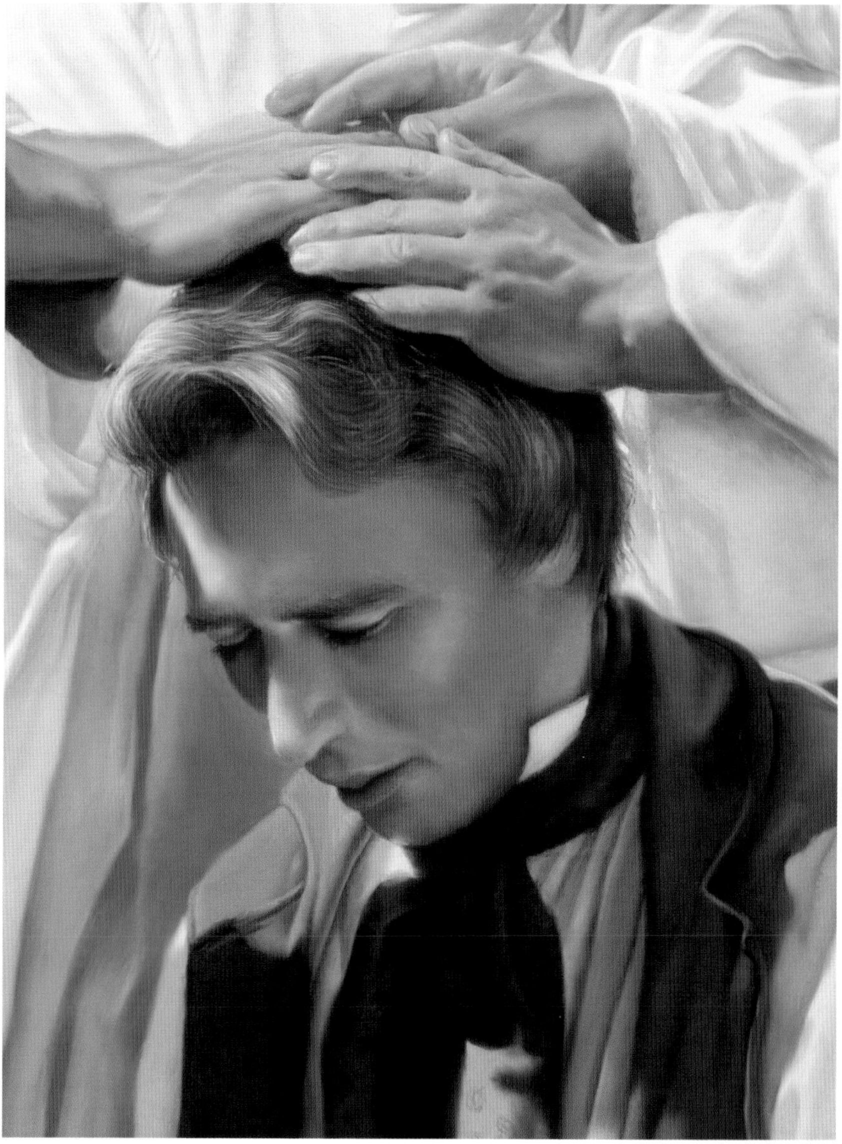

Peter, James, and John ordaining Joseph Smith to the apostleship.

Unfortunately, there are no firsthand accounts of the Melchizedek Priesthood restoration other than the mention of Peter, James, and John bestowing priesthood keys. If an 1881 Addison Everett letter can be considered reliable, then a few additional facts of the restoration of the priesthood are known. In the letter, Everett pens of overhearing a conversation between Joseph Smith and his brother Hyrum Smith regarding a time when Joseph and Oliver Cowdery were escaping from enemies in Colesville, New York. Everett describes the escape being at "night and they traveled through brush and water and mud, fell over logs, etc., until Oliver was exhausted; then Joseph helped him along through brush and water, almost carrying him. They traveled all night, and just at the break of day Oliver gave out entirely and exclaimed, 'O Lord! Brother Joseph, how long have we got to endure this thing?' They sat down on a log to rest and Joseph said that at that very time Peter, James, and John came to them and ordained them to the Apostleship."[139]

In 1882 Elder Erastus Snow gave a similar account in his general conference address: "It was at a period when they were being pursued by their enemies and had to travel all night, and in the dawn of the coming day when they were weary and worn who should appear to them but Peter, James, and John, for the purpose of conferring upon them the Apostleship, the keys of which they themselves had held while upon the earth, which had been bestowed upon them by the Savior."[140] Note that the word used by both Everett and Snow was *apostleship*, not *Melchizedek Priesthood.*

# Section 19

**D&C 19: Section Heading—What are the historical circumstances that led to another revelation intended for Martin Harris?**

In late March 1830, Joseph Smith and Joseph Knight journeyed from Colesville to Palmyra to be in the Grandin Bookstore when the first copies of the Book of Mormon were released for public sale. As they approached Palmyra, they saw Martin Harris cross the road ahead of them with "a Bunch of morman Books." Joseph Knight recalled that Martin approached them and said, "'The Book will not sell for no Body wants them.' Joseph says, 'I think they will sell well.' Says he, 'I want a Commandment.' 'Why,' says Joseph, 'fulfill what you have got.' 'But,' says he, 'I must have a Commandment.'"[141] Martin was not pacified until Joseph invited him to spend the night at the Joseph Smith Sr. log home and promised that in the home they would discuss the matter. After staying the night, the next morning Martin again asked Joseph for a "commandment." Later that day Joseph received "a commandment of God and not of Man, to Martin Harris, given by him who is Eternal" (D&C 19: Section Heading). In the commandment the Lord admonished Martin to repent, not just once but three times (see D&C 19:13–15, 20, 34–35). He was to repent of his thoughts and actions toward neighbors and his failure to pay the debt owed to Book of Mormon publisher, E. B. Grandin. If Martin ignored these admonitions, the Lord warned "misery thou shalt receive if thou wilt slight these counsels, yea, even the destruction of thyself and property" (D&C 19:33).

**D&C 19:26–27, 35—Why was Martin Harris slow in paying the printer for publishing the Book of Mormon?**

Egbert B. Grandin, a local printer, bookseller, and publisher of the *Wayne Sentinel,* initially declined "to entertain the proposal

Grandin Building, the location of the first printing of the Book of Mormon.

to print at any price" the Book of Mormon manuscript.[142] But when Martin Harris accepted the financial burden of the publication, Grandin took "the advice of several discrete, fair-minded neighbors" who assured him that his connection with the book would be only a business matter. Their advice and Martin's willingness to enter a contractual agreement led Grandin to reconsider his position. On August 25, 1829, Martin entered into a mortgage agreement with Grandin guaranteeing that before the expiration of eighteen months "from the date hereof," he would pay the requisite $3,000. In case of nonpayment of monies, sale of the described acreage would cover the cost.[143]

Martin did not make payment within the prescribed time period. Instead he dickered, bargained, and handled the transaction in his own way, seemingly unmindful of the Lord's directive to "not covet thine own property, but impart it freely to the printing of the Book of Mormon, which contains the truth and the word of God" (D&C 19:26). In the same revelation, he was forewarned that "misery thou shalt receive if thou wilt slight these counsels, yea, even the destruction of thyself and property" (D&C 19:33). Then, in no uncertain terms, the Lord said, "Pay the debt thou hast contracted with the printer. Release thyself from bondage" (D&C 19:35). Belatedly but with determination, Martin did as the Lord commanded. The contractual arrangement, however, was not fully satisfied until January 12, 1832, as certified by Truman Hemingway, the commissioner of deeds for Wayne County.

# Section 20

**D&C 20: Section Heading—Were the "Articles and Covenants of the Church" the first document in this dispensation to be canonized?**

In June 1830 at the first conference of the Church held in Fayette, New York, Joseph Smith asked that the "articles and covenants of the Church" be read aloud. After the reading, the Articles and Covenants was received by a unanimous voice as the word of God, and was thus canonized.[144]

The organization of the Church

**D&C 20: Section Heading—Where is the legal document or certificate of the incorporation of the Church?**

To date the certificate of incorporation has not been found. A few scholars contend that the beginning verses of section 20 read like a legal document and suggest that these verses may be the missing certificate of incorporation of the Church for the state of New York. In August 1879, President John Taylor invited William C. Staines to search for the certificate in local government offices in New York. Staines wrote to President Taylor of his extensive but fruitless search.[145] Later researchers also searched for the certificate but they have not been able to locate the document.

**D&C 20: Section Heading—Is section 20 a revelation from God or a series of inspired writings?**

Section 20 combines several inspired writings on Church doctrines, practices, and procedures by Joseph Smith and Oliver Cowdery. The section was written between June 1829 and the spring of 1830. The section is reminiscent of creeds or platforms of traditional Christian churches that set forth basic beliefs, standards, expectation of conduct, and responsibility of members. When combined with sections 21 and 22, section 20 forms the Constitution of the Church or what is referred to as "the Mormon Creed." It should be noted that verses 65–67 were added at a later date. These verses designate additional priesthood offices within the Church.[146] There are other additions and changes besides those mentioned.

**D&C 20:1—What significant dates in the life of Jesus Christ correlate with the timing of the organization of the Church?**

In a conference address given on April 6, 1973, President Harold B. Lee spoke of April 6 commemorating the anniversary of the organization of the Church and "the anniversary of the birth of the Savior, our Lord and Master, Jesus Christ."[147] President Spencer W. Kimball also spoke of April 6 being the date of the Savior's birth.[148] Joseph Smith wrote of the Savior being crucified on April 6: "On the 6th of April, in the land of Zion [near Independence, Missouri] . . . [we] met for instruction and the service of God, at the Ferry on Big Blue river. . . . It being just 1,800 years since the Savior laid down his life that men might have everlasting life."[149] Although the day and month of the Savior's birth and death has been spoken of by holy prophets, the year of His birth and death has not been identified.

**D&C 20:1—Why is there confusion and controversy over where the Church was organized?**

The discrepancy over where the Church was organized arises from an article printed in the LDS newspaper, *The Evening and the Morning Star*, and Orson Pratt's pamphlet titled *Interesting Account of Several Remarkable Visions, and of the Late Discovery of Ancient Americans Records.* The newspaper and pamphlet tell of the Church being organized in Manchester, New York. The writings of Joseph Smith reveal the Church was organized in Fayette, New York: "We had received a commandment to organize the Church; and accordingly we met together for that purpose, at the house of Mr. Peter Whitmer, Sen. [in Fayette, New York] (being six in number) on Tuesday, the sixth day of April, A.D., one thousand eight hundred and thirty."[150]

**D&C 20:1—At the organizational meeting on April 6, 1830, the Church was known as the Church of Christ. When did the Church become known as The Church of Jesus Christ of Latter-day Saints?**

The name of The Church of Jesus Christ of Latter-day Saints was given by the Lord in revelation to Joseph Smith on April 26, 1838 (see D&C 115:4). The Church had been known as The Church of Christ from 1830 to 1834 (see D&C 20:1) and The Church of the Latter Day Saints from 1834 to 1838. The Church is commonly but unofficially referred to as the Mormon Church and its members as Mormons because of their belief in the Book of Mormon. But use of the word *Mormon* in reference to the Church "is unsatisfactory [to] Church members because it does not convey the conviction that Jesus Christ is the head of the Church and that members strive to live Christian lives."[151]

**D&C 20:24—What are some examples of the favored position being on "the right hand of the Father" as opposed to the "left hand"?**

Throughout holy writ God uses His right hand to designate a privileged status for the righteous. For example, Jesus Christ is on the right hand of the Father (see D&C 20:24; Moro. 7:27; Acts 7:56). Those whose names are recorded in the Book of Life are promised a favored position on the right hand of God (see Mosiah 5:9; 26:23–24; Alma 5:58). The Lord further promises that through trials, "I will uphold thee with the right hand of my righteousness" (Isa. 41:10).[152] For those who merit His left hand, no such promises are given, for they chose to transgress the laws of God and ignore His command to righteousness.

**D&C 20:37—Oliver Cowdery wrote to Joseph Smith about a perceived error in the statement, "Truly manifest by their works that they have received of the Spirit of Christ unto the remission of their sins." What was Joseph's response to Oliver's perception of the error?**

"I received a letter from Oliver Cowdery, the contents of which gave me both sorrow and uneasiness," wrote Joseph. "The above quotation, he said, was erroneous, and added: 'I command you in the name of God to erase those words, that no priestcraft be amongst us!'" In response to Oliver's command, Joseph wrote to him, asking, "By what authority he took upon him to command me to alter or erase, to add to or diminish from, a revelation or commandment from Almighty God." Before the issue was solved, Joseph discovered that Oliver's perception was also held by the Whitmers. After working with and instructing Oliver and the Whitmers, Joseph penned, "I succeeded in bringing, not only the Whitmer family, but also Oliver Cowdery to acknowledge that they had been in error, and that the sentence in dispute was in accordance with the rest of the commandment. And thus was this error rooted out."[153]

## Section 21

**D&C 21:12—When did Oliver Cowdery first preach the gospel of Jesus Christ?**

Interior of the Peter Whitmer home.

The first public meeting of the fledgling Church of Christ was held on April 11, 1830, at the Peter Whitmer Sr. home in Fayette, New York. At this meeting Joseph Smith directed Oliver Cowdery to preach the gospel of Jesus Christ to those in attendance, many of whom had been meeting informally for several months before the Church was officially organized. Oliver's remarks on that occasion are viewed as the first preaching in this dispensation in a Church setting. The preaching of Oliver may have led "a number of persons" to demand "baptism and membership among the people of God."[154]

## Section 22

**D&C 22:1–2—Why was it necessary for Joseph Smith to receive an additional revelation on baptism when section 20 so clearly outlined the process?**

This revelation, received ten days after the Church was organized, explains the need for baptism by proper authority. According to Elder Orson Pratt, "In the early days of this Church there were certain persons, belonging to the Baptist denomination, very moral and no doubt as good a people as you could find anywhere, who came, saying they believed in the Book of Mormon, and that they had been baptized into the Baptist Church, and they wished to come into our Church. The Prophet Joseph had not, at that time, particularly inquired in relation to this matter, but he did inquire, and received a revelation from the Lord. . . . These Baptists had to be re-baptized: there was no other way to get into this Church."[155] The notion of baptism for those who had been previously baptized smacked against traditional Christian beliefs. A rebaptism to enter the true fold of God contradicted the writings of Francis Weyland, a leading American Baptist, who contended, "We consider ourselves not to *baptize again*, . . . but to baptize these who have never yet submitted to this ordinance."[156]

## Section 23

**D&C 23: Section Heading—Is section 23 one single revelation or a compilation of five separate revelations?**

The 1833 Book of Commandments recorded each revelation given to a specific individual as five separate revelations or chapters. The five men mentioned in the revelations were Oliver Cowdery, Hyrum Smith, Samuel H. Smith, Joseph Smith Sr., and Joseph Knight Sr. Each man was "anxious to know of the Lord what might be their respective duties in relation to this work." After inquiring of the Lord, Joseph received the five revelations that now are combined into one—section 23.[157] Of the men named, up to that point only Samuel Smith had not been the subject of a revelation given to Joseph Smith.

**D&C 23: Section Heading—What were the contributions of Samuel Smith to the Restoration?**

Samuel Smith, like other members of his family, believed in the visions of his brother Joseph. He was baptized on May 25, 1829, by Oliver Cowdery, becoming the third person baptized in this dispensation. After his baptism "he returned to his father's house, greatly glorifying and praising God, being filled with the Holy Spirit."[158] Samuel was privileged to be one of the Eight Witnesses of the Book of Mormon and one of the six original members of the Church. He is recognized as the first missionary of the Church. Although discouraged with his initial missionary labors, his labors led to the later baptisms of Brigham Young and Heber C. Kimball. Samuel received his patriarchal blessing from his father in December 1834 and was promised in that blessing, "The just shall rise up and call thee, a perfect man. . . . The testimony which thou hast borne and shall bear, shall be received by thousands, and thou shalt magnify thy calling and do honor to the Holy Priesthood."[159]

# Section 24

**D&C 24:5—Joseph Smith was admonished to write "the things which shall be given thee by the Comforter." Up to this point in time, was Joseph in the habit of writing down the revelations he received?**

It appears that Joseph Smith did not always record revelations at the time they were received.

William E. McLellin.

The Lord instructed him in July 1830 to "continue in calling upon God in my name, and writing the things which shall be given thee" (D&C 24:5). Willing to follow counsel, Joseph asked scribes to write as he dictated the revelations from God. William E. McLellin wrote of his experience as a scribe for some of the revelations: "The scribe seats himself at a desk or table, with pen, ink, and paper. The subject of enquiry being understood, the Prophet and Revelator enquires of God. He spiritually sees, hears, and feels, and then speaks as he is moved upon by the Holy Ghost, the 'thus saith the Lord,' sentence after sentence, and waits for his amanuenses to write and then read aloud each sentence. Thus they proceed until the revelator says Amen, at the close of what is then communicated." McLellin added, "I have known [Joseph], without premeditation, to thus deliver off in broken sentences, some of the most sublime pieces of composition which I ever perused in any book."[160]

### D&C 24:12—Did Oliver Cowdery receive "strength such as is not known among men"?

Elder Wilford Woodruff wrote, "I have seen Oliver Cowdery when it seemed as though the earth trembled under his feet. I never heard a man bear a stronger testimony than he did when under the influence of the Spirit. But the moment he left the kingdom of God, that moment his power fell like lightning from heaven. He was shorn of his strength, like Samson in the lap of Delilah. He lost the power and testimony which he had enjoyed, and he never recovered it again in its fulness while in the flesh, although he died in the Church."[161] It should be remembered that Oliver was promised that God would be with him "even unto the end of thy days" (D&C 24:8).

**D&C 24:15—What is the ancient symbolism associated with "casting off the dust of your feet"?**

Elder James E. Talmage wrote, "To ceremonially shake the dust from one's feet as a testimony against another was understood by the Jews to symbolize a cessation of fellowship and a renunciation of all responsibility for consequences that might follow. It became an ordinance of accusation and testimony by the Lord's instructions to His apostles. . . . In the current dispensation, the Lord has similarly directed His authorized servants to so testify against those who willfully and maliciously oppose the truth when authoritatively presented (D&C 24:15; 60:15; 75:20; 84:92; 99:4)."[162]

# 3

# Sections 25–49



## Section 25

**D&C 25:3—In what sense was Emma Smith an "elect lady"?**

Joseph Smith wrote, "I assisted in commencing the organization of 'The Female Relief Society of Nauvoo' in the Lodge Room [on March 17, 1842]. Sister Emma Smith, President, . . . I gave much instruction . . . concerning the Elect Lady, and showed that the elect meant to be elected to a certain work, &c., and that the revelation was then fulfilled by Sister Emma's election to the Presidency of the Society, she having previously been ordained to expound the Scriptures."[163]

**D&C 25:5—What was the calling given to Emma Smith?**

The main calling of Emma Smith was to be the wife of a prophet of God. Emma was told by revelation, "The office of thy calling shall be for a comfort unto my servant, Joseph Smith, Jun., thy husband" (D&C 25:5). As a wife she was to use "consoling

*An Elect Lady.*

words, in the spirit of meekness" and to cleave to Joseph and to "go with him at the time of his going and be unto him for a scribe" (D&C 25:5–6). For faithfully fulfilling her role as a wife, Emma was promised that her "husband shall support thee in the church" (D&C 25:9).

### D&C 25:5—Was Emma beloved by Joseph Smith and his family?

Emma Smith was loved and respected by her husband, Joseph, and his extended family. Joseph wrote, "My beloved Emma—she that was my wife, even the wife of my youth, and the choice of my heart. Many were the reverberations of my mind when I contemplated for a moment the many scenes we had been called to pass through, the fatigues and the toils, the sorrows and sufferings, and the joys and consolations, from time to time, which had strewed our paths. . . . Oh what a commingling of thought filled my mind for the moment, again she is here . . . undaunted, firm, and unwavering—unchangeable, affectionate Emma!"[164] Joseph's mother, Lucy Mack Smith, wrote of Emma, "I have never seen a woman in my life, who would endure every species of fatigue and hardship, from month to month, and from year to year, with that unflinching courage, zeal, and patience, which she has ever done; for I know that which she has had to endure. . . . She has breasted the storms of persecution, and buffeted the rage of men and devils, which would have borne down almost any other woman."[165]

### D&C 25:7—The revelation calls for Emma to "be ordained under [Joseph's] hand." At that time was the word "ordained" synonymous with "set apart"?

In the early days of the Church, the word *ordain* was used in conjunction with priesthood ordinations and the setting apart of women to specific callings. Through the passage of time, a distinction has developed between being "ordained" and being "set apart." Brethren are ordained to priesthood offices and set apart to preside over administrative assignments, such as stakes, wards, branches, and missions. Sisters are no longer ordained to a specific calling but are set apart for their callings. President John Taylor stated, "For the information of all interested in this subject I will say, it is not the calling of these sisters to hold the Priesthood, only in connection with their husbands, they being one with their husbands."[166]

**D&C 25:11—In what ways did Emma Smith fulfill her responsibility to select sacred hymns?**

By revelation Emma Smith was told to expound scriptures, exhort the Church, and write, learn, and select sacred hymns (see D&C 25:7, 8, 11). At a meeting of the Kirtland High Council and presidency of the Church held on September 15, 1835, it was "decided that Sister Emma proceed to make a selection of Sacred Hymns according to revelation, and that President W. W. Phelps be appointed to revise and arrange them for printing."[167] With the assistance of Phelps, Emma compiled a pocket-size hymnbook titled *A Collection of Sacred Hymns for the Church of the Latter Day Saints.* The hymnal contained ninety hymns, the first being "Know This, That Every Soul Is Free." On October 27, 1839, "the High Council of Nauvoo voted . . . that Sister Emma Smith select and publish a [second] hymn-book for the use of the Church." In accordance with the vote, Emma compiled a second hymnal in 1841 that included 304 hymns with suggested tempos.[168]

# Section 26

**D&C 26:2—In what way is the law of common consent binding upon participants?**

Elder Bruce R. McConkie wrote of the law of common consent as being "operative in every dispensation." He contended that the uplifted or raised hand in each dispensation represented the law of common consent, meaning "a vote taken" or a "token of a sacred covenant being made." For example, Moses practiced the law of common consent in one form or another (see Ex. 24:3), as did Joshua (see Num. 27:19–22), Peter (see Acts 1:26), and Mosiah (see Mosiah 29:25–26). Of this law, John Taylor asked, "Is there a monarch, potentate or power under the heavens, that undergoes a scrutiny as fine as this? No, there is not; yet this is done twice a year" at general conference in the LDS Church.[169]

Of the obligations associated with the law of common consent, President Harold B. Lee said, "When you vote affirmatively you make a solemn covenant with the Lord that you will sustain, that is, give your full loyalty and support, without equivocation or reservation, to the officer for whom you vote."[170]

## Section 27

**D&C 27: Section Heading—What historical circumstances led up to this revelation on the sacrament?**

Although Sally Knight, wife of Newel Knight, and Emma Smith, wife of Joseph Smith, had been baptized on June 28, 1830, neither woman had been confirmed by August 1830. When Newel and his wife visited Joseph and Emma in early August 1830, Joseph penned, "As neither his wife nor mine had been as yet confirmed, it was proposed that we should confirm them, and partake together of the Sacrament." Wanting to prepare for these sacred events, Joseph went to "procure some wine for the occasion." He had not gone far when a heavenly messenger appeared and made known to him this revelation on the emblems of the sacrament.[171] Joseph wrote, "In obedience to [this revelation] we prepared some wine of our own making, and held our meeting, consisting only of five, viz., Newel Knight and his wife, and myself and wife, and John Whitmer. We partook of the Sacrament, after which we confirmed the two sisters into the Church, and spent the evening in a glorious manner. The Spirit of the Lord was poured out upon us. We praised the Lord God, and rejoiced exceedingly."[172] Since 1906, water has been exclusively used in place of wine as an emblem of the sacrament.[173]

The sacrament

**D&C 27:6—Of the ancient prophets mentioned in section 27, the identity of Elias is of particular interest. What does his name represent?**

*Elias* is the Greek form of the Hebrew name "Elijah." Elias can be a proper name, such as the prophet mentioned in 1 Kings 17–2 Kings 2, but can also be a title or office for a heavenly messenger sent from God, such as John the Baptist when he conferred the Aaronic Priesthood upon Joseph Smith and Oliver Cowdery (see Matt. 17:10–13). Joseph also applied the name of "Elias" to John the Revelator (see D&C 77:14).

## Section 28

**D&C 28:6, 11–12—What was the nature of the confrontation that led to Oliver's rebuke, "Thou shalt not command him who is at thy head"?**

September 1830 was not the first time Joseph Smith and Oliver Cowdery had disagreed on religious matters. Just one month earlier, Oliver had sent a letter to Joseph about a perceived error in the wording of D&C 20:37. The disagreement in September was over Hiram Page, one of the Eight Witnesses of the Book of Mormon, who claimed that he received revelations through a "seer stone" that he wore around his neck. Page claimed to receive revelations about Zion, Restoration doctrines, and Church organization. Newel Knight wrote that Hiram Page had "quite a roll of papers full of these revelations, and many in the Church were led astray by them."[174] Among those deceived were Oliver Cowdery and the Whitmers,[175] whose deception by and confidence in Hiram Page caused Joseph Smith "great distress of mind."[176] Joseph inquired of the Lord concerning the matter and received the revelation contained in section 28, which clearly tells Oliver Cowdery that "no one shall be appointed to receive commandments and revelations in this church" except the Prophet Joseph (D&C 28:2). The revelation reminds Oliver to be like Aaron of old, declaring true commandments and revelations with power and authority unto the Church and forbearing to command Joseph (see D&C 28:4–5). Oliver was admonished to take

"Hiram Page, between him and thee alone, and tell him that those things which he hath written from that stone are not of me and that Satan deceiveth him" (D&C 28:11).

**D&C 28:14—Did Hiram Page repent of his folly?**

At a conference held on September 26, 1830, all present, including Hiram Page, "renounced the stone and its revelations." Joseph Smith described their renunciation as being "much to our mutual satisfaction and happiness." He then noted that as the conference continued, "We now partook of the Sacrament, confirmed and ordained many . . . the Holy Ghost came upon us, and filled us with joy unspeakable; and peace, and faith, and hope, and charity abounded in our midst."[177] Although Page repented of his follies, his use of the stone was not forgotten. In 1913 the First Presidency issued the following statement: "From the days of Hiram Page . . . at different periods there have been manifestations from delusive spirits to members of the Church. . . . When visions, dreams, tongues, prophecy, impressions or any extraordinary gift or inspiration, convey something out of harmony with the accepted revelations of the Church or contrary to the decisions of its constituted authorities, Latter-day Saints may know that *it is not of God*, no matter how plausible it may appear. . . . The Lord's Church 'is a house of order.'"[178]

## Section 29

**D&C 29:31–42—How does this revelation coincide with Joseph Smith's translation of the first chapters of Genesis?**

This revelation was received within days of Joseph's translation of Genesis, chapters 1–3, which tell of the Creation of the world and the Fall of Adam. Note that the doctrinal emphasis of D&C 29:31–42 parallels the doctrinal emphasis of Moses 2–4 in the Pearl of Great Price, which tell of "the spiritual and temporal aspects of the Creation as well as the cause and consequences of the Fall of Adam."[179]

**D&C 29:47—When was the "age of accountability" revealed to Joseph Smith?**

Adam-ondi-Ahman, where Adam dwelt after the Fall.

In September 1830 the Lord said, "Power is not given unto Satan to tempt little children, until they begin to become accountable before me" (D&C 29:46–47). At that time the Lord did not disclose the age when children became accountable for their actions. The age of accountability was revealed by the Lord as "eight years old" in November 1831 (see D&C 68:27). Anciently, the age of accountability was made known unto Father Abraham: "Children are not accountable before me until they are eight years old" (JST, Gen. 17:11).[180]

# Section 30

**D&C 30: Section Heading—Was section 30 three separate chapters in the Book of Commandments?**

Three chapters (30–32) of the 1833 Book of Commandments formed section 30 in the 1835 Doctrine and Covenants. The three men named in these revelations—David Whitmer, Peter Whitmer Jr., and John Whitmer—were the sons of Peter Whitmer Sr. of Fayette, New York. In the revelations, David was chastened for failing to faithfully serve in the ministry of Jesus Christ, Peter was commanded to journey with Oliver Cowdery to the borders of the Lamanites, and John was instructed to labor for the cause of Zion. Each brother was given a different yet specific assignment. To the credit of the brothers, each fulfilled his assignment.

## Section 31

### D&C 31: Section Heading—How soon after the baptism of Thomas B. Marsh was this revelation received in his behalf?

Thomas B. Marsh was baptized on September 3, 1830, in Cayuga Lake by David Whitmer. A few days later he was ordained an elder and called by revelation to preach the gospel: "Lift up your heart and rejoice, for the hour of your mission is come; and your tongue shall be loosed, and you shall declare glad tidings of great joy unto this generation" (D&C 31:3). This was the first of many missionary assignments given to Thomas (see D&C 52:22; 56:5; 75:30–31). Due to his faithfulness, other priesthood responsibilities followed. In September 1833 he was appointed president of the Big Blue Branch in Jackson County, Missouri, and in 1834 he was called to the Clay County High Council. In 1835 Thomas became president of the Quorum of the Twelve Apostles. Unfortunately, during the ensuing years his faithfulness faltered and on March 17, 1839, Thomas was excommunicated.[181] He was rebaptized in 1857.

### D&C 31:12—Did the Lord forewarn Thomas B. Marsh of the sorrow that awaited the unrepentant?

Heber C. Kimball said, "Thomas B. Marsh was once the President over the Quorum of the Twelve—over Brother Brigham, me, and others; and God saw fit to give him a revelation to forewarn him of the course he would take; and still he took that course. We told him that if he would listen to that revelation he had received, he would be saved." Thomas said of his apostasy, "I can say, in reference to the Quorum of the Twelve, to which I belonged that I did not consider myself a whit behind any of them, and I suppose that others had the same opinion; but, let no one feel too secure; for, before you think of it, your steps will slide. You will not then think nor feel for a moment as you did before you lost the Spirit of Christ; for when men apostatize, they are left to grovel in the dark." He told others who faltered, "You don't know what you are about; if you want to see the fruits of apostasy look on me."[182]

## Section 32

**D&C 32:2–3—Why was it necessary to call additional missionaries to journey with Oliver Cowdery and Peter Whitmer Jr. to the borders of the Lamanites?**

On May 28, 1830, the United States Congress passed the Indian Removal Bill, directing all Native American tribes residing in the United States to relocate west of the Missouri in the Indian Territory.[183] Large numbers of tribes complied with the Removal Bill and moved to the Midwest. Joseph Smith and his followers were very much aware of the removal of Indians to the West. In October 1830 Joseph noted that "a great desire was manifested by several of the Elders respecting the remnants of the house of Joseph, the Lamanites, residing in the west."

Portrait of an Indian chief circa 1830.

This desire stemmed from their knowledge of "the purposes of God," which were "great respecting that people." Hoping that "the time had come when the promises of the Almighty in regard to them were about to be accomplished, and that they would receive the Gospel, and enjoy its blessings," several elders wanted to preach to the tribes in the Indian Territory. Joseph said, "It was agreed that we should inquire of the Lord respecting the propriety of sending" additional missionaries with Oliver Cowdery and Peter Whitmer Jr. In answer to Joseph's inquiry, the Lord revealed that Parley P. Pratt and Ziba Peterson should accompany Oliver and Peter to the West (see D&C 32:1, 3).

## Section 33

**D&C 33:4—What specific evil corrupted the "Lord's vineyard"?**

The world of the 1830s had become corrupt "every whit" with false teachings, theories, and practices about the nature of God. The Lord revealed in this section that the prophesied corruption was complete, for apostasy or a falling away from understanding the true nature of God had penetrated the entire world. The Lord expressed an urgent need for elders to carry the message of the Restoration at this last, even the eleventh hour.[184] Elders who willingly accepted and acted upon the call to missionary service were promised the same reward or blessing given to faithful laborers of former dispensations, that of joy in the eternal realms (see Matt. 20:6).

**D&C 33:9–11—Did Ezra Thayre and Northrop Sweet accept the call to labor as missionaries?**

A bridge, dam, and mill builder in Palmyra, Ezra Thayre was baptized in October 1830 by Parley P. Pratt. A few days after Thayre's baptism, Joseph Smith received this revelation directing him to serve a mission with Northrop Sweet. Thayre accepted the directive as a revelation from God. En route from New York to Ohio he preached at several houses and baptized many into the Church. Although he is remembered for fulfilling other similar assignments, Thayre left the Church.[185] As for Sweet, he journeyed with Thayre from New York and Ohio, preaching along the route. However, like Thayre, his faithfulness waned. By 1831 Sweet had left the Church and played a key role in the formation of a religious society called "The Pure Church of Christ."[186]

## Section 34

**Section 34: Section Heading—Did Orson Pratt comment on the revelation that Joseph Smith received in his behalf?**

Section 34 was received at the behest of Orson Pratt, who was

Orson Pratt.

nineteen years old at the time. Pratt contended that the promises bestowed upon him in this revelation were "almost too great for a person of as humble origin as myself ever to attain to. After telling in the revelation that the great day of the Lord was at hand, and calling upon me to lift up my voice among the people, to call upon them to repent and prepare the way of the Lord, and that the time was near when the heavens should be shaken, when the earth should tremble, when the stars should refuse their shining, and when great destructions awaited the wicked, the Lord said to your humble servant—'Lift up your voice and prophesy, and it shall be given by the power of the Holy Ghost.' This was a particular point in the revelation that seemed to me too great for me ever to attain to, and yet there was a positive command that I should do it. I have often reflected upon this revelation, and have oftentimes inquired in my heart—'Have I fulfilled the commandment as I ought to have done? Have I sought as earnestly as I ought to obtain the gift of prophecy, so as to fulfill the requirement of heaven?' And I have felt sometimes to condemn myself because of my slothfulness, and because of the little progress that I have made in relation to this great, heavenly, and divine gift."[187]

# Section 35

**D&C 35: Section Heading—Who was the first to scribe Joseph Smith's revisions of the Bible?**

The first scribe for the Joseph Smith translation of the Bible was John Whitmer. When Whitmer accepted a missionary call to preach the gospel of Jesus Christ in Ohio, Joseph turned to Sidney Rigdon for a scribe. In December 1830 Rigdon scribed the words of Enoch, which now comprise

Moses 7 of the Pearl of Great Price.[188]

**D&C 35:13–14—The Lord promised the "weak things of the world" that they would "thrash the nations by the power of my Spirit" and that He would be their "shield and their buckler." What is a buckler?**

"To thrash" means to "tread out the grain on a threshing floor" (Hab. 3:12). "To thrash the nations" is a symbolic expression revealing that those who preach the gospel will trample wheat sheaves (or the nations of the world) to straw. As they do so, these preachers are armed with a shield and a buckler, which is a small round shield worn on the arm for added defense or protection to ensure victory. Their defense is the unwavering promise that God will protect His laborers during the great harvest (see Ps. 18:2; Prov. 2:7).

## Section 36

**D&C 36: Section Heading—How soon after the baptism of Edward Partridge did Joseph Smith receive this revelation in his behalf?**

In the winter of 1830 Edward Partridge journeyed with

Modern-day threshing floor.

Sidney Rigdon from Ohio to New York to meet Joseph Smith. After meeting the Prophet and listening to him speak of the Restoration, Partridge desired baptism, "if Brother Joseph will baptize me."[189] He was baptized by Joseph the next day, December 11, 1830. Shortly after his baptism, Partridge asked the Prophet to seek the Lord's will concerning him. The answer received was, "You are blessed, and your sins are forgiven you, and you are called to preach my gospel as with the voice of a trump" (D&C 36:1). A *trump* symbolizes "heralding or announcing something highly significant," such as sounding an alarm or signaling a battle. To Partridge the "voice of a trump" meant that he was to preach the gospel of Jesus Christ with a loud and clear voice, even with boldness.[190]

### D&C 36:6—What is meant by "this untoward generation" and "garments spotted with flesh"?

The Greek word *skolia* translates as "untoward" and means "crooked" or "perverse." An untoward generation carelessly or willfully casts aside the word of God. "Garments spotted with flesh" symbolically represents garments defiled by carnal desires and disobedience to the Lord's commands.

## Section 37

### D&C 37:3—What sacrifices were made by the New York Saints to accept the call to gather to Ohio?

In December 1830, eight months after the organization of the Church, Joseph Smith received this revelation calling upon Church members in New York to assemble in the state of Ohio to welcome Oliver Cowdery as he returned from a mission to the Lamanites. With some reluctance the Whitmers, Knights, and others left their homes in the state of New York to obey the divine directive. Peter Whitmer Sr. sold his Fayette acreage and farmhouse for $2,200 before leaving. Others also sold properties, but not at such a favorable return. "As might be expected, we were obliged to make great sacrifices of our property," penned Newel Knight.[191] But to some the words of Phoebe Carter were representative of their real sacrifice: "When the time came for my departure

I dared not trust myself to say farewell; so I wrote my good-byes to each, and leaving them on my table, ran downstairs and jumped into the carriage. Thus I left the beloved home of my childhood to link my life with the saints of God."[192] The New York Saints began arriving in Ohio as early as February 1831. As for Oliver Cowdery, he did not join them until late August 1831, about eight months after this revelation was received by Joseph Smith.

### D&C 37:3—What was the Lord's purpose in gathering the Saints to one locale?

According to Joseph Smith, one purpose of gathering the elect from among the unrepentant is to "build unto the Lord a house whereby He could reveal unto His people the ordinances of His house and the glories of His kingdom, and teach the people the way of salvation."[193] Another reason for gathering is to prepare the elect for the Second Coming of the Savior for "the signs of the coming of the Son of Man are already commenced. One pestilence will desolate after another. We shall soon have war and bloodshed. The moon will be turned into blood. I testify of these things, and that the coming of the Son of Man is nigh, even at your doors."[194]

### D&C 37:3—What did Joseph Smith say about the doctrine of gathering?

Of this doctrine Joseph Smith wrote, "All that the prophets have written, from the days of righteous Abel, down to the last man that has left any testimony on record for our consideration, in speaking of the salvation of Israel in the last days, goes directly to show that it consists in the work of gathering"[195] (see Deut. 30:1–4; Rev. 21:3; 3 Ne. 20:22; Ether 13:1–12).

### D&C 37:3—How did the New York Saints react to the doctrine of gathering?

Although the January 2, 1831, entry in the *Journal History of the Church* reads, "The Saints manifested unshaken confidence in the great work [in] which they were engaged, and all rejoiced under the blessings of the gospel," the doctrine of gathering led to divisions among the early Saints.[196] Some accepted the doctrine as the word

Modern-day Kirtland, restored to reflect what it might have looked like during the time of Joseph Smith.

of God while others refused to acknowledge the heavenly directive.

## Section 38

**D&C 38: Section Heading—How many people witnessed Joseph Smith receiving this revelation from God?**

On January 2, 1831, the third conference of the Church was held at the Peter Whitmer Sr. home in Fayette. Joseph Smith said of this conference, "The year 1831 opened with a prospect great and glorious for the welfare of the kingdom; for on the 2nd of January, 1831, a conference was held in the town of Fayette, New York, at which the ordinary business of the Church was transacted; and in addition, the following revelation was received" (D&C 38; *HC,* 1:140). Although minutes of the conference are missing, making it impossible to estimate the number in attendance, John Whitmer wrote of Joseph receiving this revelation: "The Seer enquired of the Lord in the presence of the whole congregation, and thus came the word of the Lord." This was the first recorded revelation in 1831, a year in which more recorded revelations were received than in previous or following years (see D&C 1, 38–72, 133; John Whitmer, *Book of John Whitmer*, Salt Lake City: Deseret Book, 1838, chapter 1).

**D&C 38:1—What are "seraphic hosts of heaven"?**

*Seraph*, a Hebrew verb meaning "to burn," is associated with angels who dwell near the presence of God. Seraphic hosts include "pre-earth spirits of some men and women who would dwell on earth" (D&C 109:79). Isaiah saw seraphim in his vision of God (see Isa. 6:2–7; 2 Ne. 16:2–7).[197]

**D&C 38:4—What is the meaning of the City of Holiness being taken to the "bosom of the Lord"?**

City of Holiness.

The City of Holiness flourished for 365 years or until the Lord "took it with all its inhabitants, 'to His bosom'" (Moses 7:18, 19, 68–69). The phrase "in the bosom" is a Hebrew idiom derived from the imagery of carrying lambs or children close to the bosom while wearing a long flowing robe fastened with a sash about the waist. "To be in the bosom of another" implies "an extremely close and favored relationship" (see 2 Sam. 12:8; Luke 16:22; John 1:18).[198]

**D&C 38:26—Which of the Gospel writers recorded the parable of the twelve sons?**

Although the Gospel writer Matthew recorded fourteen parables, Mark five, and Luke twenty, the parable of the twelve sons is recorded only in the Doctrine and Covenants. In this parable the Lord reveals His displeasure with those who fail to address the economic disparity among the children of God. The tenor of this parable is in keeping with the thirty-nine parables attributed to Jesus in the New Testament in that it contradicts the accepted norms of society. In the other parables of Jesus, "bad servants are rewarded, and good servants seem to be punished. His heroes are sometimes unsavory characters—an unjust judge, neighbors who do not want to be neighborly, a man who pockets someone else's treasure by purchasing his fields, a steward who cheats his master, a sinful woman, and other socially unacceptable characters."[199]

**D&C 38:32—When was the law of the Lord revealed to Joseph Smith and how does obedience to that law lead to "power from on high"?**

The law of the Lord was revealed to Joseph Smith on February 9, 1831, about eight days after he arrived in Kirtland, Ohio (see D&C 42). The promise given to those who obey the law is to be "endowed with power from on high" (D&C 38:32). The Greek word for endow is *enduo*, meaning "to be clothed." Therefore, to be endowed means to be clothed with power or priesthood from on high.

## Section 39

**D&C 39: Section Heading—What are the historic events surrounding the visit of James Covill to Joseph Smith?**

Little is known of James Covill or his visit with the Prophet Joseph. Some scholars question whether Covill was a Baptist or a Methodist preacher. A James Covill, a preacher on the Litchfield, Connecticut, circuit, appears on the Methodist records as early as 1791.[200] All that is known is that Joseph Smith received a revelation directed to Covill on January 5, 1831, three days after the third conference of the Church held at Fayette. Although it is recorded that Covill received the word of the Lord with "gladness," there is no record of his baptism (D&C 40:2).[201] It appears that Covill "rejected the word of the Lord, and returned to his former principles and people" (D&C 40: Section Heading). The Lord said of Covill, "He broke my covenant, and it remaineth with me to do with him as seemeth me good" (D&C 40:3).

## Section 40

**D&C 40:1–3—Although little is known of James Covill, why has he received so much comment by latter-day prophets?**

When Church leaders speak of James Covill, their remarks are always associated with his rejection of the word of God. Of the many Church leaders who have spoken of Covill, perhaps Joseph Fielding Smith described his failings best: "We are led to believe that in this promised blessing, this foolish man was convinced of the truth, for it is clear that the Lord revealed to him things which he and the Lord alone knew to be the truth. However, when he withdrew from the influence of the Spirit of the Lord and had time to consider the fact that he would lose the fellowship of the world, and his place and position among his associates, he failed and rejected the promises and blessings which the Lord offered him."[202]

## Section 41

**D&C 41: Section Heading—What were the "strange notions" and "false spirits" associated with early Church members in Kirtland?**

After arriving in Kirtland, Joseph Smith found the faithful members "striving to do the will of God, so far as they knew it, though some strange notions and false spirits had crept in among them."[203] One strange notion was the concept of "the family" that held "all things common" and had organized a "common stock" (Acts 4:32). John Whitmer viewed the family system "going to destruction very fast as to temporal things; for they considered from reading the scripture that what belonged to a brother, belonged to any of the brethren. Therefore they would take each other's clothes and other property and use it without leave which, brought on confusion and disappointments, for they did not understand the scripture."[204]

Numbered among the "false spirits" present in Kirtland was Black Pete, an African-American who claimed to see angels and receive letters directly from heaven. There was also Wycam Clark, who formed a schism group called the Pure Church of Christ. It was only through teaching correct principles and doctrines that Joseph was able to convince those led astray by strange notions and false spirits to abandon their preconceived notions and accept the "more perfect law of the Lord."[205]

# Section 42

## D&C 42: Section Heading—Why is section 42 viewed as two revelations instead of one?

Verses 1–73 of section 42 comprise a revelation given to the Prophet Joseph Smith on February 4, 1831. Verses 74–93 are a revelation received by Joseph two weeks later on February 23. This latter revelation was "given for the establishment of the City of Zion—New Jerusalem—which was to be built by the law of consecration and obedience to the fulness of the Gospel."[206] These two revelations were printed in the Book of Commandments as two distinct chapters: verses 1–73 comprised chapter 44, and verses 74–93 comprised chapter 47.

## D&C 42:2, 11–12, 18—What is the "law of the Lord"?

The Lord God gave the law of the Lord so that His people could become "a righteous people, without spot and blameless" (D&C 38:31) and "be endowed with power from on high" (D&C 38:32). The law of the Lord is a description of the proper way to teach and act in personal and moral situations. The proper way to teach "requires that any teacher in the Church be 'ordained by some one who has authority, and it is known to the church that he has authority'" (D&C 42:11). Teachers are to instruct others in the principles of the fulness of the gospel "by the power and influence of the Holy Ghost" (D&C 42:12).[207] President Spencer W. Kimball spoke of the solemn obligation resting on gospel teachers: "If one cannot accept and teach the program of the Church in an orthodox way without reservations, *he should not teach*. It would be the part of honor to resign his position. Not only would he be dishonest and deceitful, but he is also actually under condemnation, for the Savior said that it were better that a millstone were hanged about his neck and he be cast into the sea than that he should lead astray doctrinally or betray the cause or give offense, destroying the faith of one of 'these little ones' who believe in him."[208]

The proper way to act in personal and moral situations mirrors the Ten Commandments given to Moses, such as "Thou shalt not kill; and he that kills shall not have forgiveness in this world, nor in the world to come" (D&C 42:18). This suggests a moral standard of equality under which "all are under equal obligation to obey, and have an equal chance of obtaining the reward of obedience."[209]

### D&C 42:30–42—What is the purpose of the law of consecration?

There are many purposes of the law of consecration. They include caring for the poor and needy (see D&C 42:30), purchasing lands, building houses of worship, and creating New Jerusalem (see D&C 42:35). Other purposes are helping the Latter-day Saints overcome pride (see D&C 42:40) by becoming industrious and avoiding idleness (see D&C 42:42) and becoming one (see D&C 51:9), which means to be equal in all earthly matters (see D&C 78:3). The blessings of living the law of consecration are that the Church will "stand independent above all other creatures" (D&C 78:14) and all things will be done "with an eye single to the glory of God" (D&C 82:17–19). It should be noted that the law of consecration is not the same as the united order.

### D&C 42:46—What is the meaning of the phrase "taste of death"?

The phrase "taste of death" is also found in the Book of Mormon (see 3 Ne. 28:7, 25, 37, 38; Ether 12:17) and the New Testament (see Mark 9:1; John 8:52). Among the promises given to the righteous is that they will not taste of death, suggesting they will not experience spiritual suffering, for their death will be sweet.[210]

### D&C 42:88–92—Is it always necessary to confess "your sin" to the one or ones offended?

Elder Marion G. Romney taught, "I would assume that we are to confess all our sins unto the Lord. For transgressions which are wholly personal, affecting none but ourselves and the Lord, such confession would seem to be sufficient. For misconduct which offends another, confession should also be made to the offended one, and his forgiveness sought."[211]

By teaching correct principles Joseph was able to lead the Saints against "strange notions" and "false spirits."

# Section 43

**D&C 43: Section Heading—What impact did the false claims of Mrs. Hubble have on Church members in Kirtland?**

Mrs. Hubble claimed "to be a prophetess of the Lord, and professed" to make "great pretensions of revealing commandments, laws and other curious matters." Hubble backed her pretensions by testifying that she "knew the Book of Mormon was true, and that she should become a teacher in the church of Christ. She appeared to be very sanctimonious and deceived some who were not able to detect her in her hypoccracy [*sic*]: others however had the spirit of discernment, and her follies and abominations were made manifest." Following this manifestation and a revelation given to Joseph Smith, the Saints came to an "understanding on this subject, and unity and harmony prevailed throughout the church of God."[212] From this time forth, the Saints learned wisdom and how to treasure the truths that came from God.

# Section 44

### D&C 44: Section Heading—Why were missionaries called from their various fields of labor to attend a June 1831 conference in Kirtland?

In early June 1831, missionaries began arriving in Kirtland in response to letters directing them to attend a general conference (see D&C 44:1; 20:61). The reason given for their attendance was not stated in the letters. However, John Corrill claimed the purpose was to bless the elders with an endowment. At the conference, the purpose was soon manifested, for "the Lord displayed His power to the most perfect satisfaction of the Saints. The man of sin was revealed, and the authority of the Melchizedek Priesthood was manifested and conferred for the first time upon several of the Elders." One elder wrote, "It was clearly evident that the Lord gave us power in proportion to the work to be done, and strength according to the race set before us, and grace and help as our needs required. Great harmony prevailed; several were ordained; faith was strengthened; and humility, so necessary for the blessing of God to follow prayer, characterized the Saints."[213]

# Section 45

### D&C 45:16–23—What is the best way to prepare for the Second Coming of Jesus Christ?

The scriptures teach that the Lord will come as a "thief in the night" (see D&C 45:19; Matt. 24:43–44), suggesting many will not be prepared for His coming. According to the apostle Paul, those who are prepared watch for the signs of the times (see 1 Thess. 4:16–18; 5:1–4). "How do you prepare for the Second Coming?" President Gordon B. Hinckley was asked. His answer was, "You just do not worry about it. You just live the kind of life that if the Second Coming were to be tomorrow you would be ready. Nobody knows when it was going to happen. . . . Our responsibility is to prepare ourselves, to live worthy of the association of the Savior, to deport ourselves in such a way that we would not be embarrassed if He were to come among us. That is a challenge in this day and age."[214]

Great calamities will increase in the last days.

**D&C 45:26–27—What are the signs of the times that will occur in the latter days?**

Section 45 is filled with information about signs that will occur in the last days. Although it is suggested that this section parallels Matthew 24, there is greater information about the signs of the times in section 45 than in the Gospel of Matthew. For example, section 45 reveals that New Jerusalem will be a place of peace and safety for the righteous in the last days (see D&C 45:66–67); there will be wars and rumors of wars to such an extent that the entire earth will be in commotion (see D&C 45:26); the love of men will wax cold and iniquity will abound (see D&C 45:27); there will be earthquakes and great waves upon the seas and men will harden their hearts against the Lord God and fight each other (see D&C 45:33); there will be famines, scourges, sickness, and desolation (see D&C 45:31); and there will be many signs and wonders in the heavens and on the earth (see D&C 45:40–42).

**D&C 45:60–61—When did Joseph Smith's translation of the Old Testament end and his revisions of the New Testament begin?**

On March 7, 1831, Joseph Smith received a revelation directing him to begin translating the New Testament (see D&C 45:60–62). His work on the New Testament began the next day, March 8, with Matthew 1. At that time, his translation of the Old Testament had progressed through Genesis 19:35. During the month of March 1831, Joseph worked on Matthew and Genesis concurrently. In early April, his translation of the Old Testament ended for a brief time. As to his completing the New Testament translation, Joseph wrote, "I completed the translation and review of the New Testament, on the 2nd of February, 1833, and sealed it up" (*HC*, 1:324). He then turned his attention once again to the Old Testament.

**D&C 45:60–61—How many verses did Joseph Smith revise or change in the Old and New Testaments?**

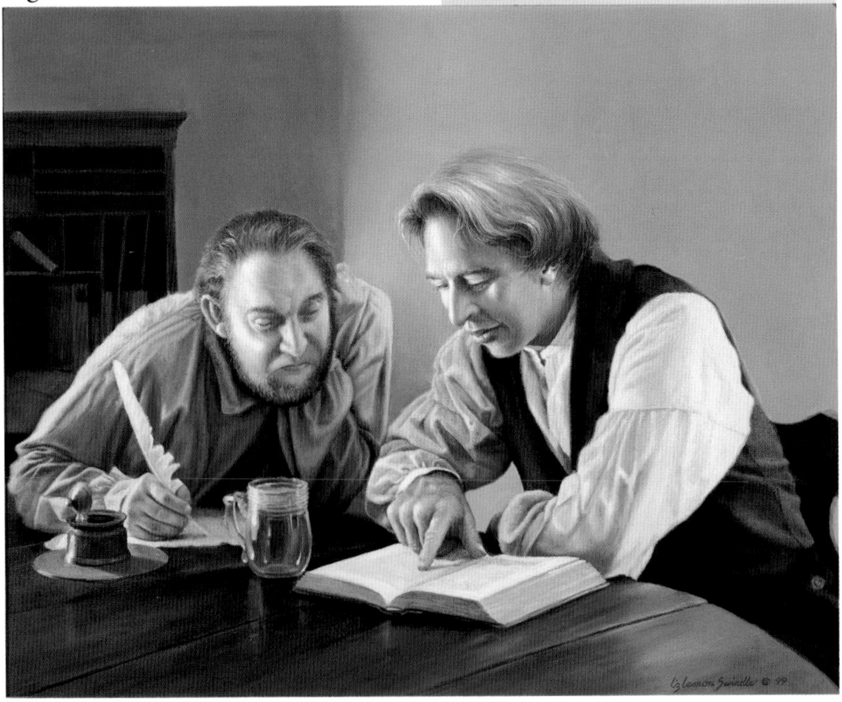

Joseph translating the Bible.

When Joseph Smith's revisions of the Old and New Testament are brought together, the statistical results of his inspired changes are as follows: "A total of 3,410 verses in the printed Joseph Smith Translation differ in textual construction from the King James Bible. Of this number 25 verses compose the visions of Moses (Moses 1), 1,289 changes are in the Old Testament, and 2,096 in the New Testament."[215]

# Section 46

**D&C 46:13–26—What are the gifts of the Spirit bestowed by God to the righteous?**

In section 46, twelve gifts of the Spirit are named. The first is the gift to know "by the Holy Ghost . . . that Jesus Christ is the Son of God, and that he was crucified for the sins of the world" (D&C 46:13). The second gift is to believe in the testimony of others that Jesus is the Savior (see D&C 46:14). The third and fourth gifts are to know "the differences of administration" (D&C 46:15) and to discern the "diversities of operations, whether they be of God" (D&C 46:16). The remaining gifts are wisdom and knowledge (see D&C 46:17–18), faith to be healed (see D&C 46:19), faith to heal (see D&C 46:20), and power to work miracles in the name of Jesus (see D&C 46:21). There are also the gifts to prophesy (see D&C 46:22), discern spirits (see D&C 46:23), speak in tongues (see D&C 46:24), and interpret tongues (see D&C 46:25).

**D&C 46:16—What is the penalty for failing to recognize the manifestations of the Spirit?**

"Nothing is a greater injury to the children of men than to be under the influence of a false spirit when they think they have the Spirit of God," said Joseph Smith. "Thousands have felt the influence of its terrible power and baneful effects. Long pilgrimages have been undertaken, penances endured, and pain, misery and ruin have followed in their train; nations have been convulsed, kingdoms overthrown, provinces laid waste, and blood, carnage and desolation are [habiliments] in which it has been clothed."[216]

# Section 47

**D&C 47:1—Where are the writings of John Whitmer about the history of the Church?**

Although John Whitmer said that he would "rather not keep the Church history, but observed—'The will of the Lord be done, and if He desires it, I wish that He would manifest it through Joseph the Seer,'"[217] he served as Church historian from 1831 through 1835. Unfortunately, the historical record kept by John proved "a mere sketch of the things that transpired." His work "consisted of eighty-five pages," including previously written revelations. Whitmer was excommunicated on March 10, 1838. Although presiding brethren at that time "demanded that he deliver the history of the Church to them he refused."[218] A copy of his history was acquired by the Church in 1893 and is now housed in the archives of the Church History Library.

# Section 48

**D&C 48: Section Heading—Why was procuring land in the greater Kirtland area on which the New York Saints could settle so important to the Saints already residing in Kirtland?**

The Lord commanded the New York Saints to gather to Ohio (see D&C 37:3; 38:32; 39:15). In response to the command, they made plans to gather to Kirtland, Ohio, to unite with other early Saints. Anticipating that dozens of families would soon be moving to Kirtland, long-term residents of the agrarian community were concerned about housing the newcomers. This revelation was given in answer to their concerns.

# Section 49

**D&C 49: Section Heading—What is the origin of the Shakers?**

The Shaker movement was begun by James and Jane Wardley and others and carried to

A Shaker community circa 1930s.

fruition by Ann Lee. At age twenty-two Lee attended a series of revival meetings conducted by James and Jane Wardley. She united with the Wardleys' "Shaking Quakers," a name first used to ridicule the group's mode of religious worship. Followers of the Wardleys believed that chanting, dancing, shaking, clapping, and whirling caused sin to fall from believers. They professed that Christ was coming to reign on earth and that His second appearance would be in the form of a woman. Sharing in that belief, Lee confessed her sins and joined in the frenzy of the dance.

After her conversion to Shakerism, Lee married in 1762 and subsequently gave birth to four children, three of whom died as infants. The loss of these children caused her much grief and led to her conviction that sexual relations and marriage was the root of all evil. Public denunciation of Lee's teachings led English authorities to imprison her, but this did not thwart her stance. By 1777 she was the recognized leader of Shakerism in England.[219]

### D&C 49: Section Heading—Did Ann Lee claim to be Jesus Christ?

Ann Lee claimed to see a vision of Adam and Eve. Biographer Nardi Reeder Campion wrote, "She watched them defy God and commit the forbidden sexual act. Then she witnessed their expulsion from the garden by an enraged Deity. All at once it became crystal clear to Ann Lee there was one single cause of humanity's separation from God: *sex*." Lee "took up her cross against the carnal gratifications of the flesh" and pronounced herself the long-awaited "female Christ." Lee purported that she was Christ's anointed successor on earth and chosen to carry His truth to the world. She became known by her followers as Ann the Word or, more affectionately, Mother Ann. She declared, "I feel the blood of Christ running through my soul and body!"[220] Lee died in September 1784 in Watervliet, New York, at age forty-eight.

### D&C 49: Section Heading—Which of the teachings of Ann Lee were still accepted by her followers in the 1830s?

The societies established by Ann Lee continued long after her demise. One such society, a virtual stronghold of Shakerism, was established in North Union, Ohio, a few miles southwest of Kirtland. This society believed in Lee's teachings that no meat should be consumed, "confession alone was necessary for forgiveness . . . and celibacy was a higher law than marriage."[221]

### D&C 49: Section Heading—Who asked Joseph Smith to inquire of the Lord concerning the doctrines of the Shakers?

Leman Copley asked Joseph Smith to inquire of the Lord concerning Shakerism. Copley, a former Shaker, "embraced the fulness of the everlasting Gospel, apparently honest-hearted, but still retain[ed] the idea that the Shakers were right in some particulars of their faith." "In order to have more perfect understanding of the subject," Joseph wrote, "I inquired of the Lord." The revelation he received called for three missionaries to labor among the Shakers—Sidney Rigdon, Parley P. Pratt, and Leman Copley. Copley wanted missionaries sent to the Shakers in North Union, but "feared to be ordained to preach

North Union closed in 1889; within thirteen years the area had been recreated as the secular city of Shaker Heights.

himself, and desired that the Lord direct in this and all matters."[222] It was only after Joseph received this revelation that Copley was willing to accompany Sidney Rigdon to North Union. They arrived in the Shaker stronghold on Saturday evening, May 7, 1831.

**D&C 49:2–3—What was the reaction of the North Union Shaker community to the message of the missionaries?**

Ashbel Kitchell, leader of the Shaker community in North Union, recorded the arrival of Rigdon and Copley in North Union: "We continued on friendly terms in the way of trade and other acts of good neighborship untill [*sic*] the spring of 1831 when we were visited on saturday [*sic*] evening by Sidney Rigdon and Leman Copley, the latter of whom had been among us; but not likeing [*sic*] the cross [the Shaker practice of celibacy] any to [*sic*] well, had taken up with Mormonism as the easier plan and had been appointed by them as one of the missionaries to convert us. They tarried all night, and in the course of the evening, the doctrines of the cross and the Mormon faith were both investigated; and we found that the life of self-denial [*sic*] corresponded better with the life of Christ, than Mormonism. . . . Thus the matter stood and we retired to rest, not knowing that they had then in possession what they called a revelation or message from Jesus Christ to us, which they intended to deliver to day [*sic*] (sabbath.) [*sic*] and which they supposed would bring us to terms."[223]

Before their message was delivered, Parley P. Pratt had joined Sidney Rigdon and Leman Copley at North Union. Kitchell then went on to report, "[Sidney Rigdon] stated that he had a message from the Lord Jesus Christ to this people; could he have the privilege of delivering it? He was answered, he could. He then said it was in writing; could he read it? He was told he might." He then read the text of section 49. The Shakers rejected the revelation as being from God.[224] Witnessing their rejection, "Parley Pratt arose and commenced shakeing [sic] his coattail." Kitchell reported, "He said he shook the dust from his garments as a testimony against us, that we had rejected the word of the Lord Jesus." Kitchell then arose and called Pratt a "filthy Beast" and severely rebuked him.[225]

# 4

# Sections 50–74



## Section 50

**D&C 50: Section Heading—Who told Joseph Smith of the false and lying spirits that manifested themselves in Church meetings in Ohio?**

Parley P. Pratt, John Murdock, and other elders reported to Joseph of spiritual aberrations being present in Church meetings. Pratt explained why they wanted to inform the Prophet of this matter: "Feeling our weakness and inexperience, and lest we should err in judgment concerning these spiritual phenomena, myself, John Murdock, and several other Elders, went to Joseph Smith, and asked him to inquire of the Lord concerning these spirits or manifestations. After we had joined in prayer in his translating room, [Joseph] dictated in our presence the following revelation:—(each sentence was uttered slowly and very distinctly and with a pause between each, sufficiently long for it to be recorded, by an ordinary writer, in long hand.) This was the manner in which all his written revelations were dictated and written. There was never any hesitation, reviewing, or reading back to keep the run of the subject" (D&C 50).[226]

**D&C 50:1–4—What were the "excessive spiritual aberrations"?**

Church historian John Whitmer wrote of "excessive spiritual aberrations" prevailing among early converts in Kirtland: "Some had visions and could not tell what they saw. Some would fancy to themselves that they had the sword of Laban, and would wield it as expert as a light dragon; some would act like an Indian in the act of scalping; some would slide or scoot on the floor with the rapidity of a serpent, which they termed sailing in the boat to the Lamanites, preaching the gospel."[227] Parley P. Pratt described these manifestations as "disgusting, rather than edifying. Some persons would seem to swoon away, and make unseemly gestures, and be drawn or disfigured in their countenances. Others would fall into ecstacies [*sic*], and be drawn into contortions, cramps, fits, etc. Others would seem to have visions and revelations, which were not edifying, and which were not congenial to the doctrine and spirit of the gospel."[228]

**D&C 50:44—The main theme of this revelation is pastoral—sheep, shepherds, flocks, lambs, and so on. Is pastoral imagery a repetitive theme in the Doctrine and Covenants?**

Although "shepherds abiding in their fields" describes the pastoral economy of ancient Israelites, it has few parallels to the nineteenth-century America in

Shepherd in the Făgăraş Mountains of Romania.

which Joseph and the early Saints lived. Yet the pastoral symbolism is found in several revelations contained in the Doctrine and Covenants: "I am the good shepherd" (D&C 50:44), "the Lamb, who was slain" (D&C 76:39; 135:4), "feed my sheep" (D&C 112:14) and "take care of your flocks" (D&C 88:72). Further references are to "the Lamb's Book of Life" (D&C 132:19), "the marriage of the Lamb" (D&C 58:11), "the supper of the Lamb" (D&C 65:3), and "the song of the Lamb" (D&C 133:56). This suggests a biblical influence on modern-day scriptures and shows that pastoral imagery is timeless.

## Section 51

**D&C 51:1—Why did Bishop Edward Partridge need divine guidance to distribute land in the greater Kirtland area among the New York Saints?**

When the New York Saints began arriving in Kirtland, their first and surely their most immediate need was temporal. To meet the needs of the New York Saints, the Saints in Ohio were asked to divide their land with

Bishop Edward Partridge.

their "eastern brethren" (D&C 48:2). Bishop Edward Partridge was assigned to distribute the proffered land among the New York Saints (see D&C 48:2–5). Worried about his ability to fulfill this task to the satisfaction of all concerned, Partridge sought direction from the Lord through the Prophet Joseph. Some of those who witnessed Joseph dictate this revelation recorded that his "countenance shone."[229]

## Section 52

**D&C 52:2, 42—What are "lands of inheritance"?**

Lands of inheritance were located in Jackson County, Missouri, and were given to specific Latter-day Saints as part of the united firm, or united order, for this life and the next.[230]

**D&C 52:37—In this revelation several elders were called and appointed to share news of the Restoration of the gospel of Jesus Christ. The exception was Heman Basset. Who was Basset?**

In 1830 sixteen-year-old Heman Basset was residing with a hundred individuals known collectively as the "family," who shared all things equally on the Isaac Morley farm in Kirtland. In October 1830 he, along with many of the "family," was baptized. When missionaries left the greater Kirtland area, false spirits were detected among the new converts and "many strange visions were seen."[231] Levi Hancock observed Heman Basset "behav[ing] like a baboon. He said he had a revelation he had received in Kirtland from the hand of an angel, he would read it and show pictures of a course of angels declared to be Gods, then would testify of the truth of the work and I believed it all, like a fool."[232] Despite his shortcomings Basset was ordained an elder in spring of 1831. During the June 1831 conference, Joseph said to him, "Heamon basset you sit still the Devil wants to sift you." [233] Basset did not heed the warning. By revelation the Lord told Joseph, "in consequence of transgression, let that which was bestowed" upon Basset be taken from him (D&C 52:37).

# Section 53

**D&C 53: Section Heading—What had Sidney Gilbert done to prepare himself to be an agent for the Church?**

By 1817 Algernon Sidney Gilbert was a storeowner in Painesville, Ohio. From 1820 to 1827 he was an entrepreneur, buying and selling properties in Ohio and Michigan, with commercial interests in trading centers near Lake Ontario and the Erie Canal. By 1827 Gilbert and Newel K. Whitney had entered a mercantile partnership and opened a small store in Kirtland under the name of N. K. Whitney and Company. It was while engaged in this business enterprise that both men were converted to Mormonism in 1830. Gilbert lived only four years after his baptism. During these years the Lord recognized his talents, his unique financial background, and the contribution he would make to the Church as an agent: "I have heard your prayers. . . . Take upon you mine ordination, even that of an elder . . . and also to be an agent unto this church . . . Take your journey with my servants" (D&C 53:1, 3–5).[234]

# Section 54

**D&C 54: Section Heading—What were the difficult circumstances in Thompson, Ohio, that led to this revelation?**

"At this time," John Whitmer recorded, "the Church at Thompson Ohio was involved in difficulty, because of the rebellion of Leman Copley. Who would not do as he had previously agreed. Which thing confused the whole church."[235] At issue was a contractual agreement between the New York Saints and Leman Copley, a landowner in Thompson, Ohio.

Cemetery located on the old Leman Copley farm.

Copley had entered a contractual agreement that permitted the New York Saints to settle on his property. Initially, settling on Copley's land went as planned. But "in a short time Copley broke the engagement."[236] Adding to the difficulty, Copley became disgruntled with Mormonism and insisted that the New York Saints leave his property.

**D&C 54:10—What is the meaning of "They who have sought me early shall find rest to their souls"?**

According to Joseph F. Smith, the proper interpretation of this phrase is to enter into "the knowledge and love of God, having faith in His purpose, and in his plan to such an extent that we know we are right, and that we are not hunting for something else, we are not disturbed by every wind of doctrine or by the cunning and craftiness of men who lay in wait to deceive."[237]

## Section 55

**D&C 55: Section Heading—What led to the conversion of William W. Phelps?**

On April 9, 1830, William W. Phelps purchased a Book of Mormon from Parley P. Pratt and "sat up all night to compare the Book of Mormon with the Bible." He then exclaimed, "I am going to join that church; I am convinced that it is true."[238] In a letter to Oliver Cowdery, Phelps wrote, "From the first time I read this volume of volumes, even till now, I have been struck with a kind of sacred joy at its title page. . . . What a wonderful volume!"[239] On May 11, 1831, the *Ontario Phoenix*, one of three newspapers Phelps edited, announced his removal from New York. Phelps moved to Kirtland to offer his time and talents to the Church. Of his arrival in town, Joseph Smith wrote, "William W. Phelps and his family arrived among us—'to do the will of the Lord,' he said: so I inquired of the Lord concerning him and received" a revelation.[240] In the revelation, Phelps was told, "Thou art called and chosen; and after thou hast been baptized by water . . . then thou shalt be ordained by the hand of my servant Joseph Smith, Jun., to be an elder unto this church. . . . And on whomsoever you shall lay your hands, if they are contrite before me, you shall have power to give the Holy Spirit" (D&C 55:1–3). He was baptized on June 10, 1831, and ordained an elder by Joseph Smith.

## Section 56

**D&C 56:5—Why did Ezra Thayre fail to serve the appointed mission with Thomas B. Marsh?**

Although Ezra Thayre had served a mission with Northrop Sweet in 1831, he did not accept the missionary call extended to him on June 7, 1831, to be the missionary companion of Thomas B. Marsh (see D&C 33:1–2). Marsh was correct in assuming that Thayre "could not get ready to start on his mission as soon as he [Marsh] would." The failure of Thayre to put his personal affairs in order stems from his role in the controversy between Leman Copley and the New York Saints. Other than his involvement in the Copley affair, Thayre's transgressions are difficult to document. Thayre repented of his transgression and on January 25, 1832, was called to serve a mission with Marsh. This time, he faithfully fulfilled the mission assignment (see D&C 75:31).[241]

## Section 57

**D&C 57: Section Heading—When did Joseph Smith learn that the land of Zion was near the "line running directly between Jew and Gentile"?**

"When will Zion be built up in her glory, and where will Thy temple stand, unto which all nations shall come in the last days?" Joseph Smith asked of God, just as ancient prophets had done in an earlier age (see Isa. 2:2–3; 35:1; Ps. 87:1–3).[242] Joseph recorded the divine answer: "I received, by a heavenly vision, a commandment in June [1831] following, to take my journey to the western boundaries of the State of Missouri, and there designate the very spot which was to be the central place for the commencement of the gathering together of those who embrace the fullness of the everlasting Gospel." In Jackson County, Missouri, in June 1831, Joseph said, "[The Lord] manifested Himself unto us, and designated, to me and others, the very spot upon which He designed to commence the work of the gathering, and the upbuilding of an 'holy city,' which should be called Zion."[243]

### D&C 57: Section Heading—Who identified Independence, Missouri, as the ancient site of the Garden of Eden?

On May 19, 1838, Joseph Smith identified Spring Hill, Missouri, as Adam-ondi-Ahman, or the valley where Adam dwelt. On March 30, 1873, Brigham Young said that Joseph taught him "the Garden of Eden was in Jackson County, Missouri." Previous to this remark, Brigham Young identified "the American continent" as the land of the Garden of Eden.[244] Joseph Fielding Smith, wrote, "The Garden of Eden was on the American continent located where the City Zion, or the New Jerusalem, will be built."[245]

### D&C 57:3—What immediate events followed Joseph Smith's designating the "very spot" for the city of Zion?

"Being no longer at a loss to know where the exact spot for the building of the temple and the city of Zion was," Newel Knight wrote, "we immediately prepared for our labors [which included laying] the first log as a foundation for Zion in Kaw township [now in Kansas City], twelve miles west of Independence. The log was carried by twelve men, in honor of the twelve tribes of Israel." To Newel, "This was truly a season of joy and rejoicing to all the Saints, who took part in, or witnessed the proceedings."[246]

Independence, Missouri, circa 1909.

On August 3, 1831, Joseph Smith "laid a stone at the Northeast corner of the contemplated Temple in the name of the Lord Jesus of Nazareth. After all present had rendered thanks to the great ruler of the universe, Sidney Rigdon pronounced [that] Spot of ground wholly dedicated unto the Lord forever."[247] The temple lot was dedicated that very day by Joseph. "The scene," said Joseph, "was solemn [and] impressive." To him, "It was a season of joy to those present, and afforded a glimpse of the future, which time will yet unfold to the satisfaction of the faithful."[248]

**D&C 57:4—What was the "line running directly between a Jew and Gentile"?**

The line was the border of the state of Missouri. In this instance, *Jew* was a reference to the Lamanites or Native Americans living beyond the border of Missouri in Indian Territory on land designated for them by the United States government. This was in accordance with a policy specifying the establishment of a "permanent Indian frontier." From 1825 to 1840, the United States encouraged the removal of "Indians from east of this line and assign[ed] them to reservations on the Great Plains. It was anticipated that non-Indian settlers would . . . remain east of the ninety-fifth meridian, thus solving the problem of conflict with the Indians."[249]

**D&C 57:13—What was Oliver Cowdery's role in printing Church literature?**

William W. Phelps was appointed to be the Church printer and Oliver Cowdery was called to assist him in copying, correcting, and selecting text, that "all things may be right before me, as it shall be proved by the Spirit through him" (D&C 57:13). Oliver was given the responsibility to select and write "books for schools in this church, that little children also may receive instruction before me as is pleasing unto me" (D&C 55:4). Oliver reviewed, prepared, and assisted Phelps in the publication of the revelations, first in *The Evening and the Morning Star* and later for inclusion in the Book of Commandments. He also served as the editor of the *Messenger and Advocate* from 1834 to 1835 and again in 1836.

# Section 58

**D&C 58:15—What is "blindness of the heart"?**

According to scholar Daniel H. Ludlow, "'Blindness of heart' means affections not guided by the light of the Spirit. Those who place their affection upon wrong objects, such as belong to the world, in preference to those that pertain to the Kingdom of God,

Independence, Missouri, circa 1855.

are blind at heart, no matter how clear the physical or mental vision may be" (see Matt. 10:37).[250]

### D&C 58:43—Why is recognition of the Savior and His Atonement such an integral part of the repentance process?

The repentance process would not be possible without Jesus Christ and His great sacrifice. Elder Richard G. Scott said, "Recognition of the Savior is the most important step to forgiveness of sin, for a conviction of his true identity brings forgiveness which is the ultimate peace in the repentance process." Other parts of the process include sorrow for wrongdoing, abandonment of sin, confession of transgression, and restitution to those wronged. Throughout the repentance process Elder Scott encourages obedience to the commandments of God, stating, "Full obedience brings the complete power of the gospel into your life."[251]

### D&C 58:50—Why was Sidney Rigdon's "description of the land of Zion" unacceptable to Joseph Smith?

A later revelation claimed that Sidney's writing was unacceptable because "he exalted himself in his heart" (D&C 63:55). According to Joseph Smith, the building impediments that Sidney Rigdon described in his depiction of the land of Zion would vanish, for "when it is recollected what the Prophets have said concerning Zion in the last days; how the glory of Lebanon is to come upon her; the fir tree, the pine tree, and the box tree together, to beautify the place of His sanctuary, that He may make the place of His feet glorious. Where for brass, He will bring gold; and for iron, He will bring silver; and for wood, brass; and for stones, iron; and where the feast of fat things will be given to the just; yea, when the splendor of the Lord is brought to our consideration for the good of His people, the calculations of men and the vain glory of the world vanish, and we exclaim, 'Out of Zion, the perfection of beauty, God hath shined'" (see Isa. 60; Ps. 50:2).[252]

### D&C 58:57—When was the land of Missouri consecrated and dedicated to the Lord?

On August 3, 1831, the Prophet Joseph asked Sidney Rigdon to consecrate and dedicate the land of Zion. Details of the event include a series of questions asked by Sidney Rigdon of those present at the dedication:

"Do you receive this land for the land of your inheritance with thankful hearts, from the Lord?"

Answer from all:—"We do."

"Do you pledge yourselves to keep the law of God in this land which you never have kept in your own lands?"

"We do."

"Do you pledge yourselves to see that others of your brethren who shall come hither do keep the laws of God?"

"We do."

After prayer, Sidney Rigdon said, "I now pronounce this land consecrated and dedicated unto the Lord for a possession and inheritance for the Saints, and for all the faithful servants of the Lord to the remotest ages of time. In the name of Jesus Christ, having authority from Him. Amen."[253]

# Section 59

**D&C 59:3–4—Whose death preceded this revelation and may have been the reason the revelation was given to Joseph Smith?**

Polly Knight, wife of Joseph Knight Sr., was close to death as she journeyed from Kirtland to Missouri in 1831. Her son Newel Knight recalled, "She would not consent to stop traveling; her only, or her greatest desire was to set her feet upon the land of Zion, and to have her body interred in that land. I went on shore and brought lumber to make a coffin in case she should die before we arrived at our place of destination—so fast did she fail. But the Lord gave her the desire of her heart, and she lived to stand upon that land."[254] Of her death Joseph Smith recorded, "On the 7th, I attended the funeral of Sister Polly Knight, the wife of Joseph Knight, Sen. This was the first death in the Church in this land, and I can say, a worthy member sleeps in Jesus till the resurrection."[255]

**D&C 59:12—What are "oblations"?**

From the time of Adam, man has offered oblations.

According to scholars Smith and Sjodahl, "In the Mosaic dispensation, an oblation, or offering, was anything presented to God to atone for sins, to merit favors, or to express gratitude for favors received. The firstlings of the flock, first fruits, tithes, incense, the shewbread, all these were oblations or offerings; some prescribed by law, some entirely voluntary." The Lord God commands the faithful to offer oblations on His holy day. Oblations include tithes, offerings, and other donations that are freely given. The "Sabbath Day" or "Day of the Lord" is a "very proper day upon which to remember such obligations."[256]

## Section 60

**D&C 60:5–6—Why was the route the elders took to reach Kirtland significant enough to warrant a revelation from God?**

Following a Church conference in Jackson County, Missouri, on August 8, 1831, "elders who had been appointed to return to the East desired to know how they should proceed, and by what route and manner they should travel" (D&C 60: Section Heading). By revelation, the elders were told to "take your journey speedily for the place which is called St. Louis" (D&C 60:5). From there, they were to travel two by two, preaching "my gospel among the congregations of the wicked" as they journeyed eastward (D&C 60:13). This suggests that there were individuals along the specific route wanting to hear the good news of the gospel of Jesus Christ and the Restoration. Exceptions to this travel guideline were Joseph Smith, Sidney Rigdon, and Oliver Cowdery, who were instructed to journey to Cincinnati before returning to Kirtland (see D&C 60:6). In obedience to the directive, Joseph and those named hired a stagecoach and driver in the hub city of St. Louis to transport them to Cincinnati and

McIlwaine's Bend on the Missouri River, where W. W. Phelps saw the destroyer, near present-day Miami, Missouri.

from there to Kirtland. Eighteen days after leaving Independence, Joseph and his close associates arrived at their destination.[257]

# Section 61

### D&C 61: Section Heading—Who saw the destroyer riding upon the waters of the Missouri River?

At the close of the first conference held in Jackson County, Missouri, Joseph Smith and several brethren began their journey back to Kirtland, paddling canoes on the Missouri River. After three days of paddling, the traveling party reached McIlwaine's Bend in the river, where "many of the dangers so common upon the western waters, manifested themselves." At the bend, William W. Phelps had an open vision of the destroyer "in his most horrible power, ride upon the face of the waters." "Others," wrote Joseph, "heard the noise but saw not the vision." By revelation Joseph learned that his traveling party and those who would journey to the land of Zion thereafter should not travel via the river, but journey by land, camping along the way.[258]

**D&C 61:4–6—Have the dangers once prevalent on the Missouri River lessened with the passage of time?**

Through the years the dangers associated with the Missouri River have manifested themselves again and again. For example, on June 7, 1903, the river flooded and destroyed crops at an estimated damage of five to seven million dollars.[259] In 1927, in response to continuous flooding, the United States Congress adopted the army engineer's plan that called for an appropriation of $325 million for flood control in these regions. In that same year the Red Cross reported setting up 149 major concentration centers for care of the refugees driven from their homes in the flooded region. The number of refugees assisted with emergency relief was 607,236.

**D&C 61:38—By observing the many prophesied signs that will appear before the Second Coming of the Savior, is it possible to calculate when Jesus Christ will return?**

Joseph Smith taught, "Jesus Christ never did reveal to any man the precise time that He would come. Go and read the Scriptures, and you cannot find anything that specifies the exact hour He would come; and all that say so are false teachers."[260]

# Section 62

**D&C 62: Section Heading—Did the elders who met Joseph Smith's traveling party at Chariton, Missouri, remain faithful to the gospel of Jesus Christ?**

On August 13, 1831, at Chariton, Missouri, Joseph Smith and those traveling with him to Kirtland met elders—Hyrum Smith, John Murdock, Harvey Whitlock, and David Whitmer—en route to the land of Zion. After "joyful salutations with which brethren meet each other, who are actually 'contending for the faith once delivered to the Saints,'" Joseph received the revelation now contained in section 62. In the revelation, these elders were told to rejoice, for the "testimony which ye have borne is recorded in heaven for the angels to look upon; and they rejoice over you, and your sins are forgiven you" (D&C 62:3).[261] Unfortunately, of the four elders mentioned, only two remained faithful—Hyrum Smith and John Murdock. Harvey Whitlock lost his fellowship in 1835. He wrote to the Prophet Joseph on September 28 of that year: "I have fallen from that princely station where unto our God has called me. . . . I have sunk myself . . . in crimes of the deepest dye." He then declared himself to be "a poor, wretched, bewildered, way-wanderer to eternity."[262] Whitlock was forgiven and on January 30, 1836, the First Presidency of the Church authorized his rebaptism and ordination to the office of high priest. In 1838 Whitlock forsook the Church again and never returned to fellowship. As for David Whitmer, he succumbed to smoldering apostate sentiments in 1836. By 1837 he was associated with a small but influential group of Kirtland Saints who rebelled against the Prophet's leadership, believing him to be in error. He was excommunicated on April 13, 1838, in Far West, Missouri. For the next fifty years, Whitmer remained aloof from the society of the Saints.[263]

# Section 63

**D&C 63:16—What doctrinal insights does the Doctrine and Covenants give on biblical passages not found in the Joseph Smith Translation of the Bible?**

Like the Book of Mormon, the Doctrine and Covenants restores or adds truths by expanding and interpreting biblical passages. For example, Matthew 5:28 reads: "But I say unto you, that whosoever looketh on a woman to lust after her hath committed adultery with her already in his heart." The Doctrine and Covenants adds that those who lust after women shall not have the Spirit of God, will deny the faith, and will know fear (D&C 63:16). Another example is Matthew 7:13–14: "Enter ye in at the strait gate: for wide is the gate, and broad is the way, that leadeth to destruction, and many there be which go in thereat: Because strait is the gate, and narrow is the way, which leadeth unto life, and few there be that find it." In the Doctrine and Covenants, the way to receive the greatest gift of God—

exaltation—is explained as journeying on the strait and narrow way. Those who enter and pursue the narrow way receive Jesus Christ and inherit the blessings of God. Those who enter and pursue the broad gate know much sorrow, for their path leads to destruction and damnation.

**D&C 63:36–48—How can Latter-day Saints avoid the judgments of God that will be poured out upon the nations of the earth?**

"In these infant days of the Church, there was a great anxiety to obtain the word of the Lord upon every subject that in any way concerned our salvation," wrote Joseph Smith. Of much concern in 1831 were prophesies about the forthcoming judgments of God. Brigham Young explained, "We read that war, pestilence, plagues, famine, etc., will be visited upon the inhabitants of the earth." To avoid such judgments, Brigham Young advised the Saints, "If distress through the judgments of God comes upon this people, it will be because the majority have turned away from the Lord. Let the majority of the people turn away from the Holy Commandments which the Lord has delivered to us, and cease to hold the balance of power in the Church, and we may expect the judgments of God to come upon us."[264] What was needed then and now is to stand in holy places with the companionship of the Holy Ghost: "We cannot have the companionship of the Holy Ghost—the medium of individual revelation—if we are in transgression or if we are angry or if we are in rebellion against God's chosen authorities."[265]

## Section 64

**D&C 64: Section Heading—Did Joseph Smith make revisions in each book of the Bible?**

The meaning of *translation* in this case is "a revision of the Bible by inspiration or revelation as the Lord had commanded." Acting as scribe for most of the Bible translation was Sidney Rigdon. His work "seems to have consisted in writing on sheets on paper that which was dictated by Joseph Smith. Joseph would read directly from the Bible and through the spirit of inspiration note the need for a revision of a text." Rigdon wrote the biblical text for Genesis 1–24 and Matthew 1 through John 5 on manuscript pages. For other areas of the Bible translation, "only the passages to be revised were noted" on the manuscript pages. Of books comprising the Old Testament, all were revised according to the pattern mentioned except Ruth, Ezra, Esther, Lamentations, Haggai, Malachi, and the Song of Solomon. Of the books comprising the New Testament, only the second and third epistles of John had no revisions.

The number of verses Joseph Smith changed or revised in the King James Version of the Bible were:

**Old Testament**
Genesis—662
Exodus—66
Psalms—188
Isaiah—178
**New Testament**
Matthew—483
Mark—349
Luke—563
John—159
Romans—118
1 Corinthians—68
Hebrews—47
Revelation—75[266]

## D&C 64:15–17—Why was the Lord angry with Ezra Booth, Isaac Morley, and Edward Partridge?

The Lord was angry with these brethren because they "sought evil in their hearts" (D&C 64:16). Isaac Morley and Edward Partridge repented, but Ezra Booth, who wanted "power to smite men and make them believe," did not. When he found that this was not the way of the Lord, he was disappointed and turned away from Joseph Smith. Fellowship was withdrawn from Booth on September 6, 1831.[267] Six days later, on September 12, he published the first in a series of nine letters deriding Joseph Smith and Mormonism in the *Ohio Star*, a newspaper printed in Ravenna, Ohio.

## D&C 64:23—What other words are synonymous with "tithing"?

According to scholar Daniel H. Ludlow, "'Sacrifice' and 'tithing' seem to be used as synonymous terms here, for the law of tithing had not yet been introduced. . . . The mention of tithing here is prophetic, indicating

The Tithing Office as it would have appeared.

a restoration of that lesser law, instead of the greater."[268] Other words viewed as synonymous with *tithing* at this time were *donations*, *offerings*, and *gifts*. The law of tithing was introduced by revelation on July 8, 1838, at Far West, Missouri.

## Section 65

**D&C 65:2—What was Joseph Smith's role in the prophecy about the stone being cut out without hands?**

As to Joseph Smith's role in the divine construction of the kingdom to be "cut out without hands" (Dan. 2:34), he said, "I calculate to be one of the instruments of setting up the kingdom of Daniel by the word of the Lord, and I intend to lay a foundation that will revolutionize the whole world."[269] Of this kingdom, President Spencer W. Kimball said, "This is the kingdom, set up by the God of heaven, that would never be destroyed nor superseded, and the stone cut out of the mountain without hands that would become a great mountain and would fill the whole earth."[270] At the dedication of the Boise Idaho Temple, President Gordon B. Hinckley said, "Father, the little stone which thou didst cut out of the mountain without hands is rolling forth to fill the earth. Guide and strengthen the messengers of the truth."[271]

**D&C 65:2—What is the interpretation of the image that Nebuchadnezzar saw in his dream?**

The head of gold symbolized the Near East or the empire ruled by Nebuchadnezzar. The silver breast and arms symbolized the

Persian Empire. When Babylon was overthrown by King Cyrus in 539 BC, the Persian monarch assumed control over the Near East, lands once ruled by Nebuchadnezzar and his successors. The brass belly and thighs represented the empires of Alexander the Great and his successors. The iron legs symbolized the Roman Empire. The feet, a mixture of iron and clay, represented a time when monarchs or regional leaders competed for land once held by ancient world leaders.

# Section 66

**D&C 66: Section Heading—What were the five questions that William McLellin wanted God to answer?**

William McLellin was baptized on August 20, 1831, by Hyrum Smith. That evening, he recalled, "The Enemy of all righteousness made a mighty struggle to persuade me that I was deceived until it seemed to me sometimes that horror would overwhelm me." McLellin was comforted when Newel Knight, "by the spirit of God was enabled to tell me the very secrets of my heart and in a degree to chase darkness from my mind."[272] After this incident McLellin journeyed to Ohio to meet the Prophet Joseph Smith. He lived with Joseph for about three weeks, "and from my acquaintance then and until now I can truly say I believe him to be a man of God, a prophet, a seer and revelator to The Church of Christ."[273] His belief led McLellin to ask Joseph to inquire of the Lord about a few questions that troubled him. McLellin wrote, "I went before the Lord in secret, and on my knees asked him to reveal the answer to five questions through his Prophet, and that too without his having any knowledge of my having made such a request." He then went to Joseph and asked to receive a blessing. Joseph wrote, "In seeking this blessing he did so with full desire to know the will of the Lord concerning himself." The subsequent revelation commended and reproved the actions of McLellin (see D&C 66:1–3). Yet he later wrote, "I now testify in the fear of God, that every question which I had thus lodged in the ears of the Lord of Sabbath, were answered to my full and entire satisfaction."[274]

# Section 67

**D&C 67:5–8—Who accepted the Lord's challenge to write revelations or commandments as if from God?**

At the November 1831 conference at Hiram, Ohio, William E. McLellin voiced concern about the grammatical wording of the revelations to be printed in the Book of Commandments. In response to McLellin's concerns, the Lord challenged him to write a commandment (see D&C 67:5–8). McLellin accepted the challenge. Joseph Smith wrote, "The wisest man [McLellin], in his own estimation, having more learning than sense, endeavored to write a commandment like unto one of the least of the Lord's." McLellin failed to write even one command. Those attending the conference "witnessed this vain attempt of a man to imitate the language of Jesus Christ, [and it] renewed their faith in the fulness of the Gospel, and in the truth of the commandments and revelations which the Lord had given to the Church" through Joseph Smith.[275]

# Section 68

**D&C 68: Section Heading—Although this revelation was given at the request of specific brethren, does the directive have universal application?**

At the close of the November 1–2, 1831, conference in Hiram, Ohio, Orson Hyde, Luke Johnson, Lyman E. Johnson, and William E. McLellin asked Joseph Smith to seek "the will of the Lord concerning themselves, and their ministry." In response, Joseph inquired of the Lord in behalf of these brethren. Joseph learned through revelation that Orson Hyde was called "to proclaim the everlasting gospel, by the Spirit of the living God, from people to people, and from land to land, in the congregations of the wicked, in their synagogues" (D&C 68:1). Luke Johnson, Lyman Johnson, and William E. McLellin were told, "Go ye into all the world, preach the gospel to every creature, acting in the authority which [the Lord] has given you, baptizing in the name of the Father, and of the Son, and of the Holy Ghost" (D&C 68:8).

## Section 69

**D&C 69: Section Heading—Why were the three thousand copies of the Book of Commandments not published as planned?**

Oliver Cowdery and John Whitmer were commissioned to carry revelatory manuscripts from Kirtland to Independence to be typeset and printed on a press operated by William W. Phelps. By the summer of 1833, the printing of the revelations was nearing completion, although none had yet been bound in book form. On July 20, 1833, a mob entered Phelps's printing establishment and destroyed the printing press. Mary Elizabeth Rollins saw men carrying sheets of paper from the printing establishment and heard them yelling, "Here are the Mormon Commandments." Mary wrote, "When they spoke of the commandments I was determined to have some of them. Sister said if I went to get any of them she would go too, but said 'they will kill us.' While their backs were turned, prying out the gable end of the house, we went, and got our arms full, and were turning away, when some of the mob saw us and called on us to stop, but we ran as fast as we could. Two of them started after us. Seeing a gap in a fence, we entered into a large cornfield, laid the papers on the ground, and hid them with our persons. The corn was from five to six feet high, and very thick; they hunted around considerable, and came very near us but did not find us."[276]

## Section 70

**D&C 70:1–5—What was the Literary Firm? What was the involvement of this firm in publishing sacred writings of the Church?**

Joseph Smith's interest in publishing the "New Translation" of the Bible and the revelations was a focal point for conferences held in the John Johnson farmhouse at Hiram, Ohio, on November 12–13, 1831. At one conference Joseph recognized the brethren who had contributed to the sacred writings of the Church: "Br. Oliver has labored with me from the beginning in writing &c Br. Martin has labored with me from the beginning, brs. John [Whitmer] and Sidney also for a considerable time." Due to the diligence of those named "in bringing to light by the grace of God these sacred things," they were appointed to manage like undertakings according to the laws of the Church and the commandments of the Lord. These brethren became the nucleus or original members of the Literary Firm.[277] As such, they were to consecrate, manage, print, and distribute revelations so "that the revelations may be published, and go forth unto the ends of the earth" (D&C 72:21). They were to be "stewards" of the sacred writings and were promised proceeds from the sale of these writings for their temporal use.

# Section 71

**D&C 71: Section Heading—Who was primarily responsible for the "unfriendly feelings" that arose against the Church in the fall of 1831?**

At that time the severest critic was Ezra Booth, a former Methodist minister who had joined the Church but since turned his

The John Johnson home.

heel against the Lord's anointed servant. Booth penned nine letters defaming Joseph Smith and Mormonism that were printed in the *Ohio Star* at Ravenna, Ohio. Of the critical letters Joseph Smith wrote, "By their coloring, falsity, and vain calculations to overthrow the work of the Lord, exposed [Booth's] weakness, wickedness and folly, and left him a monument of his own shame, for the world to wonder at."[278] By revelation the Lord told Joseph and Sidney Rigdon to stop revising the Holy Bible in order to proclaim the gospel of Jesus Christ.

Joseph said, "Knowing now the mind of the Lord, that the time had come that the Gospel should be proclaimed in power and demonstration to the world, from the Scriptures, reasoning with men as in days of old, I took a journey to Kirtland, in company with Elder Sidney Rigdon on the 3rd day of December, to fulfil [*sic*] the above revelation."[279] For more than a month Joseph and Sidney preached in the Ohio towns of Shalersville, Ravenna, and others. As to the success of their labors, Joseph wrote, "We did much towards allaying the excited feelings which were growing out of the scandalous letters then being published in the *Ohio Star*, at Ravenna, by the before-mentioned apostate, Ezra Booth."[280]

## Section 72

### D&C 72:7–8—How did Newel K. Whitney respond to his call to be a bishop?

"Staggering under the weight of the responsibility that was about to be placed upon him," Newel K. Whitney said to the Prophet Joseph, "Brother Joseph, I can't see a Bishop in myself." Joseph answered, "Go and ask the Lord about it." Newel asked God and "heard a voice from heaven say, 'Thy strength is in me.'"[281] In June 1832 Joseph Smith wrote of Bishop Whitney, "He is Chearfull [*sic*] and patient and a true Brother to me."[282]

## Section 73

### D&C 73:3–4—Where is the revelation found that commands Joseph Smith to translate the Bible?

According to scholars Robert L. Millet and Kent P. Jackson,

there is not a specific revelation commanding Joseph Smith to make revisions or to translate the Bible. Millet and Jackson wrote, "Though we do not have in our possession a specific revelation instructing Joseph Smith to begin a careful study of the Bible (as a means of restoring many of the plain and precious parts), yet we do have numerous statements by the Prophet and the Lord indicating its value and overall import."[283] Note that section 73 reveals the Lord's approval of the Bible translation by indicating "it is expedient" for them "to translate again . . . [and] to continue the work of translation until it be finished" (D&C 73:3–4).

## Section 74

**D&C 74: Section Heading—Why was it necessary to include an explanation of 1 Corinthians 7:14 in the Doctrine and Covenants?**

To explain the reasons why this passage was included in the Doctrine and Covenants, it is necessary to understand that questions had arisen among the early Saints about marriages between believers and unbelievers. These same questions were addressed in the ancient Greek city of Corinth during the days of the apostle Paul. Some contended that "when the husband, or wife, had been converted, he, or she, ought to abandon the unconverted partner as unclean and contaminating." Paul countered by arguing that "the conversion of one of the partners has brought a sanctifying influence into the family." Although Paul preached that "Christians were forbidden to marry outside the [early] Church," he taught that marriages entered into before conversion to Christianity were not to be severed (see 2 Cor. 6:14).[284] This revelation coincides with the teachings of the apostle Paul.

Paul teaching the gospel.

# 5 Sections 75–99

## Section 75

**D&C 75: Section Heading—Which elders encountered difficulty in bringing men to an understanding of the gospel message?**

Prior to this revelation Joseph Smith wrote, "The Elders seemed anxious for me to inquire of the Lord that they might know His will, or learn what would be most pleasing to Him for them to do, in order to bring men to a sense of their condition; for, as it was written, all men have gone out of the way, so that none doeth good, no, not one."[285] This suggests that many if not all elders encountered those unwilling to accept the gospel of Jesus Christ. Two such elders were Orson Pratt and Samuel Smith. Pratt wrote of journeying with Smith in the spring of 1832 "without purse or scrip" and "going from house to house, teaching and preaching in families, and also in the public congregations of the people." He penned, "Wherever we were received and entertained, we left our blessing; and wherever we were rejected, we washed our feet in private against those who rejected us, and bore testimony of it unto our Father in heaven." Yet Pratt concluded, "[We] went on our way rejoicing, according to the commandment."[286]

## Section 76

**D&C 76: Section Heading—Who wrote the most detailed account of the events that transpired as Joseph Smith and Sidney Rigdon were being shown the Visions of Glories?**

In retrospect Joseph Smith and Sidney Rigdon wrote little of what they saw or heard of the Visions of Glories. In wanting to explain his reason for not revealing more, Joseph said, "I could explain a hundred fold more than I ever have of the glories of the kingdoms manifested to me in the vision, were I permitted, and were the people prepared to receive them."[287] The most detailed account of events that transpired during the Visions of Glories was written by Philo Dibble. He wrote of entering "the room while the vision was being received." He witnessed, "Joseph and Sidney were in the spirit and saw the heavens open, there were other men in the room, perhaps twelve, among whom I was one during a part of the time—probably two-thirds of the time,—I saw the glory and felt the power, but did not see the vision." Dibble recorded, "Joseph would, at intervals, say: 'What do I see?' as one might say while looking out the window and beholding what all in the room could not see. Then he would relate what he had seen or what he was looking at. Then Sidney replied, 'I see the same.' Presently Sidney would say, 'what do I see?' and would repeat what he had seen or was seeing, and Joseph would reply, 'I see the same.'" Dibble reported that "this manner of conversation was repeated at short intervals to the end of the vision, and during the whole time not a word was spoken by any other person. Not a sound nor motion made by anyone but Joseph and Sidney, and it seemed to me that they never moved a joint or limb during the time I was there, which I think was over an hour, and to the end of the vision. Joseph sat firmly and calmly all the time in the midst of a magnificent glory, but Sidney sat limp and pale, apparently as limber as a rag, observing which, Joseph remarked, smilingly, 'Sidney is not used to it as I am.'"[288]

**D&C 76: Section Heading—Why did Brigham Young struggle to accept the doctrines presented in these visions? Does the reason stem from lingering beliefs in traditional Christian views of life and death?**

Joseph Smith said of the Visions of Glories, "Nothing could be more pleasing to the Saints upon the order of the kingdom of the Lord, than the light which burst upon the world through the foregoing vision. Every law, every commandment, every promise, every truth, and every point touching the destiny of man, from Genesis to Revelation, where the purity of the scriptures remains unsullied by the folly of men, go to show the perfection of the theory [of different degrees of glory in the future life] and witnesses the fact that that document is a transcript from the records of the eternal world. . . . every honest man is constrained to exclaim: '*It came from God*.'" But not every Ohio Saint agreed.[289] Brigham Young struggled at first to accept doctrines presented in the Visions of Glories: "My traditions were such, that when the Vision came first to me, it was directly contrary and opposed to my former education. I said, Wait a little. I did not reject it; but I could not understand it. I then could feel what incorrect tradition had done for me. Suppose all that I have ever heard from my priest and parents—the way they taught me to read the Bible—had been true, my understanding would be diametrically opposed to the doctrine revealed in the Vision. I used to think and

Brigham Young.

pray, to read and think, until I knew and fully understood it for myself, by the visions of the Holy Spirit."[290]

**D&C 76: Section Heading—Why did Joseph Smith rephrase section 76 in poetic verse?**

On February 1, 1843, in the *Times and Seasons*—an LDS newspaper printed in Nauvoo, Illinois—William W. Phelps addressed his poem, "Go with Me," to Joseph Smith. A few stanzas read:

Go with me, will you go
to the saints that have died,

To the next, better world,
where the righteous reside;

Where the angels and spirits
in harmony be

In the joys of a vast paradise?
Go with me. . . .

Go with me, will you go
to the mansions above,

Where the bliss and the knowledge,
the light, and the love,

And the glory of God,
do eternally be?—

Death, the wages of sin, is not
there: Go with me.[291]

In response to Phelps, Joseph rephrased section 76 in poetic verse. The following are a few of the stanzas from "The Answer: A Vision," penned by Joseph:

I will go, I will go,
to the home of the Saints,

Where the virtue's the value,
and life the reward;

But before I return
to my former estate,

I must fulfill the mission
I had from the Lord. . . .

I, Joseph, the prophet,
in spirit beheld,

And the eyes of the inner
man truly did see

Eternity sketch'd in a vision
from God,

Of what was, and now is,
and yet is to be. . . .

But the great things of God,
which he show'd unto me,

Unlawful to utter,
I dare not declare;

They surpass all the wisdom
and greatness of men,

And only are seen, as has Paul,
where they are.[292]

**D&C 76:1–10—Why did Joseph Smith want the Saints to give "strict attention" to the plan of salvation as presented in the vision of glories?**

"The great plan of salvation is a theme which ought to occupy our strict attention, and be regarded as one of heaven's best gifts to mankind," Joseph Smith said.[293] In the Visions of Glories, Joseph learned that there are three kingdoms in eternity—celestial, terrestrial, and telestial. Those who merit the celestial kingdom overcome the carnalities of this world by faith and are "sealed by the Holy Spirit of promise . . . [these are] they who are the church of the Firstborn" (D&C 76:53–54). Those who merit the terrestrial kingdom are not valiant in their testimony of Christ. Of them, President Spencer W. Kimball said, "There are many people in this Church today who think they live, but they are dead to the spiritual things. And I believe even many who are making the pretenses of being active are also spiritually dead. Their service is much of the letter and less of the spirit."[294] Those who merit the telestial kingdom "cannot come where God and Christ dwell, worlds without end."[295] Joseph Smith wanted his followers to choose a course in life that led to eternal happiness and exaltation in the celestial kingdom of God.

### D&C 76:26, 43—What is the meaning of "Lucifer," "Perdition," and "sons of perdition"?

The name Lucifer means "light bearer" or "shining one." The name Perdition means "loss" or "destruction." When the two names are put together, the interpretation is that Lucifer, or the light bearer, fell from his exalted position to that of perdition, which is one of great loss and destruction (see Rev. 12:1–11; Moses 4:1–4). Sons of perdition are men who embraced the gospel of Jesus Christ, understood the plan of salvation, unlocked the mysteries of eternity, and received priesthood power to overcome all things, yet "prostituted that power and turned away from that which they knew to be true, denying the Son of God and putting Him to open shame." For their rebellious behavior, they became sons of perdition, meaning "doomed to suffer the wrath of God reserved for the devil and his angels."[296] They committed the unpardonable sin, which is to deny the Holy Ghost. Of such men Joseph Smith said, "After a man has sinned against the Holy Ghost, there is no repentance for him. He has got to say that the sun does not shine while he sees it; he has got to deny Jesus Christ when the heavens have been opened unto him, and to deny the plan of salvation with his eyes open to the truth of it; and from that time he begins to be an enemy."[297]

**D&C 76:107—Why will the resurrected Lord appear in red apparel at His Second Coming?**

One symbolic interpretation of the color red is as the symbol of victory. The Second Coming is victorious, yet the color represents much more. The Savior's red apparel also symbolizes His atoning blood and sacrifice for mankind, for He trod "the wine-press alone, even the wine-press of the fierceness of the wrath of

An interpretation of Christ in a red robe at His Second Coming.

Almighty God" (D&C 76:107; 88:106). He descended below all things to take upon Himself our sins and sorrows. With His precious blood He brought salvation to fallen man (see 2 Ne. 9:44; Jacob 1:19; 2:2; Alma 5:22). He also comes in dyed garments as the God of justice who trampled the wicked (D&C 133:48–51). Thus, the red apparel represents the mercy and justice of God, a pure, unselfish victory.

## Section 77

**D&C 77:1—What valuable insights did Joseph Smith learn about the earth becoming a sea of glass?**

While engaged in revising the King James Version of the Bible, Joseph Smith uncovered the meaning of "some of the figurative and symbolical writings of John in the Book of Revelation."[298] One mystery concerned the earth becoming a "sea of glass" (D&C 77:1). Joseph said, "When the earth was sanctified and became like a sea of glass, it would be one great urim and thummim, and the Saints could look in it and see as they are seen."[299] Brigham Young added, "This earth will become a celestial body—be like a sea of glass, or like a urim and thummim; and when you wish to know anything, you can look in this earth and see all the eternities of God. We shall make our home here, and go on our missions as we do now."[300] Brigham Young further stated, "It will not then be an opaque body as it now is, but it will be like the stars of the firmament, full of light and glory: it will be a body of light. John compared it, in its celestialized state, to a sea of glass."[301] Such a state will occur when the earth is renewed and becomes a celestial sphere.

**D&C 77:2—When a revelation is given using symbolic images of beasts and other figures, how can we know the meaning associated with the symbolic images?**

Joseph Smith taught, "Whenever God gives a vision of an image, or beast, or figure of any kind, He always holds Himself responsible to give a revelation or interpretation of the meaning thereof, otherwise we are not responsible or accountable for our belief in it."[302]

**D&C 77:6—What is the significance of the seven seals that bind the book seen in vision by John the Revelator?**

The book John the Revelator saw consisted of seven parchments, the number seven conveying completeness (see Rev. 5). Each parchment was separately bound with seals representing seven periods of the earth. As the parchment unrolled a seal was broken. As it continued to unroll, other seals were broken until all had been revealed.[303] Thus, the dispensations and history of the world will be made known in its completeness starting from the beginning and moving toward the end by opening the seals in sequential order.

**D&C 77:8—Who are the four angels mentioned in Revelation 7:1?**

The identities of the four angels mentioned in Revelation 7:1 have not been revealed. According to scholar Daniel H. Ludlow, "These angels seem to fit the description of the angels spoken of in the parable of the wheat and the tares," who pled with the Lord to be sent forth to reap the field (see Matt. 13:24–43; D&C 86:17). The Lord told the angels to let the wheat and the tares grow together until the time of harvest, meaning the end of the world (see Matt. 13:38–40).[304]

# Section 78

**D&C 78: Section Heading—Why was it necessary in early editions of the Doctrine and Covenants to refer to men and places by unusual names and titles?**

Elder Orson Pratt taught, "The names that were incorporated when it [the Doctrine and Covenants] was printed, did not exist there when the manuscript revelations were given, for I saw them myself. Some of them I copied. And when the Lord was about to have the Book of Covenants given to the world it was thought wisdom, in consequence of the persecutions of our enemies in Kirtland and some of the regions around, that some of the names should be changed."[305] The following is an alphabetical listing of names and titles used to identify individuals and places in early editions of the Doctrine and Covenants:

Ahashdah—Newel K. Whitney (78:9; 82:11; 96:2; 104:39, 40, 41)

Alam—Newel K. Whitney (82:11)

Baneemy—mine elders (105:27)

Baurak Ale—Joseph Smith (103:21, 22, 35; 105:16, 27)

Cainhannoch—New York (104:81)

Enoch—Joseph Smith (78:1, 4)

Gazelam—Joseph Smith (78:9; 82:11; 104:26, 43, 45, 46)

Horah—Oliver Cowdery (82:11)

Laneshine house—printing office (104:28, 29)

Mahalaleel—Sidney Rigdon (82:11)

Mahemson—Martin Harris (82:11; 104:24, 26)

Olihah—Oliver Cowdery (82:11; 104:28, 29, 34)

Ozondah—mercantile establishment (104:39, 40, 41)

Pelagoram—Sidney Rigdon (78:9; 82:11; 104:20, 22)

Seth—Joseph of Egypt (96:7)

Shalemanasseh—Martin Harris (82:11)

Shederlaomach—Frederick G. Williams (92:1, 2; 104:27, 29)

Shinehah—Kirtland (82:12, 13)

Shinehah—print (104:58)

Shinelane—printing (104:63)

Shule—ashery (104:39)

Tahhanes—tannery (104:20)

Talents—dollars (104:69, 73)

Zombre—John Johnson (96:6; 104:24, 34)

These names and titles appeared only in sections 78, 82, 92, 96, 103, 104, and 105. The unusual names and titles were eliminated in the 1981 Doctrine and Covenants.

### D&C 78:15—What is the meaning of "Ahman"?

Elder Orson Pratt explained that in the pure language, or the language of Adam, *Ahman* is the name of God. *Son Ahman* is the name given to the Son of God, Jesus Christ.[306] Because *Ahman* is part of the name of the place where Adam dwelt, Pratt concludes that *Adam-ondi-Ahman* means "the Valley of God."[307]

Adam-ondi-Ahman in Daviess County, Missouri.

# Section 79

### D&C 79:1—How successful were Jared Carter's missionary labors?

From 1831 to 1834, Jared Carter's missionary labors were exemplary. Of preaching in his hometown of Benson, Vermont, Carter wrote, "I commenced holding meetings and the Lord was with me. . . . Baptized 27 in number."[308] To his credit, Carter accepted with enthusiasm his second missionary call to the East. All reports suggest that he successfully fulfilled this assignment. "I remember the goodness of the Lord to me in the mission that I have lately been to in the East," Carter penned. "The Lord has permitted me to administer the gospel to 79 souls and many others by my instrumentality have been convinced of this most glorious work."[309]

# Section 80

### D&C 80:1—In what way did the missionary call of Stephen Burnett differ from the call extended to Jared Carter?

On January 25, 1832, eighteen-year-old Stephen Burnett was called by revelation to serve a mission with Ruggles Eames (see D&C 75:35). It is assumed that this mission was not fulfilled, because two months later (in March 1832) Burnett was called to be a missionary companion to Eden Smith and to "go ye and preach my gospel, whether to the north or to the south, to the east or to the west, it mattereth not, for ye cannot go amiss" (D&C 80:2–3). The assignment given Burnett shows that "there are times and circumstances in which it matters very much where an individual is called to serve and other times when the area of assignment is not as important."[310] The difference between the calls of Burnett and Carter is that Carter's assignment was to a specific locale—the eastern states—whereas Burnett's assignment had no state borders.

## Section 81

**D&C 81: Section Heading—Was the subject of this revelation changed from Jesse Gause to Frederick G. Williams in the manuscript copies or in the printed editions?**

There are two extant manuscript copies of this revelation: one in the Kirtland Revelation Book and the other in the library/archives of the Community of Christ (RLDS). In both copies the name of Jesse Gause is crossed out and the name of Frederick G. Williams written above. The published copies also show Frederick G. Williams as the subject. The First Presidency was organized on March 18, 1833, with Frederick G. Williams replacing Jesse Gause as a counselor to the Prophet Joseph Smith.[311]

**D&C 81: Section Heading—Why is the faithfulness of Jesse Gause questioned?**

On March 8, 1832, Joseph Smith wrote, "Chose this day and ordained brother Jesse Gause and Broth[er] Sidney [Rigdon] to be my counsellers of the ministry of the presidency of the high Priesthood."[312] One week later the Prophet received a revelation confirming Jesse Gause as a member of the presidency and giving further directions to his office and calling (see D&C 81: Section Heading). President Gause functioned in his calling for six months in Kirtland before serving a mission with Zebedee Coltrin. While on the mission, President Gause entered the Shaker community of North Union, Ohio, and there petitioned his wife, Minerva, to unite with him in Mormonism. She refused. He left North Union and continued his missionary journeys until Coltrin departed for Kirtland. President Gause continued his journey but was never heard of again. He was excommunicated on December 3, 1832.

**D&C 81:1—By 1832, what was the relationship of Joseph Smith to Frederick G. Williams?**

Frederick G. Williams was serving as a justice of the peace in Kirtland when missionaries arrived in Ohio. He listened and accepted their gospel message in October 1830. After being baptized and ordained an elder, Williams accompanied the missionaries to Missouri. After a ten-month absence he returned to his family in Kirtland. Soon thereafter he was called to be a counselor to Joseph Smith (see D&C 81:1–3). The love of the Prophet for his counselor is best illustrated by Joseph's

Frederick G. Williams.

naming his newborn son Frederick Granger Williams Smith. President Williams served as a personal scribe for Joseph and as an editor of the *Northern Times*, an LDS newspaper. Joseph wrote of him, "Brother Frederick G. Williams is one of those men in whom I place the greatest confidence and trust, for I have found him ever full of love and brotherly kindness. He is not a man of many words, but is ever winning, because of his constant mind. He shall ever have place in my heart."[313]

# Section 82

**D&C 82:3—What is the expected result of the phrase "Unto whom much is given much is required"?**

"Jesus made it plain that each will be required to given an accounting only for the talents or gifts he has received," taught Elder LeGrand Richards (see Matt. 25:14–40). "No man can say that he has received nothing. Even though it be but one talent, he will be expected to develop that talent so that when his Lord comes, he will be able to return it with profit. . . . Can you imagine any greater justification for 'weeping and gnashing of teeth,' than to learn from your Lord, when called to give an accounting for your life here upon the earth, that while you had been faithful in your spirit existence and had kept your first estate, you had failed in your second estate [?]"[314]

**D&C 82:10—What historical events led to the promise "I the Lord am bound when ye do what I say; but when ye do not what I say, ye have no promise"?**

On April 26, 1832, two days after Joseph Smith and other brethren had arrived in Jackson County, Missouri, "a difficulty or hardness which had existed between Bishop Partridge and Elder [Sidney] Rigdon, was amicably settled."[315] A general council of the Church followed. During the morning session of the council, Joseph was acknowledged as president of the High Priesthood, a position granted him on January 25, 1832, at Amherst, Ohio. In the afternoon session, Joseph received this revelation, which promises the faithful that the Lord is "bound when ye do what I say; but when ye do not what I say, ye have no promise" (D&C 82:10).

# Section 83

**D&C 83:1–4—What historical events led to this revelation that outlines the responsibilities of husbands and fathers to support their families?**

On April 28–29, 1832, Joseph Smith visited Saints residing near the Big Blue River in Kaw Township, a few miles west of Independence, Missouri. Of his visit Joseph wrote, "[I] received a

Sections 84–98 and 101 were received by Joseph Smith while in Kirtland.

welcome only known by brethren and sisters united as one in the same faith, and by the same baptism, and supported by the same Lord." He concluded, "It is good to rejoice with the people of God."[316] One day later, April 30, as Joseph sat in council with the Saints, he received a revelation advising them that women and children have claim upon their husbands and fathers for support and widows and orphans have claim upon the Church for support.

# Section 84

**D&C 84: Section Heading—What historical circumstances led to Joseph Smith receiving this revelation that clarifies priesthood responsibilities?**

Between September 1832 and December 1833, sixteen revelations were given to the Prophet Joseph Smith in Kirtland, Ohio (D&C 84–98 and 101). Of these revelations, section 84 is the most quoted. The historical circumstances that surround this revelation were recorded by Joseph Smith: "The Elders during the month of September began to return from their missions to the Eastern States, and present the histories of their several stewardships in the Lord's vineyard; while together in these seasons of joy, I inquired of the Lord, and received on the 22nd and 23rd of September, the following revelation on Priesthood."[317] Of the enduring power of the priesthood, Joseph Smith said, "The Priesthood is an everlasting principle, and existed with God from eternity, and will to eternity, without beginning of days or end of years."[318]

**D&C 84:9–10—Why is Jeremy mentioned in relation to a priesthood descendent line when his name does not appear in any such line in the Old Testament?**

The only mention of Jeremy in a priesthood line of authority was revealed to Joseph Smith in 1832 (see D&C 84:9–10). From that revelation, it is known that Jeremy received his priesthood "under the hand of Gad." Jeremy then conferred that priesthood upon Elihu. Perhaps more information on Jeremy, Gad, and Elihu will be known when "those things which never have been revealed from the foundation of the world, but have been kept hid from the wise and prudent, shall be revealed" (D&C 128:18).

**D&C 84:33—What does "magnifying their calling" entail?**

"What does it mean to magnify a calling?" President Thomas S. Monson asked. He answered, "It means to build it up in dignity and importance, to make it honorable and commendable in the eyes of all men, to enlarge and strengthen it, to let the light of heaven shine through it to the view of other men. And how does one magnify a calling? Simply by performing the service that pertains to it."[319]

**D&C 84:33–41—What is the oath and covenant of the priesthood?**

By being ordained to the priesthood, a worthy male accepts the "covenant of the priesthood," which is to magnify his calling in the priesthood; to commit to "live by every word that proceedeth forth from the mouth of God"; and to keep the commandments (see D&C 84:33–44).

The "oath of the priesthood" is the Lord's solemn promise that "if man does as he promises, then all that the Father hath shall be given unto him."[320] To live worthy to receive "all that the Father hath" is "to inherit the same power, the same glory and the same exaltation, until you arrive at the station of a God, and ascend to the throne of eternal power, the same as those who have gone before."[321]

**D&C 84:71—Was the promise "[poison] shall not hurt them" fulfilled?**

In May 1832 Joseph and his traveling companion, Newel K. Whitney, who was recovering from a fractured leg, took lodging in Greenville, Indiana. Of their stay in Greenville, Joseph recalled, "I frequently walked out in the woods, where I saw several fresh graves; and one day when I rose from the dinner table, I walked directly to the door and commenced vomiting most profusely. I raised large quantities of blood and poisonous matter, and so great were the muscular contortions of my system, that my jaw in a few moments was dislocated. This I succeeded in replacing with my own hands, and made my way to Brother Whitney (who was on the bed), as speedily as possible; he laid his hands on me and administered to me in the name of the Lord, and I was healed in an instant. . . . Thanks be to my heavenly Father for his interference in my behalf at this critical moment, in the name of Jesus Christ. Amen."[322]

# Section 85

**D&C 85: Section Heading—Section 85 contains part of a letter Joseph Smith wrote to W. W. Phelps on November 27, 1832. What portion of the letter was not included in section 85?**

On November 27, 1832, in Kirtland, Ohio, Joseph Smith wrote a letter to W. W. Phelps, a resident of Independence, Missouri. A portion of that letter was canonized as section 85. The remainder of the letter reads, "I say brother, because I feel so from the heart, and although it is not long since I wrote a letter unto you, yet I feel as though you would excuse me for writing this, as I have many things which I wish to communicate. Some things which I will mention in this letter, which are lying with great weight on my mind. I am well, and my family also; God grant that you may enjoy the same, and yours, and all the brethren and sisters who remember to inquire after the commandments of the Lord, and the welfare of Zion and such a being as myself; and while I dictate this letter, I fancy to myself that you are saying or thinking something similar to these words:—'My God, great and mighty art Thou, therefore show unto Thy servant what shall become of those who are essaying to come up unto Zion, in order to keep the commandments of God, and yet receive not their inheritance by consecrations, by order of deed from the Bishop, the man that God has appointed in a legal way, agreeably to the law given to organize and regulate the Church, and all the affairs of the same.' Brother William, in the love of God, having the most implicit confidence in you as a man of God, having obtained this confidence by a vision of heaven, therefore I will proceed to unfold to you some of the feelings of my heart, and to answer the question."[323] What follows is included in section 85.

**D&C 85:7—In his letter to W. W. Phelps, Joseph Smith criticizes Bishop Edward Partridge for the manner in which he conducted Church affairs in Jackson County, Missouri, and threatens to "send one mighty and strong" to replace him. Did Joseph send someone to solve the problems in Jackson County?**

Bishop Edward Partridge was able to resolve the problems that caused difficulty among Church members in Jackson County. Therefore, the need to send "one mighty and strong . . . to set in order the house of God, and to arrange by lot the inheritances of the saints" was unnecessary (D&C 85:7). Through time, however, some Latter-day Saints have interpreted the sending of "one mighty and strong" as a future event. This has led to "no end of needless speculation due to a misunderstanding of what is written."[324] To counteract those who claim to be the prophesied "one mighty and strong," on November 13, 1905, the First Presidency issued a proclamation refuting such claims.[325]

### D&C 85:8—What is the meaning of "steady the ark of God"?

The phrase "steady the ark of God" refers to an ancient event that occurred when the ark of the covenant was being transported (see 2 Sam. 6:1–11). As the ark began to topple from its wagon, Uzzah tried to steady the ark to prevent it from falling. In so doing, he was struck dead, for "the ark was the tangible object that symbolized the presence of God, his throne, his glory, [and] his divine majesty." However well-meaning Uzzah's intentions, he "approached casually what could only be approached under the strictest conditions."[326]

# Section 86

### D&C 86:1–7—What is the interpretation of the parable of the wheat and the tares recorded in the Doctrine and Covenants?

On December 6, 1832, while engaged in revising the New Testament, Joseph Smith received a more complete interpretation of the parable of the wheat and the

Gathering tares from wheat at Bethel circa 1900.

tares than was recorded in the Gospel of Matthew. This interpretation is as follows: the field is the world (see D&C 86:2), apostles sow seeds (see D&C 86:2), and Satan sows tares that choke the wheat (see D&C 86:3). Being driven into the wilderness represents the apostasy, a time when the fulness of the gospel of Jesus Christ and His priesthood power were taken from the earth (see Rev. 12:12–17; D&C 86:3). The tenderness of the wheat represents a weakness of faith (see D&C 86:4), the reapers represent angels who are anxious to reap the field or world (see D&C 86:5), and the harvest represents gathering the righteous (see D&C 86:7).

"The harvest and the end of the world have an allusion directly to the human family in the last days," Joseph Smith wrote. "The Son of Man shall send forth His angels, and gather out of His kingdom all things that offend, and them which do iniquity, and shall cast them into a furnace of fire, there shall be wailing and gnashing of teeth.' We understand that the work of gathering together of the wheat into barns, or garners, is to take place while the tares are being bound over, and [incident to] preparing for the day of burning; that after the day of burnings, the righteous shall shine forth like the sun, in the Kingdom of their Father."[327]

## Section 87

**D&C 87: Section Heading—Critics of Joseph Smith point out that this revelation was not published until after the Civil War. What historical evidence suggests that Joseph Smith received this prophecy on war in 1832?**

The revelation known as the "prophecy on war" was not included in the Doctrine and Covenants until 1876. However, it should be noted that Church leaders knew of this prophecy in the early 1830s. The revelation was recorded in the Kirtland Revelation Book on December 25, 1832. Elder Orson Pratt wrote, "When I was a boy, I traveled extensively in the United States and the Canadas, preaching this restored Gospel. I had a manuscript copy of this revelation [D&C 87], which I carried in my pocket, and I was in the habit of reading it to the people among whom I traveled and preached. As a general thing the people regarded it as the height of nonsense, saying the Union was too strong to be broken; and I, they said, was led away, the victim of an impostor. I knew the prophecy was true, for the Lord had spoken to me and had given me revelation."[328] The "prophecy on war" was first published in 1851 by Franklin D. Richards in the first edition of the Pearl of Great Price.

**D&C 87:1–4—Was Joseph Smith aware of the nullification crisis dominating political discussion in the United States when he received the "prophecy on war"?**

In 1832 the nullification crisis, spawned by rising tensions between the Northern and Southern states, dominated the political scene of the United States. At the center of the controversy was South Carolina, whose Southern residents contended that they were at a great economic disadvantage due to the protective tariff of 1828, which imposed heavy duties on foreign goods favoring the industrial North and compromising the rural South. This tariff, coupled with an antislavery mentality in the North, led threatened Southern legislators in South Carolina to pass the Ordinance of Nullification, declaring that sovereignty resided with the states.

In November 1832 South Carolina revoked the national Tariff Act of 1828, declaring it null and void. The national posturing that followed threatened war between the states. It is assumed that Joseph Smith was well aware of the nullification crisis before he received the "prophecy on war." He stated in 1843, "I prophesy, in the name of the Lord God, that the commencement of the difficulties which will cause much bloodshed previous to the coming of the Son of Man will be in South Carolina. It may probably arise through the slave question. This a voice declared to me, while I was praying earnestly on the subject, December 25th, 1832" (D&C 130:12–13). However, to Joseph there was

Soldiers in action during the Civil War.

more than war threatening the union. He wrote, "Appearances of troubles among the nations became more visible this season than they had previously been since the Church began her journey out of the wilderness. The ravages of the cholera were frightful in almost all the large cities on the globe. The plague broke out in India."[329]

# Section 88

### D&C 88: Section Heading—Why is section 88 referred to as the "olive leaf"?

The association of "olive leaf" with this revelation comes from a letter Joseph Smith wrote on January 14, 1833, to William W. Phelps; it reads in part, "I send you the 'olive leaf' which we have plucked from the Tree of Paradise, the Lord's message of peace to us; for though our brethren in Zion indulge in feelings towards us, which are not according to the requirements of the new covenant, yet, we have the satisfaction of knowing that the Lord approves of us, and has accepted us, and established His name in Kirtland for the salvation of the nations; for the Lord will have a place whence His word will go forth, in these last days, in purity; for if Zion will not purify herself, so as to be approved of in all things, in His sight, He will seek another people; for His work will go on until Israel is gathered."[330] Enclosed with the letter were the "Olive Leaf Revelations," aptly named, for an olive branch symbolizes peace. These revelations were received on at least three different dates—December 27 and 28, 1832, and January 3, 1833.

### D&C 88:5—What is the Church of the Firstborn?

References to the Church of the Firstborn are found in the New Testament (see Heb. 12:23) and in the Doctrine and Covenants (see D&C 76:54, 67, 71, 94; 77:11; 78:21; 93:22; 107:19). The title Church of the Firstborn refers to those who inherit exaltation. As exalted beings, they receive an "inheritance of the firstborn," for they are "joint heirs with Jesus in all that the Father" has given him (Gal. 3:26; 4:7).[331]

### D&C 88:70, 117—What is the purpose of solemn assemblies?

The term *solemn assemblies* appears eight times in the Doctrine and Covenants (see D&C 88:70, 117; 95:7; 108:4; 109:6, 10; 124:39; 133:6). Of these sacred assemblies, President Spencer W. Kimball said, "Solemn assemblies have been known among the Saints since the days of Israel. They have been of various kinds but generally have been associated with the dedication of a temple or a special meeting appointed for the sustaining of a new First Presidency or a meeting for the priesthood to sustain a revelation."[332]

### D&C 88:76—What are the promised blessings associated with fasting?

Promised blessings directly linked to fasting are a strengthened testimony (see Alma 5:45–56); revelations from God (see D&C 1:34); the spirit of prophecy (see Alma 17:3); power to resist temptations (see 1 Cor. 7:5); and power to heal the sick (see Mark 9:17–29). "The greatest of all benefits from fasting," taught President David O. McKay, "is the spiritual strength derived by the subjection of physical appetite to the will of the individual."[333]

Participating in a monthly fast day was not practiced in the Church on a regular basis until 1852, "when the first Thursday of each month was set aside as a day of sacrifice. This continued until 1896, when the First Presidency changed the [fast] day from Thursday to the first Sunday of the month."[334]

### D&C 88:93—What is the "great sign in heaven" that will appear before the Second Coming of Jesus Christ?

Jesus referred to the "great sign in heaven" as the "sign of the Son of Man" (Matt. 24:30). The nature of the sign has not been revealed. In 1843, a Mr. Redding of Ogle County, Illinois, claimed to see the great sign. Joseph Smith discounted Mr. Redding's claim and wrote in the *Times and Seasons*, "Notwithstanding Mr. Redding may have seen a wonderful appearance in the clouds one morning . . . he has not seen the sign of the Son of Man, as foretold by Jesus; neither has any man, nor will any man, until after the sun shall have been darkened and the moon bathed in blood; for the Lord hath not shown me any such sign."[335]

## D&C 88:118—What were the gospel messages taught in the School for the Elders?

The School for the Elders began in the winter of 1834–1835 and continued in the winter of 1835–1836. Of the school Joseph Smith wrote, "Our school for the Elders was now well attended, and with the lectures on theology [Lectures on Faith], which were regularly delivered, absorbed for the time being everything else of a temporal nature. The classes, being mostly Elders gave the most studious attention to the all-important object of qualifying themselves as messengers of Jesus Christ, to be ready to do His will in carrying glad tidings to all that would open their eyes, ears and hearts."[336]

# Section 89

## D&C 89: Section Heading—What historical events led Joseph Smith to inquire of the Lord concerning dietary issues?

"I think I am as well acquainted with the circumstances which led to the giving of the

Joseph Smith studied for the School of the Prophets.

Word of Wisdom as any man in the Church," said Brigham Young, "although I was not present at the time to witness them. The first school of the prophets was held in a small room situated over the Prophet Joseph's kitchen, in a house which belonged to Bishop Whitney. . . . The brethren came to that place for hundreds of miles to attend school in a little room probably no larger than eleven by fourteen. When they assembled together in this room after breakfast, the first [thing] they did was to light their pipes, and, while smoking, talk about the great things of the kingdom, and spit all over the room, and as soon as the pipe was out of their mouths a large chew of tobacco would then be taken.

Often when the Prophet entered the room to give the school instructions he would find himself in a cloud of tobacco smoke. This, and the complaints of his wife at having to clean so filthy a floor, made the Prophet think upon the matter, and he inquired of the Lord relating to the conduct of the Elders in using tobacco, and the revelation known as the Word of Wisdom was the result of his inquiry."[337]

**D&C 89:2—Was acceptance of the Word of Wisdom gradual or immediate?**

Elder Zebedee Coltrin told of Joseph Smith reading the "Word of Wisdom" revelation to those attending the School of the Prophets. After hearing the revelation, twenty out of the twenty-one present "immediately threw their tobacco and pipes into the fire."[338] Yet acceptance of the Word of Wisdom by the general Church membership was gradual. As the decades passed, the Word of Wisdom became a controversial topic among Church members. On September 9, 1851, about eighteen years after the revelation was received by Joseph Smith, Brigham Young proposed that all Latter-day Saints live the Word of Wisdom. His proposal was unanimously accepted as a binding commandment upon

In addition to the things we should avoid, the Word of Wisdom prescribes how various foods should be used.

Church members.[339] However, the general membership failed to keep this commandment at that time.

Repeated admonitions by Church leaders met with varying degrees of acceptance. In 1913 President Joseph F. Smith explained, "The reason undoubtedly why the Word of Wisdom was given—as not by 'commandment or restraint' [*sic*] was that at that time, at least, if it had been given as a commandment, it would have brought every man, addicted to the use of these noxious things under condemnation; so the Lord was merciful and gave them a chance to overcome, before he brought them under the law."[340] At the October 1942 general conference, the First Presidency urged Latter-day Saints to "quit trifling with this law [the Word of Wisdom] and so to live it that we may claim its promises."[341]

## Section 90

### D&C 90:4—What are the "oracles of God"?

An oracle is a "revelation" or "a person through whom revelations are given." To "receive the oracles of God" is "to obtain the powers of revelation and to accept the prophets who reveal the mind of the Lord."[342] To "reject an oracle of God" is "to stumble and fall when the storms descend, and the winds blow, and the rains descend" (D&C 90:5).

## Section 91

### D&C 91:2—What is the Apocrypha?

The word *Apocrypha* means "of doubtful or questionable origin." It also means "hidden, obscure, and esoteric." "The Apocrypha" is used to describe "fourteen books which were part of early Greek and Latin versions of the Bible but were not part of the Hebrew Bible." These books are said to be a history of the Hebrews from Old Testament times to New Testament times. Through the years, the Apocrypha has been included in Catholic scriptures and in editions of the King James Version of the Bible. Since the early nineteenth century, the Apocrypha has been excluded from most Protestant Bibles.[343]

While translating/revising biblical text, Joseph Smith referred to a Bible that contained apocryphal writings. When Joseph inquired as to the worth of revising the apocryphal writings, he received the revelation contained in section 91. In this revelation Joseph was told not to translate the Apocrypha, for it contained falsehoods "which are interpolations by the hands of men"—meaning some of the writings and word phrases were not found in the original manuscripts (D&C 91:2).

## Section 92

**D&C 92:1—What was the purpose of the united order?**

The united order, also known as the united firm, managed the financial and commercial interests of the Church. The main purpose of the united order was to generate revenue for the financial operations of the Church. Those who managed the order had "equal claims on the properties, for the benefit of managing the concerns of [their] stewardships" (D&C 82:17). The united order had oversight of the mercantile establishments of the Gilbert, Whitney, and Company store in Independence, Missouri, and of the N. K. Whitney and Company store in Kirtland, Ohio.[344]

N. K. Whitney and Company store in Kirtland, Ohio.

**D&C 92:1—What is the order of Enoch?**

The order of Enoch is another name for the united order or united firm. On April 26, 1832, Joseph Smith, Oliver Cowdery, Martin Harris, Sidney Rigdon, Newel K. Whitney, and a few others were invited to form the order of Enoch (see D&C 82:11). By revelation, they were told to welcome Frederick G. Williams as a "lively member" and to receive him as "equal with thee [Joseph Smith] in holding the keys of this last kingdom" (D&C 90:6; 92:2).

## Section 93

**D&C 93:6–18—What is the record of John?**

The record of John is a record that was kept by John the Baptist. Of this record, Elder Orson Pratt said, "The records of John, him who baptized the Lamb of God, are yet to be revealed. We are informed in the book of Doctrine and Covenants [D&C 93:18] . . . that the fullness of the record of John, is to be revealed to the Latter-day Saints."[345]

**D&C 93:19–20—What is the proper way to worship God?**

The word *worship* stems from "two Anglo-Saxon words: *weorth*, worthy, and *scipe*, state or condition." Since God is in a "state of glory," meaning "brightness" and "luster," to enter into His glory is to be approved of God. Therefore, to receive the glory of God is to receive the favor granted those who merit His divine approbation.

According to President Spencer W. Kimball, to enter a state of glory requires proper worship of God, which includes "a prayerful heart, a hungering after righteousness, a forsaking of sins, and obedience to the commandments of God."[346] To those who willingly proffer such reverential worship, "the Lord pours out more and more light until there is finally power to pierce the heavenly veil and to know more than man knows. A person of such righteousness has the priceless promise that one day he shall see the Lord's face and know that he is."[347]

**D&C 93:51—What is the "acceptable year of the Lord"?**

The "acceptable year of the Lord" is the proper or designated time in the divine order of God for a certain work to be accomplished (see D&C 93:51; Isa. 61:2; Luke 4:19). In section 93, the phrase "acceptable year of the Lord" refers to the nearness of the Second Coming of Jesus Christ and a time to prepare for that glorious event.

# Section 94

**D&C 94:1—What was the center place of the "city of the stake of Zion" in Kirtland?**

On March 23, 1833, a committee was appointed to purchase acreage for the purpose of building a stake of Zion in Kirtland. After the requisite acreage had been purchased, it was surveyed beginning at the site where the Kirtland Temple would one day be built. This site was to be the center of Zion.

# Section 95

**D&C 95:3—In what manner did the Lord God reveal His plan for building the Kirtland Temple?**

Blueprints for the Kirtland Temple.

On June 3, 1833, a council of high priests convened at Kirtland to discuss building a small temple. According to Lucy Mack Smith, "In this council, Joseph requested that each of the brethren should give his views with regard to the house; and when they had all got through, he would give his opinion concerning the matter. They all complied with his request. Some were in favor of building a frame house, but others were of a mind to put up a log house. Joseph reminded them that they were not building a house for a man, but for God; 'and shall we, brethren,' said he, 'build a house for our God, of logs? No, I have a better plan than that. I have a plan of the house of the Lord, given by himself; and you will soon see by this, the difference between our calculations and his idea of things.'"[348] Joseph then told of a vision received by the First Presidency of the Church—Joseph Smith, Sidney Rigdon, and Frederick G. Williams. Williams's recollection of this vision was that a model of the building appeared "within viewing distance. . . . After we had taken a good look at the exterior, the building seemed to come right over us."[349]

In spite of the descriptive vision related by members of the First Presidency, the Kirtland Saints did not begin to build a temple. The Lord rebuked them for neglecting and delaying construction (see D&C 95:3); four days after this rebuke, George A. Smith hauled the first load of stone for the construction of the temple.

**D&C 95:4—What is the Lord's "strange act"? How does the Lord prepare for His "strange act"?**

One purpose for building the Kirtland Temple was to prepare the apostles so that the Lord could "bring to pass [his] strange act" (D&C 95:4; Isa. 28:21). In the latter days, God's "strange act" reveals "His marvelous plan of salvation and [makes] war upon an apostate church which is boasting of its intimate relations with Deity."[350] To prepare for this imminent war or the battle that lies ahead, the Lord's servants must be endowed with power from on high or receive a gift or bequest from God. To be endowed in the Kirtland era meant to be washed and anointed and receive an abundance of the Spirit of the Lord.

Brigham Young explained what an endowment from God meant to the Lord's servants: "Your endowment is, to receive all those ordinances in the house of the Lord, which are necessary for you, after you have departed this life, to enable you to walk back to the presence of the Father, passing the angels who stand as sentinels, being enabled to give them the key words, the signs and tokens, pertaining to the holy Priesthood, and gain your eternal exaltation in spite of earth and hell."[351]

## Section 96

**D&C 96:2—What was the process in selecting a manager to oversee Church properties in 1833?**

On June 4, 1833, high priests met in conference at Kirtland to consider "what disposition to make of the [Peter] French farm"—a farm on which the Kirtland Temple would be built. The council also considered the distribution of other properties that had been purchased for the Church. Although the council could agree on the use of the properties, they could not agree on a manager for the properties and expressed a willingness to let Joseph Smith ask God. In answer to Joseph's inquiry, the Lord directed the high priests to give Bishop Newel K. Whitney charge over the French farm and to assign to faithful brethren lots from other properties for building of the city of Zion.

## Section 97

**D&C 97: Section Heading—Was Joseph Smith aware of mob activity in Missouri when he wrote a letter counseling Church leaders to refrain from revenge in Jackson County?**

On July 20, 1833, extreme violence erupted against the Saints in Jackson County. The printing press owned and operated by William W. Phelps was destroyed, Latter-day Saints were driven from their homes, and Church leaders Edward Partridge and Charles Allen were tarred and feathered at the central square in Independence. Joseph Smith received the revelation known as section 97 about two weeks after the violence. At that time he was not aware of the extreme persecution.

In his letter of August 6, 1833, Joseph answered questions about the School in Zion and counseled Saints on a variety of topics. Parley P. Pratt, in recalling this particular revelation, wrote, "The revelation was not complied with by the leaders and Church in Missouri, as a whole; notwithstanding many were humble and faithful. Therefore, the threatened judgment was poured out to the uttermost."[352]

**D&C 97:1–3—Who directed the School for the Elders in Missouri?**

In late summer of 1838, a School for the Elders was organized in Missouri under the direction of Parley P. Pratt. About sixty elders met once a week for instruction. According to Pratt, "The place of meeting was in the open air, under some tall trees, in a retired place in the wilderness, where we prayed, preached and prophesied, and exercised ourselves in the gifts of the Holy Spirit. Here great blessings were poured out, and many great and marvelous things were manifested and taught." Of his teaching Pratt recalled, "The Lord gave me great wisdom, and enabled me to

Parley P. Pratt directed the School of the Elders.

teach and edify the Elders, and comfort and encourage them in their preparations for the great work which lay before us. I was also much edified and strengthened."[353]

## Section 98

**D&C 98:2—Why were the Saints told to be patient in afflictions?**

Seventeen days after Latter-day Saints were mobbed in Jackson County, Joseph Smith received a revelation counseling them to "bear it patiently and revile not against them, neither seek revenge" (D&C 98:23). Perhaps the purpose was more far-reaching than the obvious answer of not stooping to vengeance. The answer had much to do with seeking redress for wrongs perpetuated against the Saints in the framework of the Constitution of the United States. Joseph said, "The Constitution of the United States is a glorious standard; it is founded in the wisdom of God. It is a heavenly banner. . . . I am the greatest advocate of the Constitution of the United States there is on the earth."[354] Joseph contended that the principles of the Constitution enabled the Saints to right the wrongs they had suffered in Missouri.

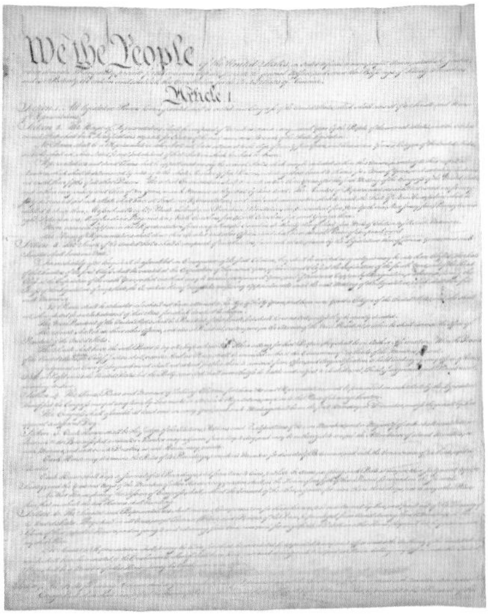

According to Joseph Smith, "The Constitution of the United States of America is a glorious standard."

# Section 99

## D&C 99:1—In what ways was John Murdock prepared to serve a mission in 1833?

John Murdock served a mission with Zebedee Coltrin from April 1833 to April 1834, laboring primarily in New York. Prior to leaving on this mission, he wrote of seeing a glorious vision of the Savior: "I saw the form of a man, most lovely, the visage of his face was sound and fair as the sun. His hair a bright silver grey, curled in most majestic form; His eyes a keen penetrating blue, and the skin of his neck a most beautiful white, and he was covered from the neck to the feet with a loose garment, pure white; Whiter than any garment I have ever before seen. His countenance was most penetrating, and yet most lovely."[355]

## D&C 99:2—What was the quest that John Murdock made to find a religion espousing the fulness of the gospel of Jesus Christ?

As a youth John Murdock turned to prayer and meditation

in hopes of finding a church that practiced the gospel of Jesus Christ. He united with the Lutheran Dutch Church, but "soon found they did not walk according to the scriptures." He next joined the Presbyterian Ceder Church, but "soon became dissatisfied with their walk, for I saw it was not according to the scriptures." He then united with the Baptists, but "finding their walk not to agree with their profession, I withdrew myself from them." He turned to the Methodist faith and was often asked to preach, but discovered "when I did not please them I would have to be silent among them awhile." By 1827 he had joined the Campbellites, but as many of its members denied the "gift and power of the Holy Ghost," Murdock lost interest and concluded "all the Sects were out of the way." In winter 1830 he learned that "four men had arrived in Kirtland from the state of New York, who were preaching, baptizing and building up the church after the ancient order." He journeyed twenty miles to see the new preachers for himself. These men introduced him to the Book of Mormon. Murdock received the book as the word of the Lord

John Murdock.

and was baptized on November 5, 1830, by Parley P. Pratt. "This was the third time I had been immersed," he wrote, "but I never before felt the authority of the ordinance, but I felt it this time and felt as though my sins were forgiven."[356]

**D&C 99:7–8—In what ways did John Murdock show his faithfulness to the gospel of Jesus Christ throughout his life?**

John Murdock served a mission in 1833–1834 and marched with Zion's Camp in 1834. He served on two high councils in Missouri, as a bishop of the Nauvoo 5th Ward, and as a member of the stake presidency at Lima,

Illinois. In the Salt Lake Valley he served as a high councilor and as bishop of the Salt Lake 14th Ward. In 1851 Murdock accepted a mission call to Australia, journeying nearly eight thousand miles to fulfill the calling. In 1854 he was ordained a patriarch by Heber C. Kimball. For the next thirteen years he gave many patriarchal blessings before his death at age seventy-nine.

# 6

# Sections 100–124

## Section 100

**D&C 100: Section Heading—What was Joseph Smith doing in Perrysburg, New York, in 1833?**

On October 5, 1833, Joseph Smith, Sidney Rigdon, and Freeman A. Nickerson departed from Kirtland on a missionary journey to Upper Canada. En route, they stopped in several eastern villages and towns to proclaim the gospel of Jesus Christ. On October 12, seven days after leaving Ohio, they arrived in the town of Perrysburg, New York. In this town Joseph Smith received a revelation informing him that "Zion must be chastened yet for a season, although she would finally be redeemed."[357]

## Section 101

**D&C 101:23–34—What promises will be given to those who live in the Millennium?**

Promises given to those who live in the millennial era are glorious and beyond the capacity of mortal man to fully conceive. These promises are that: 1) all will see the Savior (see D&C 101:23); 2) "the wicked will be destroyed" (D&C 101:24); 3) "the earth will become new" (D&C 101:25); 4) all "people and animals will live in peace" (D&C 101:26); 5) righteous desires will be granted (see D&C 101:27); 6) Satan will be bound and have no power to tempt the people (see D&C 101:28); 7) "there will be no sorrow or death" (D&C 101:29); 8) all will grow old before being changed from mortality to immortality (see D&C 101:30–31); and 9) "the Lord will reveal all things about earth and heaven" (D&C 101:32–34).[358]

**D&C 101:88–89—Why was it important for Latter-day Saints to appeal to the federal government to redress their wrongs in the state of Missouri?**

Joseph Smith advised all Latter-day Saints who had suffered wrongs in Missouri to "employ every lawful means to seek redress of your enemies." He encouraged them to "appeal unto the executive; and when the executive fail you, appeal unto the president; and when the president fail you, and all laws fail you, and the humanity of the people fail you, and all things else fail you but God alone, and you continue to weary Him with your importunings, as the poor woman did the unjust judge [Luke 18:1–8], He will not fail to execute judgment upon your enemies, and to avenge His own elect that cry unto Him day and night."[359] The reason for this lengthy appellate process was that "there is a just law of retribution, as fixed and eternal as are the other laws of the Almighty, the day must come when there shall be adjustments made before a Just Magistrate who will not be cowed by the threats of mobs" (D&C 6:33; 2 Cor. 9:6).[360]

**D&C 101:99—Why were the Saints told to hold claim to their lands in Jackson County when they were not permitted to dwell in that county?**

At the time of the revelation, the exiled Saints of Jackson County had been driven from their lands across the Missouri River to Clay County. Yet they were commanded to "hold claim" upon their lands even though "they should not be permitted to dwell thereon" (D&C 101:99). Joseph Smith expounded on this revelation by writing to these Saints, "I would inform you that it is not the will of the Lord for you to sell your lands in Zion, if means can possibly be procured for your sustenance without. Every exertion should be made to maintain the cause you have espoused."[361] He added, "Let your sufferings be what they may, it is better in the eyes of God that you should die, than that you should give up the land of Zion, the inheritances which you have purchased with your moneys;

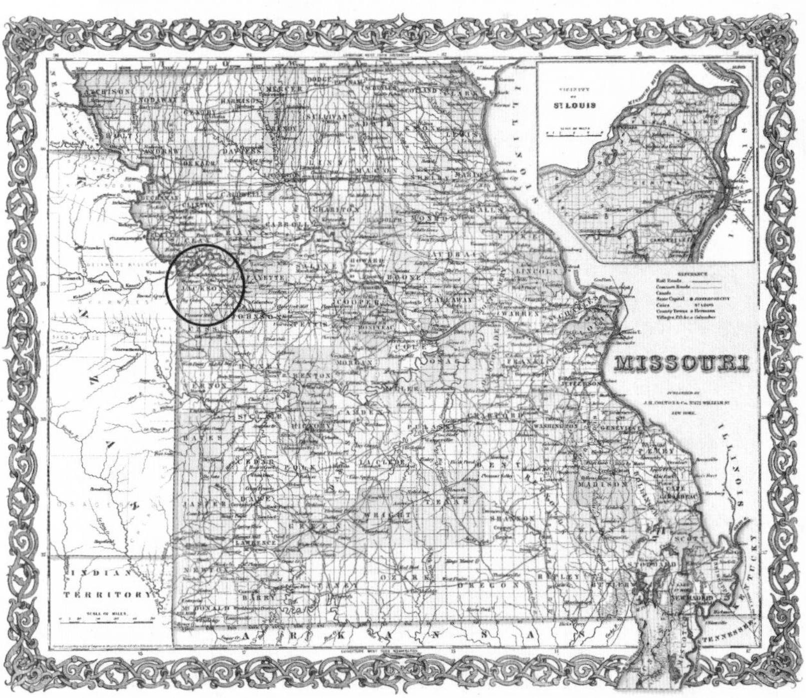


Joseph Smith commanded the Saints to "hold claim" upon their lands in Jackson County.

for every man that giveth not up his inheritance, though he should die, yet, when the Lord shall come, he shall stand upon it, and with Job, in his flesh he shall see God. Therefore, this is my counsel, that you retain your lands, even unto the uttermost."[362] The emphasis of the letter is the promise that when the Lord comes in glory, the Saints will again possess their land. To sell the land before the Second Coming was considered "a very sore and grievous sin" in the eyes of God (D&C 101:98).

# Section 102

## D&C 102: Section Heading—How did the first high council differ from other councils today?

The differences between the first high council and other such councils today are first, the First Presidency was the presiding authority of that first council, and second, the first council had jurisdiction outside of the stake. It was not until high councils were organized within stakes that stake presidencies presided over their discussions and deliberations.

### D&C 102:2—Was the primary purpose of the first high council judicial or legislative?

On February 17, 1834, Joseph Smith organized the first high council at Kirtland, Ohio. Reviewing the minutes of the organizational meeting reveals the nature of the first high council as being primarily judicial. Of the judgment that rested with this council, Joseph said, "No man is capable of judging a matter, in council, unless his own heart is pure; and that we are frequently so filled with prejudice, or have a beam in our own eye, that we are not capable of passing right decisions. . . . Our acts are recorded, and at a future day they will be laid before us, and if we should fail to judge right and injure our fellow-beings, they may there, perhaps, condemn us; there they are of great consequence, and to me the consequence appears to be of force, beyond anything which I am able to express."[363]

### D&C 102:9–23—When did Joseph Smith expand the judicial procedure of the Kirtland high council to mirror the judicial procedure of ancient councils during the days of the apostle Peter?

On February 17, 1834, Joseph Smith declared that he received a vision expanding the function of the high council in Kirtland. According to the Kirtland High Council Minute Book, "Bro. Joseph then said he would show the order of councils in ancient days as shown to him by vision. The law by which to govern the council in the Church of Christ. Jerusalem was the seat of the Church Council in ancient days. The apostle, Peter, was the president of the Council and held the keys of the Kingdom of God on the earth was appointed to this office by the voice of the Savior and acknowledged in it by the voice of the Church. . . . It was not the order of heaven in ancient councils to plead for and against the guilty as in our judicial Courts (so called) but that every counsellor when he arose to speak, should speak precisely according to evidence and according to the teaching of the Spirit of the Lord; that no counsellor should attempt to screen the guilty when his guilt was manifest. That the person accused before the high council had a right to one half the members of the council to plead his cause in order that his case might be fairly presented before the President that a decision might be rendered according to truth and righteousness . . . Bro. Joseph said that this organization was an ensample to the high priests in their Councils abroad."[364]

## Section 103

**D&C 103: Section Heading—Who informed Joseph Smith of the persecution that raged against the Latter-day Saints in Jackson County?**

During the first week of November 1833, Latter-day Saints were driven from their homes and lands in Jackson County. Parley P. Pratt recalled, "On the first of February we [Pratt and Lyman Wight] mounted our horses, and started in good cheer to ride one thousand or fifteen hundred miles through a wilderness country. We had not one cent of money in our pockets on starting." When Pratt and Wight arrived in Kirtland, they reported to Joseph Smith and the Kirtland High Council, telling of the atrocities faced by the Saints in Jackson County. They wanted "to know, if possible, how and by what means Zion was to be redeemed."[365] It was revealed to Joseph Smith on December 16, 1833, that he would lead "the strength of mine house" to redeem the land of Zion (see D&C 101:55–60). Joseph led and organized a quasi-military organization known as Zion's Camp with the specific purpose of marching to Jackson County to redeem Zion even by blood if necessary.[366]

**D&C 103:13—Will Latter-day Saints return to Jackson County in the future to build a new Zion?**

Brigham Young assured Latter-day Saints that Zion would yet be built in Jackson County: "Are we going back to Jackson County? Yes. When? As soon as the way opens up. Are we all going? O no! of course not. The country is not large enough to hold our present numbers."[367] He also said, "A portion of the Priesthood will go and redeem and build up the centre Stake of Zion."[368]

### D&C 103:15—How was Zion's Camp organized?

Zion's Camp was comprised of two divisions, one under the leadership of Joseph Smith and a smaller contingent under the leadership of Hyrum Smith and Lyman Wight. The divisions were divided into companies of twelve men. Each company elected its own captain who, in turn, arranged each man in his company according to his "post and duty." Some were assigned to be cooks, firemen, watermen, waggoners, horsemen, and commissaries, while others were appointed captains over fifties and hundreds according to the ancient order of Israel.[369]

### D&C 103:22—Who appointed Joseph Smith to be commander in chief of the armies of Israel?

On February 24, 1834, Joseph Smith informed the Kirtland High Council that "he was going to Zion, to assist in redeeming it. He called for the voice of the Council to sanction his going which was given without a dissenting voice." He was then nominated and seconded as the commander in chief of the armies of Israel—the leader of a quasi-military organization known as Zion's Camp.[370]

### D&C 103:29–34—How long did it take to recruit volunteers for Zion's Camp?

Joseph Smith was told through revelation, "Let my servant Joseph Smith, Jun., say unto the strength of my house, my young men and the middle aged—Gather yourselves together unto the land of Zion, upon the land which I have bought with money that has been consecrated unto me" (D&C 103:22). In response to this revelation, volunteers for Zion's Camp were sought in nearly every branch of the Church. It took more than two months and the recruiting efforts of eight Church leaders to gather a sufficient number of men, supplies, and money before the camp was ready to march toward Independence, Missouri.

### D&C 103:34—When did the march to Missouri begin?

An advance party of twenty men left Kirtland on May 1, 1834, to prepare the first

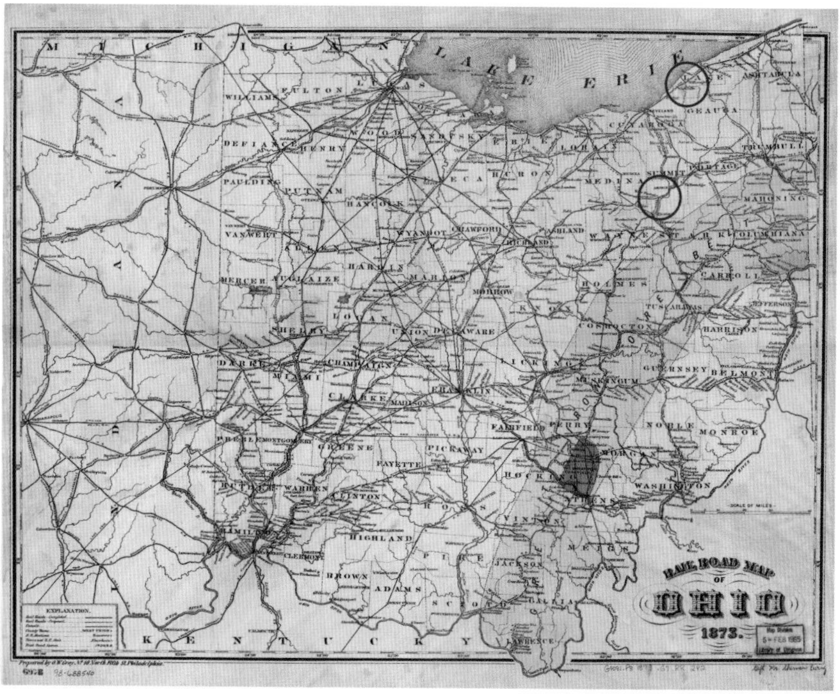


Kirtland and New Portage to the southwest, where Zion's Camp was organized.

campsite at New Portage, Ohio, where an organized branch of the Church with some fifty members was located. Joseph Smith and the main body of eighty-five men left Kirtland on May 5, arriving in New Portage on May 6. The next day, May 7, was spent organizing the camp, which now consisted of more than one hundred and thirty men accompanied by twenty-five baggage wagons. Before the camp reached Missouri, it numbered two hundred and five men under arms with a small number of women and children.

# Section 104

**D&C 104:78—What economic problems beset the Church and its leaders in 1834?**

On April 23, 1834, the First Presidency and several high priests met to discuss the urgency of indebtedness plaguing Church leaders. Although the nature and number of creditors is not sufficiently identified, the issue of debt was real and the outcome uncertain.

Joseph Smith was not immune from his own financial concerns at this time. Knowing something of Joseph's financial problems, Brigham Young said, "Joseph was doing business in Kirtland, and it seemed as though all creation was upon him, to hamper him in every way, and they drove him from his business, and it left him so that some of his debts had to be settled afterwards." Years later, in hopes of settling any debts that Joseph may have accrued, Brigham Young said, "We have sent East to New York, to Ohio, and to every place where I had any idea that Joseph had ever done business, and inquired if there was a man left to whom Joseph Smith, jun., the Prophet, owed a dollar, or a sixpence. If there was we would pay it. But I have not been able to find one. I have advertised this through every neighborhood and place where he formerly lived, consequently I have a right to conclude that all his debts were settled."[371]

## Section 105

**D&C 105: Section Heading—Did danger heighten as volunteers in Zion's Camp neared Jackson County, Missouri?**

After crossing Little Fishing River on June 19, 1834, Joseph Smith selected a campsite near the Big Fishing River. There, his camp was assaulted by a mob of some three hundred Missourians. "Swearing vengeance," the mob began cannonading the Mormon position. When it appeared that the mob had overpowered the volunteers of Zion's Camp, Joseph Smith recalled, "We discovered a small black cloud rising in the west, and in 20 minutes, or thereabouts, it began to rain and hail. . . . The storm was tremendous; wind and rain, hail and thunder met them in great wrath, and soon softened their direful courage and frustrated all their designs to 'kill Joe Smith and his army.'"[372] After the attackers left the field of battle, volunteers in Zion's Camp found a welcome relief from the storm in a Baptist meetinghouse located on the bluff above the encampment.

**D&C 105: Section Heading—Why is section 105 referred to as the "Fishing River revelation"?**

Joseph Smith sought guidance from the Lord while encamped at Fishing River and received this revelation. In the revelation Joseph was told that the Saints were not blameless for the problems that had beset them in Jackson County: "Behold, I say unto you, were it not for the transgressions of my people, speaking concerning the church and not individuals, they might have been redeemed even now" (D&C 105:2). Their transgressions included being "full of all manner of evil"; failing to "impart of their substance, as becometh saints, to the poor and afflicted among them"; and not uniting according "to the union required by the law of the celestial kingdom" (D&C 105:3–4). As a "consequence of the transgressions of my people," said the Lord, "it is expedient in me that mine elders should wait for a little season for the redemption of Zion" (D&C 105:9). Following the revelation, Joseph informed volunteers of Zion's Camp that they would no longer prosecute war with the Missourians. The camp was disbanded on June 25, 1834, and volunteers were discharged on July 2.

### D&C 105: Section Heading—Did the volunteers in Zion's Camp value their experiences in the camp?

Very few volunteers wrote memoirs of their experiences in Zion's Camp. Two exceptions

Through a vicious storm of rain, hail, and thunder, Zion's Camp was preserved from the Missourian mob.

are Brigham Young and Wilford Woodruff. Brigham Young said, "When I returned from that mission [Zion's Camp] to Kirtland, a brother said to me, 'Brother Brigham, what have you gained by this journey?' I replied, 'Just what we went for; but I would not exchange the knowledge I have received this season for the whole of Geauga County; for property and mines of wealth are not to be compared to the worth of knowledge.'"[373] Wilford Woodruff wrote, "We gained an experience that we never could have gained in any other way. We had the privilege of beholding the face of the prophet, and we had the privilege of travelling a thousand miles with him, and seeing the workings of the Spirit of God with him, and the revelations of Jesus Christ unto him and the fulfillment of those revelations."[374]

**D&C 105:14—Who tried to mitigate a peaceful solution between the leaders of Zion's Camp and the Jackson County mob/militia?**

It was Sheriff Cornelius Gillium of Clay County who attempted to mitigate a peaceful solution to the growing hostilities. He entered the Saints' encampment near Fishing River in mid-June 1834. His purpose in coming was to instruct the leaders of Zion's Camp about the hostile disposition of residents in Jackson County toward the Mormons. Joseph Smith gave Sheriff Gillium permission to address the camp after he had marched a company of men into a grove and formed a circle around the sheriff. The sheriff then addressed the men "by saying that he had heard that Joseph Smith was in the camp, and if so he would like to see him." Joseph then replied, "I am the man." Joseph later recalled, "This was the first time that I had been discovered or made known to my enemies since I left Kirtland. Gillium then gave us instruction concerning the manners, customs, and dispositions of the people, and what course we ought to pursue to secure their favor and protection, making certain inquiries, to which we replied, which were afterwards published."[375]

## Section 106

**D&C 106: Section Heading—What was the relationship between Oliver Cowdery and Warren A. Cowdery?**

Warren A. Cowdery, a farmer and physician in Freedom, New York, was the older brother of Oliver Cowdery. Warren was less inclined to accept new religious teachings than was his brother Oliver. However, when Oliver gave him proof sheets of the Book of Mormon, Warren perused the copies with faith and a growing sense of belief. He was baptized in late 1831.

**D&C 106:1—In what way did the baptism of Warren Cowdery forward the work of the Lord in Freedom, New York?**

On a missionary journey to the East in 1834, Joseph Smith stopped in Freedom, New York. In that town, he was welcomed into the home of Warren A. Cowdery. Of his host, Joseph wrote, "We were blessed with a full enjoyment of temporal and spiritual blessings, even all we needed, or were worthy to receive."[376] During his stay, a branch of the Church was organized with Cowdery as the presiding officer. As such, Cowdery was given responsibility for Church members in the towns of Freedom, Genesee, Avon, and Livonia. Although the area was vast, Cowdery was equal to the assignment. In this revelation the Lord assured him, "The laborer is worthy of his hire," suggesting that he had the necessary talents to fulfill his assignment as the presiding officer of the Freedom Branch (see D&C 106:3).[377]

**D&C 106:8—What other contributions did Warren Cowdery make to the Church?**

Possessing many of the same talents as his brother Oliver, Warren served as a scribe and as an assistant recorder for the Church. He kept council minutes, made entries in Joseph's diary, penned an historical record of the Church, and scribed patriarchal blessings. He also assisted in writing the dedicatory prayer for the Kirtland Temple (see D&C 109). He served as a high councilor and as an agent for Joseph Smith and Sidney Rigdon in the printing office and book bindery in Kirtland. He succeeded his brother Oliver as editor of the *Messenger and Advocate*. Yet he became disaffected with Church leaders in 1838 and lost his membership, as did Oliver.

# Section 107

**D&C 107: Section Heading—Why were the newly called Quorum of the Twelve Apostles in need of comfort and encouragement in March 1835?**

On March 28, 1835, feeling unprepared and unworthy as the weight of their calling rested upon them, the Quorum of the Twelve Apostles petitioned Joseph Smith in a letter to "inquire of God for us" and to obtain a revelation, if appropriate, that would comfort them. They concluded their letter, "We therefore feel to ask of him whom we have acknowledged to be our Prophet and Seer, that he inquire of God for us, and obtain a revelation, (if consistent) that we may look upon it when we are separated, that our hearts may be comforted. Our worthiness has not inspired us to make this request, but our unworthiness. We have unitedly asked God our Heavenly Father to grant unto us through His Seer, a revelation of His mind and will concerning our duty the coming season, even a great revelation, that will enlarge our hearts, comfort us in adversity, and brighten our hopes amidst the powers of darkness."[378] After receiving their letter, Joseph wrote to the Twelve, "In compliance with the above request, I inquired of the Lord, and received for answer the following" fifty-eight verses in section 107. The remaining verses were revealed at a later time.[379]

**D&C 107:1–12—What are the basic functions of the priesthood of God?**

The basic functions of the priesthood are administered through priesthood offices. There are three offices in the Aaronic Priesthood—deacon, teacher, and priest. Deacons warn and teach (see D&C 20:59; 107:85; 1 Tim. 3:8-13). Teachers watch over the Church (see D&C 20:53–58; 107:86; Eph. 4:11–12; 1 Cor. 12:28). Priests preach, teach, expound, baptize, administer the sacrament, and ordain worthy men to the Aaronic Priesthood (see D&C 20:46–52: 107:87–88; Heb. 10:11, Acts 6:7).

In the Melchizedek Priesthood, there are five offices—elder, high priest, patriarch, seventy, and apostle. Elders administer in spiritual matters, ordain worthy men to priesthood offices, bestow the gift of the Holy Ghost, and conduct meetings (see D&C 20:38–45; 107:12, 89; Acts 14:23; James 5:14; 1 Pet. 5:1). High priests preside in wards and stakes and administer in spiritual and temporal affairs (see D&C 107:12, 71; 124:134; Heb. 5:1, 2, 6; 7:11). Patriarchs give inspired blessings (see D&C 124; Acts 21:8). Seventies preach the gospel throughout the world (see D&C 107:25, 45; 124:139; Luke 10:1). Apostles serve as special witnesses of Jesus Christ to the world (see D&C 107:23, 24, 58; Matt. 16:19; Eph. 4:11–14).

## Section 108

### D&C 108: Section Heading—Why was Lyman Sherman released as a president of the seventies?

Lyman Sherman was released as a president of the seventies due to his previous ordination to the office of high priest. On December 26, 1835, soon after his release, Sherman said to Joseph Smith, "I have been wrought upon to make known to you my feelings and desires, and was promised that I should have a revelation which should make known my duty."[380] The Prophet received a revelation for Sherman that very hour. In the revelation the Lord said, "Your sins are forgiven you, because you have obeyed my voice in coming up hither this morning to receive counsel of him whom I have appointed" (D&C 108:1). Sherman was also told to "wait patiently until the solemn assembly shall be called of my servants, then you shall be remembered with the first of mine elders" (D&C 108:4). His call to the apostleship was extended in a January 16, 1839, letter signed by Joseph Smith, Sidney Rigdon, and Hyrum Smith. Sherman was never ordained to the apostolic priesthood due to his death in January 1839 at age thirty-four.[381]

## Section 109

### D&C 109: Section Heading—When did work on the Kirtland Temple commence?

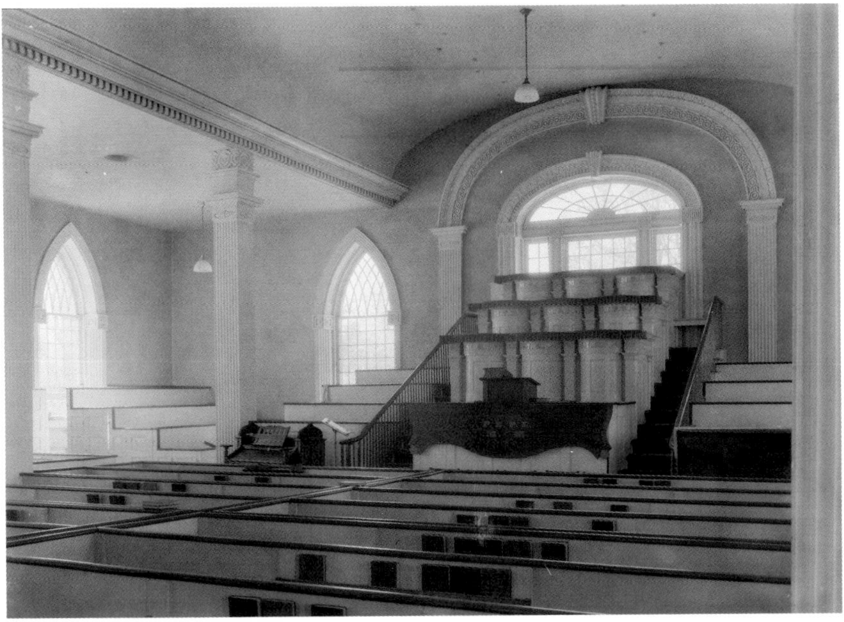

Interior of the Kirtland Temple.

Work on the Kirtland Temple commenced on June 5, 1833, when "George A. Smith hauled the first load of stone" and Hyrum Smith declared, "[I will] strike the first blow upon the house."[382] By summer 1833, nearly every able-bodied Latter-day Saint had contributed time and labor to forward construction of the temple. From cutting stones to felling trees, they worked night and day at a hurried pace to construct an edifice that would glorify God. The women of the Church were as committed to building the house of the Lord as were the men. "Our wives were all the time knitting, spinning and sewing, and, in fact, I may say doing all kinds of work," said Heber C. Kimball. Lucy Mack Smith explained the reason: "There was but one mainspring to all our thoughts and actions, and that was, the building of the Lord's house."[383]

**D&C 109: Section Heading—Who wrote the dedicatory prayer for the Kirtland Temple?**

The dedicatory prayer was written prior to the dedication of the Kirtland Temple under the direction of Joseph Smith, assisted by Sidney Rigdon, Oliver Cowdery, Warren Cowdery, and Warren Parrish.

**D&C 109:22—Is the phrase "thine angels have charge over them" a reference to guardian angels or other angelic beings?**

According to Elder John A. Widstoe, "Undoubtedly angels often guard us from accidents and harm, from temptation and sin. They may properly be spoken of as guardian angels. Many people have borne and may bear testimony to the guidance and protection that they have received from sources beyond their natural vision. Without the help that we receive from the constant presence of the Holy Spirit, and from possibly holy angels, the difficulties of life would be greatly multiplied. The common belief, however, that to every person born into the world is assigned a guardian angel to be with that person constantly, is not supported by available evidence. It is a very comforting thought, but at present without proof of its correctness. An angel may be a guardian angel though he come only as assigned to give us special help. In fact, the constant presence of the Holy Spirit would seem to make such a constant, angelic companionship unnecessary."[384]

**D&C 109:25–33—What opposition did Latter-day Saints face as they built the Kirtland Temple?**

The joy of the Saints over the rising temple walls was countered by a growing mob element in Kirtland. Although friends readily defended Joseph Smith and the Restoration, each stone added to the temple walls seemed to agitate nearby neighbors. By the winter of 1833–1834, mobs in Kirtland had threatened to tear down the walls and kill the Prophet. "Our enemies were raging and threatening destruction upon us," Heber C. Kimball said. "We had to guard night after night, and . . . were obliged to lie with our fire locks in our arms, to preserve Brother Joseph's life."[385] Men did not remove their work clothes and "gave no sleep to their eyes, nor slumber to their eyelids," to protect the temple walls and the life of the Prophet Joseph.[386] In spite of mobs and threats, the temple construction moved steadily forward.

**D&C 109:79—Why are the days following the Kirtland Temple dedication referred to as the "Pentecostal season"?**

Festivities celebrated in ancient Judah fifty days after Passover—or, as the Greeks called it, *Pentekoste*—were called the Feast of Weeks (see Ex. 34:22; Deut. 16:10), the Feast of Harvest (see Ex. 23:16), and the Day of the First Fruits (see Num. 28:26). In early Christianity, Pentecost was a day when manifestations of the Spirit of God were evident (see Acts 2:1–17). In the Kirtland Temple dedicatory prayer, Joseph Smith asked God to let the "anointing" of worthy brethren "be fulfilled upon them, as upon those on the day of Pentecost" (D&C 109:35–36). Joseph's petition was granted, for "the Savior made His appearance to some, while angels ministered to others, and it was a Pentecost and an endowment indeed, long to be remembered."[387]

### D&C 109:79—What spiritual manifestations occurred at the Kirtland Temple dedication?

"The ceremonies of that dedication may be rehearsed, but no mortal language can describe the heavenly manifestations of that memorable day," wrote Eliza R. Snow. However, she went on to pen, "Angels appeared to some,

Kirtland Temple circa 1971.

while a sense of divine presence was realized by all present." Elder Orson Pratt also wrote of the dedication, "God was there, his angels were there, the Holy Ghost was in the midst of the people, the visions of the Almighty were opened to the minds of the servants of the living God; the v[e]il was taken off from the minds of many; they saw the heavens opened; they beheld the angels of God; they heard the voice of the Lord; and they were filled from the crown of their heads to the soles of their feet with the power and inspiration of the Holy Ghost."[388]

The dedication of the Kirtland Temple marked the beginning of the greatest Pentecostal season in the Church. It is estimated that between January 21 and May 1, 1836, more Latter-day Saints beheld visions and spiritual manifestations than at any other time in the history of the Church. For example, during meetings held in the Kirtland Temple, Latter-day Saints claimed to see the Savior Jesus Christ and angels or messengers sent from God. Some reported communing with heavenly messengers while others professed to prophesy and speak in tongues.[389]

**D&C 109:79—Who wrote of seeing the glory of the Lord rest upon the Kirtland Temple like a great cloud?**

Oliver Cowdery wrote, "I saw the glory of God, like a great cloud, come down and rest upon the house, and fill the same like a mighty rushing wind. I also saw cloven tongues, like as of fire rest upon many . . . while they spake with other tongues and prophesied."[390]

Kirtland Temple circa 2009.

# Section 110

## D&C 110: Section Heading—What events led to Joseph Smith and Oliver Cowdery seeing a vision of the Savior, Moses, Elias, and Elijah?

On April 3, 1836, one week after the Kirtland Temple was dedicated, Joseph wrote, "Attended meeting in the Lord's House, and assisted the other Presidents of the Church [the First Presidency and quorum presidents] in seating the congregation, and then became an attentive listener to the preaching from the stand. Thomas B. Marsh and David W. Patten spoke in the forenoon to an attentive audience of about one thousand persons. In the afternoon, I assisted the other Presidents in distributing the Lord's Supper to the Church, receiving it from the Twelve, whose privilege it was to officiate at the sacred desk this day. After having performed this service to my brethren, I retired to the pulpit, the veils being dropped, and bowed myself, with Oliver Cowdery, in solemn and silent prayer." After the prayer, a vision of the Savior appeared, followed by a vision of Moses, Elias, and Elijah.[391]

## D&C 110:2—What is the "breastwork of the pulpit" that the Lord Jesus Christ stood on when appearing to Joseph Smith and Oliver Cowdery?

In the Kirtland Temple there are two stands or pulpit structures on the main floor—one at the west side for leading officers of the Melchizedek Priesthood and the other at the east side for leading officers of the Aaronic Priesthood. Each of these pulpit structures had a *breastwork*, which literally means "a temporary fortification." In this case it was a railing about four feet high.

Breastwork in the Kirtland Temple.

**D&C 110:11–16—What are the blessings and responsibilities associated with the priesthood keys given to Joseph Smith and Oliver Cowdery by Moses, Elias, and Elijah?**

Joseph Smith wrote that on April 3, 1836, while he and Oliver Cowdery were kneeling in prayer at the Melchizedek Priesthood altars located on the first floor of the Kirtland Temple, "The veil was taken from our minds, and the eyes of our understanding were opened. We saw the Lord standing upon the breastwork of the pulpit, before us; and under his feet was a paved work of pure gold." When that vision closed, the heavens again opened. Moses appeared and committed unto Joseph and Oliver "the keys of the gathering of Israel from the four parts of the earth, and the leading of the ten tribes from the land of the north." Next came Elias, who bestowed the keys of "the dispensation of the gospel of Abraham" (D&C 110:1–2, 11–13), which is the blessings of the Abrahamic covenant and the responsibilities associated with that covenant (see Abr. 2:9–11). And then "another great and glorious vision" was opened unto Joseph and Oliver. Elijah appeared and bestowed priesthood keys to turn "the hearts of the fathers to the children, and the children to the fathers" (see D&C 110:15).

# Section 111

**D&C 111:1—Why did Joseph Smith journey to Salem, Massachusetts, in 1836?**

Completing the Kirtland Temple and sending financial aid to the exiled Saints of Jackson County left many in Kirtland and the Church as a whole in debt. Hoping to solve this escalating financial problem, Joseph Smith and others listened to and then embraced the boasts of convert Jonathan Burgess, who claimed "knowledge of a large amount of money secreted in the cellar of a certain house in Salem, Massachusetts, which had belonged to a widow," who was then deceased. The excitement generated by these claims and the hope of finding hidden money led Joseph Smith, Hyrum Smith, Sidney Rigdon, and Oliver Cowdery to journey to Salem, Massachusetts.[392]

**D&C 111:7—How long did Joseph Smith and his traveling companions stay in Salem?**

Joseph Smith and the other brethren stayed in Salem for a month, "teaching the people from house to house, and preaching publicly, as opportunity presented; visiting occasionally, sections of the surrounding country, which are rich in the history of the Pilgrim Fathers of New England, in Indian warfare, religious superstition, bigotry, persecution, and learned ignorance."[393]

**D&C 111:10—What amount of the purported hidden money did Joseph Smith and his traveling companions find?**

Although much preaching was done in Salem, the main reason for the month-long stay of Joseph Smith and the other brethren in the seaport town was monetary. In a letter written by Joseph to his wife, Emma, he told of finding the house where the purported treasure was hidden in a cellar: "With regard to the great object of our mission, you will be anxious to know. We have found the house since Brother Burgess left us, very luckily and providentially, as we had one spell been most discouraged. The house is occupied, and it will require much care and patience to rent or buy it. We think we shall be able to effect it; if not now, within the course of a few months."[394] Such was not the case, and no hidden money was found by Joseph or the other brethren.

# Section 112

**D&C 112:1—Why was Heber C. Kimball's mission call to England significant to the development of the Church?**

At a time when the spirit of speculation in property of all kinds was "prevalent throughout the whole nation," speculation took root among the Saints in Kirtland, Ohio. The fruits of such speculation, such as evil-surmising and fault-finding, followed in quick succession. According to Joseph Smith, "It seemed as though all the powers of earth and hell were combining their influence in an especial manner to overthrow the Church at once, and make a final end." Joseph witnessed many become disaffected with the Church as if Mormon-

Four ships were lost at one time near Liverpool, England, in 1839. Ocean travel was still a risky venture in the 1800s.

ism was the sole cause of such evil. He lamented, "No quorum in the Church was entirely exempt from the influence of those false spirits who are striving against me for the mastery; even some of the Twelve were so far lost to their high and responsible calling, as to begin to take sides." It was then that the Lord revealed to His Prophet that something must be done for the salvation of the Church, since many were succumbing to the spirit of speculation and leaving the Church. Accordingly, Heber C. Kimball was sent to England to open the work abroad in foreign lands in hope of converting many to the gospel of Jesus Christ. On or about the first of June 1837, Kimball was "set apart by the spirit of prophecy and revelation, prayer and laying on of hands, of the First Presidency, to preside over a mission to England, to be the first foreign mission of the Church of Christ in the last days."[395]

**D&C 112:1—Why was Thomas B. Marsh troubled in 1837 about members of his quorum?**

On the evening of July 23, 1837, Thomas B. Marsh was concerned that some members in the Quorum of the Twelve were disobeying the Lord's commands. In response to his concern, Joseph dictated as Marsh wrote, "The word of the Lord unto Thomas B. Marsh, concerning the Twelve Apostles of the Lamb" (D&C 112: Section Heading). Through revelation the Lord told Marsh to "pray for thy brethren of the Twelve. Admonish them sharply for my name's sake, and let them be admonished for all their sins . . . I, the Lord, will feel after them, and if they harden not their hearts . . . they shall be converted, and I will heal them" (D&C 112:12–13). The Lord admonished the Twelve to "exalt not yourselves [and] rebel not against my servant Joseph" (D&C 112:15).[396]

**D&C 112:15—Who said that Joseph Smith was foreordained in eternity to preside over this dispensation?**

Brigham Young said, "It was decreed in the counsels of eternity, long before the foundations of the earth were laid, that he [Joseph Smith] should be the man, in the last dispensation of this world, to bring forth the word of God to the people, and receive the fulness of the keys and power of the Priesthood of the Son of God. The Lord had his eye upon him, and upon his father, and upon his father's father, and upon their progenitors clear back to Abraham, and from Abraham to the flood, from the flood to Enoch, and from Enoch to Adam. He has watched that family and that blood as it has circulated from its fountain to the birth of that man. He was foreordained in eternity to preside over this last dispensation."[397]

## Section 113

**D&C 113: Section Heading—How many revelations did Joseph Smith receive in Far West, Missouri?**

In 1838 seven revelations recorded in the Doctrine and Covenants were received by Joseph Smith at Far West, Missouri. Three revelations were received in March or April (see D&C 113–115) and four were received in July (see D&C 117–120).

**D&C 113: Section Heading—What historical events led to the revelation contained in section 113?**

The history of section 113 is linked to the arrival of Joseph Smith's brother Samuel Smith and his family in Far West. As Joseph was walking with his brother in Far West, Elias Higbee and other brethren approached them. These brethren had questions about the interpretation of verses in Isaiah 11 and looked to Joseph Smith for answers.[398] It is not known which brother asked about the first Isaiah passages, but it is known that Elias Higbee asked the last. The answers given are viewed as direct revelations from God.

### D&C 113:1–2—Why is Jesus Christ referred to in the book of Isaiah as the "Stem of Jesse"?

The ancestral line of Jesse is the royal line of kings that began with King David. The word *stem* is a reference to Jesus Christ's "being of the lineage of King David, the son of Jesse" (see Jer. 23:5–6; 33:15–17; Acts 2:30; 13:22–23; Rom. 1:3; Luke 1:32).[399]

### D&C 113:7—What were Elias Higbee's contributions to the Church?

Soon after joining the Church in Cincinnati, Ohio, Elias Higbee moved his family to Jackson County, Missouri. Mobs in 1833 forced their removal to Clay County, where Higbee was given his first of several leadership assignments in the Church. He was a high councilor in Clay County before serving as a clerk, historian, recorder, and high councilor in Far West. In 1838 he was driven from Missouri by mobs and sought safety in Illinois, where he continued to take a prominent role in ecclesiastical affairs. On March 9, 1839, he was appointed to determine which properties in Illinois and Iowa should be purchased for the Saints. On October 6, 1839, he was appointed to accompany the Prophet Joseph to Washington, DC, to present Latter-day Saint grievances against the state of Missouri before Congress and the president of the United States, Martin Van Buren.

Higbee remained at the national capitol to lobby for redress of Missouri wrongs long after the Prophet's departure. On February 26, 1840, he wrote to the Prophet, "I feel now that we have made our last appeal to all earthly tribunals; that we should now put our whole trust in the God of Abraham, Isaac, and Jacob. We have a right now which we could not heretofore so fully claim—that is of asking God for redress and redemption, as they have been refused us by man."[400] At that point Higbee left Washington and returned to Nauvoo, Illinois. His most important assignment in Nauvoo was serving as a member of the Nauvoo Temple committee. He died in June 1843 of cholera at age forty-seven. Joseph wrote of his death, "His loss will be universally lamented, not only by his family, but by a large circle of brethren who have long witnessed his integrity and uprightness, as well as a life of devotedness to the cause of truth."[401]

### D&C 113:10—When did Orson Hyde dedicate the ancient lands of Israel for the return of the "scattered remnants" of Judah?

On Sunday morning, October 24, 1841, Elder Orson Hyde ascended the Mount of Olives and offered a prayer dedicating and consecrating the land of Israel "for the gathering together of Judah's scattered remnants, according to the predictions of the holy Prophets—for the building up of Jerusalem again . . . and for rearing a Temple in honor of [the Lord's] name." Hyde petitioned the Lord to remember the posterity of Abraham, Isaac, and Jacob and to give them "this land for an everlasting inheritance."[402]

## Section 114

### D&C 114:1—What led David W. Patten to investigate the truthfulness of Mormonism?

In his youth David Patten journeyed alone from New York to southeastern Michigan, where he built a home in the woods. From that secluded area Patten journeyed to attend Methodist meetings, even though he wrote, "I was looking for the Church of Christ to arise in its purity, according to the promise of Christ and [believed] that I should live to see it."[403] A letter from his brother John—then living in Indiana—telling of the Restoration led Patten to travel more than three hundred miles to converse with him. Convinced of the truthfulness of the new religion, Patten was baptized by his brother. He was then ordained an elder on June 17, 1832, and was called to serve a mission in Michigan. By fall of 1833 Patten had served three missions. On February 15, 1835, he was ordained an apostle of the Lord Jesus Christ and blessed: "O God, give this, Thy servant, a knowledge of Thy will, may he be like one of old, who bore testimony of Jesus; may he be a new man from this day forth."[404]

### D&C 114:1—Why didn't David W. Patten fulfill the mission call extended in this revelation?

On April 17, 1838, Joseph Smith received a revelation admonishing David Patten to settle his business affairs in Missouri and prepare to serve a mission the following spring. Although Patten had begun to make the necessary preparations, in October 1838, threats against Latter-day Saints in Missouri turned his attention from preparing for missionary service to defending "not only the property of the Saints but also their lives." Patten led "seventy-five volunteers against the mob of thirty or forty, hoping to rout them without bloodshed" and free three LDS prisoners. During the ensuing fray at Crooked River, Patten was shot and died the next day. Joseph Smith said of him, "[David W. Patten] died as he had lived, a man of God, and strong in the faith of a glorious resurrection, in a world where mobs will have no power or place."[405]

## Section 115

### D&C 115:7—Did Far West become the prophesied "holy and consecrated land" unto the Lord?

A site was selected and dedicated and cornerstones laid for the building of a temple in Far West. Revelations now published in the Doctrine and Covenants were received by Joseph Smith at that LDS community (see D&C 113–120). A stake in Zion was organized and for a short time the community served as headquarters of the Church. Although Far

The temple site in Far West, Missouri.

West could be called a "holy and consecrated land" by these acts, the building of the temple did not go forward.

**D&C 115:19—Who were some of the disaffected who denied the faith in 1838 and rejected the "keys of this kingdom and ministry" as being in the hands of Joseph Smith?**

When Joseph Smith arrived in Far West on March 14, 1838, many of the brethren "with open arms welcomed us to their bosoms."[406] The disillusioned remained aloof but secretly whispered innuendos that disclosed their contempt. Numbered among the disaffected was Oliver Cowdery, who said, "*Give me my freedom or take my life!* I shall no longer be bound by the chains of hell. I shall speak out when I see a move to deceive the ignorant."[407] David Whitmer was also among the disaffected. He falsely claimed that Joseph had abandoned the primitive faith: and drifted "into error and spiritual blindness."[408] As such slanderous hearsay spread, attempts to establish truth were summarily dismissed. Solomon Hancock's unwavering testimony—"Brother Joseph is not a fallen prophet, but will yet be exalted and become very high"—went almost unnoticed amid vexatious lawsuits, name-calling, and the betrayal of Joseph Smith by such former leaders as Oliver Cowdery and David Whitmer.[409]

# Section 116

**D&C 116: Section Heading—What was Joseph Smith's purpose in going to Spring Hill or Adam-ondi-Ahman?**

Joseph Smith said that his purpose in going to Wight's Ferry in Spring Hill was to select and lay "claim to a city plat near said ferry in Daviess County . . . which the brethren called 'Spring Hill,' but by the mouth of the Lord it was named Adam-ondi-Ahman, 'because, said he, it is the place where Adam shall come to visit his people, or the Ancient of Days shall sit, as spoken of by Daniel the Prophet'" (D&C 116).[410] This site is located on the north side of the Grand River, about twenty-five miles north of Far West, Missouri.[411]

**D&C 116:1—When was Adam-ondi-Ahman first mentioned in scripture?**

Section 116 is the first mention of Adam-ondi-Ahman in holy writ. However, the name Adam-ondi-Ahman was familiar to Latter-day Saints before the revelation was received by Joseph Smith on May 19, 1838. For example, the hymn "Adam-ondi-Ahman" by W. W. Phelps was sung at the Kirtland Temple dedication in March 1836.

# Section 117

**D&C 117: Section Heading—Why is section 117 considered the most unique revelation Joseph Smith received in Far West?**

After the Independence Day celebrations of 1838, Church leaders in Far West announced that a three-day conference would be held July 6–8, 1838. On the final day of that conference, Joseph Smith presented the revelations he had received in Far West. Of the revelations, section 117 is the most unique,

Tower Hill at Adam-ondi-Ahman.

for it names specific individuals and problems that beset them. For example, in this revelation the Lord admonished William Marks and Newel K. Whitney to settle their business affairs in Kirtland and journey to Missouri. Although the command to journey to Missouri was previously given to all Saints in Kirtland, Marks and Whitney delayed their departure. For tarrying behind, both Marks and Whitney were commanded to repent of their "covetous desires" and journey "from the land of Kirtland" before it snowed (D&C 117:1–5).[412]

### D&C 117:8—What are the "plains of Olaha Shinehah"?

The "plains of Olaha Shinehah" are the lands where Adam dwelt (D&C 117:8). According to scholar Hoyt Brewster, "The name Olaha Shinehah may be, and in all probability is, from the language of Adam." Olaha Shinehah is also the name used to designate the "sun" (Abr. 3:13). Scholar Janne M. Sjodahl contends that "Olaha is . . . a variant of the word Olea, which is 'the moon'" (Abr. 3:13). If such is the case, the plains of Olaha Shinehah are the "Plains of the Moon and the Sun."[413]

### D&C 117:11—What is the Nicolaitane Band?

In the New Testament era, Nicolaitanes were followers of Nicolas, one of seven disciples appointed to supervise the distribution of food and goods to the poor (see Acts 6:5). Christian tradition suggests that Nicolas failed to fulfill his appointment and apostatized. Tradition further suggests that Nicolas established a religious sect with followers known as Nicolaitanes. Nicolaitanes held that "it was lawful to eat things sacrificed to idols, and to commit fornication" in direct opposition to the decrees of God (see Acts 15:20, 29). False beliefs and immoral actions spawned by such beliefs led to impurities within early Christianity.[414] Elder Bruce R. McConkie equated Nicolaitanes with "members of the Church who [are] trying to maintain their church standing while continuing to live after the manner of the world" (see Rev. 2:6, 15).[415]

### D&C 117:11—Why is the term "Nicolaitane Band" associated with Bishop Newel K. Whitney?

There was an expressed concern that Bishop Newel K. Whitney was becoming like Nicolas of old and turning from his sacred calling to a life of worldliness. Apparently Bishop Whitney was "setting his heart on the things of the world, he was then showing a disposition similar to the Nicolaitan band of old."[416] Fortunately, he repented.

**D&C 117:12—What did Oliver Granger do to keep his name "in sacred remembrance from generation to generation"?**

One month after Oliver Granger arrived in Missouri, Joseph Smith received a revelation instructing him to return to Kirtland and represent the First Presidency in settling Church debts (see D&C 117:12–15). Granger complied with the revelation and performed his assignment with such satisfaction to the Church's creditors that one wrote, "Oliver Granger's management in the arrangement of the unfinished business of people that have moved to the Far West, in redeeming their pledges and thereby sustaining their integrity has been truly praiseworthy, and has entitled him to my highest esteem, and ever grateful recollection."[417] A letter signed by the First Presidency on May 13, 1839, attested to Granger's business skills: "We have always found President Oliver Granger to be a man of the most strict integrity and moral virtue; and in fine, to be a man of God. . . . We have entrusted vast business concerns to him, which have been managed skillfully to the support of our characters and interest as well as that of the Church."[418]

# Section 118

**D&C 118:1—Why did the Twelve Apostles hold a conference in Far West immediately following a three-day general conference in July 1838 in Far West?**

At the three-day conference held in Far West on July 6–8, 1838, Joseph Smith received a revelation in response to the supplication "Show us thy will O Lord concerning the Twelve."[419] The revelation that followed informed the Twelve that they should meet in conference to fill vacancies in their quorum (see D&C 118:1). The designated conference was held with Thomas B. Marsh presiding and David W. Patten, Brigham Young, Parley P.

Pratt, and William Smith attending. Two resolutions were presented and acted upon at the conference: "Resolved 1st. That the persons who are to fill the places of those who are fallen [William E. McLellin, Luke S. Johnson, John F. Boynton, and Lyman E. Johnson], be immediately notified to come to Far West" and "Resolved 2nd. That Thomas B. Marsh notify Wilford Woodruff, that Parley P. Pratt notify Orson Pratt, and that President Rigdon notify Willard Richards, who is now in England."[420]

**D&C 118:2, 4—Why did Thomas B. Marsh fail to lead his quorum on the prophesied mission to the British Isles?**

On July 8, 1838, the Lord revealed to Joseph Smith that the apostles were to leave Missouri in the spring and cross "the 'great waters'" and there "promulgate my gospel" in Great Britain, where missionary work had commenced in 1837 through the labors of Heber C. Kimball and others (see D&C 118:4). The Lord specified that the apostles should "take leave of my saints in the city of Far West, on the twenty-sixth day of April next, on the building-spot of my house" (D&C 118:5). Thomas B. Marsh anticipated leading his quorum to foreign lands. However, due to his apostasy he never led his quorum abroad. In an 1857 letter addressed to Heber C. Kimball, Marsh wrote of his deep regret: "A mission was laid upon me & I have never filled it and now I fear it is too late but it is filled by another, I see, the Lord could get along very well without me and He has lost nothing by my falling out of the ranks; But O what have I lost?"[421]

**D&C 118:4—How successful were the Twelve in their missionary labors in Great Britain?**

Nine members of the Twelve responded to the call "to go over the great waters." Wilford Woodruff described their success: "We went to England, and we baptized, in the year 1840, something like seven thousand people, and established churches in almost all the principal cities in the kingdom. Brother Pratt established a branch in Edinburgh, Scotland. Brother Kimball, George A. and myself built up a branch in London, and

New York Harbor circa the mid-1800s.

several branches in the south of England. We baptized eighteen hundred persons in the south of England in seven months; out of that number two hundred were preachers belonging to different denominations of that land. We opened an emigration office, published the Book of Mormon and gathered many to Zion. God was with us, and I may say that He has been in all the labors of this Church and kingdom."[422]

**D&C 118:5—Did the Twelve return to Far West on April 26, 1839, to begin their mission to England?**

Brigham Young said, "Many of the authorities considered, in our present persecuted and scattered condition, the Lord would not require the Twelve to fulfil his words to the letter, and, under our present circumstances, he would take the will for the deed; but I felt differently and so did those of the Quorum who were with me. I asked them, individually, what their feelings were upon the subject. They all expressed their desires to fulfil the revelation. I told them the Lord God has spoken, and it was our duty to obey and leave the event in his hands and he would protect us." On the morning of April 26, 1839, Brigham Young and others of the Twelve "arrived at the Temple Lot at Far West, they were accompanied and met by a number of the Saints who remembered the significance of that date." At that site, five members of the Quorum of the Twelve—Brigham Young, Heber C. Kimball, Orson Pratt, John Taylor, and John E. Page—ordained two other brethren to their quorum: Wilford Woodruff and George A. Smith. Then "the Twelve prayed in the order of their standing in the Quorum; and a song was sung. A stone near the southeast corner of the Lord's house was rolled into place under the direction of Alpheus Cutler, the master workman. When the business at hand had been disposed of, they departed for Quincy, taking their families with them." [423] Their mission to England had officially begun and would continue as they voyaged across the ocean to reach the British Isles (see D&C 118:4).

# SECTION 119

**D&C 119:1–5—In what way could the payment of tithes as defined in the Doctrine and Covenants be compared with the payment of tithes in the Old Testament?**

The payment of tithes was an oft-repeated principle developed throughout the Old Testament, particularly in relation to the law of Moses (see Lev. 27:20–32; Num. 18:25–28; Deut. 26:12–14). For instance, Abraham paid tithes to Melchizedek (see Gen. 14:18–20; Alma 13:14–15) and Jacob covenanted to pay a tenth of all the Lord had given him (see Gen. 28:20–22). Malachi wrote of Jehovah's displeasure when the payment of tithes is neglected: "Will a man rob God? Yet ye have robbed me. . . . in tithes and offerings" (Mal. 3:8).

Tithing is also an oft-repeated principle in our day. On July 8, 1838, Joseph Smith was told by revelation that the Saints were to pay "one-tenth of their interest [increase] annually, and this shall be a standing law unto them forever" (D&C 119:4).

**D&C 119:4—When was tithing recognized as a commandment binding upon the Saints in the last days?**

On August 2, 1833, the Lord revealed that the Kirtland Temple

Cedar City Tithing Office. As the Saints settled Utah, many if not all the communities had a tithing office where the Saints paid their tithes.

was to "be built speedily, by the tithing of my people. Behold, this is the tithing and the sacrifice which I, the Lord, require at their hands" (D&C 97:11–12). In this instance, tithing is equated with any contribution or offering. It was not until July 8, 1838, that tithing was defined as "one-tenth of their interest annually."

The law of tithing was given in answer to Joseph Smith's prayer—"O Lord! Show unto thy servant how much thou requirest of the properties of thy people for a tithing."[424] After this revelation was read to the Saints, several who had lived the law of consecration and had given of their surplus yearly to the Church began to complain. Yet tithing remained a law unto the Church (see D&C 119:3–4).[425]

# Section 120

## D&C 120: Section Heading—How was tithing distributed in the early days of the Church?

Joseph Smith received a revelation regarding the disposition of tithed properties, which consisted of the agreement of "a council, composed of the First Presidency of my Church, and of the bishop and his council, and by my high council; and by my own voice" (D&C 120:1).[426] Today the distribution process is still guided by the Lord and His servants: "The collection of tithing is the responsibility of the bishop in each ward. Tithes are presented confidentially to him or his counselors. He forwards the tithes collected locally to Church headquarters where a committee consisting of the First Presidency, the Presiding Bishopric, and the Quorum of the Twelve Apostles supervise the distribution and expenditure of tithing funds (D&C 120). These funds are used for such purposes as the building and maintenance of meetinghouses, temples, and other facilities, as well as for the partial support of the missionary, educational, and welfare programs of the Church."[427]

# Section 121

## D&C 121: Section Heading—Why did Joseph Smith send his wife an epistle addressed to Bishop Edward Partridge and the Church?

On March 25, 1839, Joseph Smith addressed a letter "To the Church of Latter-day Saints at Quincy, Illinois, and Scattered Abroad, and to Bishop Partridge in Particular." Although the letter was addressed to Bishop Partridge and the Church, it was sent to Emma Smith with instructions that family members read the letter and share it with Church members. In the attached letter Joseph wrote, "I have sent an Epistle to the church directed to you because I wanted you to have the first reading of it and then I want Father and Mother to have a coppy of it keep the original yourself as I dictated the matter myself and shall send an other as soon as possible." He pled, "May the grace of God the Father, and of our Lord and Savior Jesus Christ, rest upon you all, and abide with you forever. May knowledge be multiplied unto you by the meorcy of God. And may faith and virtue, and knoledge and temperance, and pationce and Godliness, and Brotherly kindness and charity be in you and abound, that you may not be barron in anything, nor unfrutefull."[428] The lengthy letter was signed by Latter-day Saint prisoners in Liberty Jail—Joseph Smith, Hyrum Smith, Lyman Wight, Caleb Baldwin, and Alexander McRae. Portions of the letter were later published as sections 121–123. Less than half of the letter is included in the Doctrine and Covenants.[429]

## D&C 121: Section Heading—What was the design of Liberty Jail?

Liberty Jail was built in 1833 of rough-hewn limestone. The two-story structure was approximately twenty-two square feet. It had an outer and an inner wall separated by a "twelve-inch space filled with loose rock." The interior of the building was divided into an upper and a lower room, the lower being a dungeon lit only by two small windows grated with iron bars. On December 1, 1838, Joseph Smith was incarcerated in the jail and was confined for four months and five days.

A cutaway recreation of Liberty Jail.

During confinement Joseph was allowed to be in the upper and lower rooms of the structure.[430]

**D&C 121:1—What is the meaning of the phrase "Thy pavilion [is] thy hiding place"?**

A *pavilion* is a type of covering—a canopy or tent. The Lord's pavilion covers His presence like a veil that can be rent only by the pleading of the righteous. Joseph Smith pled with the Lord to part His pavilion so that the cries of His servant could be heard (see D&C 121:1, 4).[431] In a similar manner, King David pled with the Great Jehovah to come out from His dark hiding place, "his pavilion round about him" (Ps. 18:11). According to scholars Hyrum Smith and Janne Sjodahl, by using the phrase "Thy pavilion is thy hiding place," Joseph poetically "entreats the Lord to manifest Himself in His power for the salvation of the Saints from their enemies."[432]

**D&C 121:43—What does reproving betimes with sharpness mean?**

The word *betimes* is often interpreted to mean "occasionally" or "sometimes." This is not the primary meaning, however—*betimes*

Joseph in Liberty Jail.

also means "at an early time, in good time, in due time, while there is yet time, before it is too late, in a short time, soon, speedily."[433] When *betimes* is coupled with *reprove*, it means to correct actions at an early time.

President Heber J. Grant said, "How I wish that no man holding the Priesthood of the living God was ever guilty of allowing any words to fall from his lips that he could not repeat in the presence of his mother. Then he would be, to a very great extent, in that straight and narrow path that leads to life eternal."[434] Elder M. Russell Ballard said, "Those who hold the priesthood must never forget that they have no right to wield priesthood authority like a club over the heads of others in the family or in Church callings. . . . Any man who . . . seeks to use the priesthood in any degree of unrighteousness in the Church or in the home simply does not understand the nature of his authority. Priesthood is for service, not servitude; compassion, not compulsion; caring, not control."[435] The Lord warns that those whose actions cause the withdrawal of His Spirit will be left unto themselves "to kick against the pricks," a *prick* being a sharp goad used to prod animals (D&C 121:38; Acts 9:5). When an animal kicks at a goad, the animal is injured. Likewise, those who kick or rebel against gospel truths become "victims of their own misdirected actions."[436]

# Section 122

**D&C 122:6—Is the phrase "with a drawn sword thine enemies tear thee from the bosom of thy wife, and thy tender offspring" autobiographical or theoretical?**

All phrases in this verse are autobiographical. While under strong guard Joseph Smith was allowed to enter his home in Far West. "I found my wife and children in tears, who feared we had been shot by those who had sworn to take our lives, and that they would see me no more," wrote Joseph. "When I entered my house, they clung to my garments, their eyes streaming with tears, while mingled emotions of joy and sorrow were manifested in their countenances. I requested to have a private interview with them a few minutes, but this privilege was denied me by the guard. I was then obliged to take my departure. . . . My partner wept, my children clung to me, until they were thrust from me by the swords of the guards. I felt overwhelmed while I witnessed the scene, and could only recommend them to the care of that God whose kindness had followed me to the present time, and who alone could protect them, and deliver me from the hands of my enemies, and restore me to my family."[437]

**D&C 122:9—Does "Thy days be known, and thy years shall not be numbered less" suggest the Lord will not shorten or lengthen mortality?**

"I am confident that there is a time to die," President Spencer W. Kimball said. "I am not a fatalist. I believe that many people die before 'their time' because they are careless, abuse their bodies, take unnecessary chances, or expose themselves to hazards, accidents, and sickness. . . . I am positive in my mind that the Lord has planned our destiny. We can shorten our lives, but I think we cannot lengthen them very much. Sometime we'll understand fully, and when we see back from the vantage point of the future, we shall be satisfied with many of the happenings of this life which seemed so difficult for us to comprehend."[438]

## Section 123

**D&C 123:4—Why was it important that Church leaders gather libelous publications against Joseph Smith and Mormonism?**

At the May 4–6, 1839, conference held near Quincy, Illinois, Almon W. Babbitt, Erastus Snow, and Robert B. Thompson were appointed to gather all libelous publications that maligned any aspect of Mormonism.[439] "This gathering of information was not to be confined to the deeds committed in Missouri, but should reach out to embrace the wickedness, falsehoods, and deeds of those who fought the truth throughout all time," wrote Joseph Fielding Smith. The purpose of gathering the libelous publications was to have in Church possession evidence of the cruelties hurled against truths of God and His servants (see D&C 123:5).

**D&C 123:5—What is "the whole concatenation of diabolical rascality"?**

While imprisoned in Liberty Jail, Joseph Smith wrote, "The whole concatenation of diabolical rascality and nefarious and murderous impositions that have been practised upon this people" (D&C 123:5). In this instance, *concatenation* was referred to as connections (like links in a chain) to describe the suffering of the Latter-day Saints at the hands of wicked men.[440] Although such rascality was unbecoming of even the vilest of men, the First Presidency of the Church in April 1911 wrote of a positive outcome from the evil intent: "It is impossible to take up all the misrepresentations given to the world by anti-'Mormon' preachers and writers. They have one merit. They stir up interest in what is called the 'Mormon' question. People are led thus to investigate and many of them find out the truth, and unite with the people who are so greatly maligned."[441]

## Section 124

**D&C 124:3—What is the meaning of "corners" of the earth?**

The word *corners* in this scriptural passage is a reference to the outer edge or place where the judgment of God will reach.[442]

**D&C 124:3—Who was the "honorable president-elect"at this time?**

Joseph Smith was directed by the Lord to "make a solemn proclamation of my gospel" and send it to "all the kings of the world" even the "honorable president-elect" (D&C 124:2–3). William Henry Harrison had been elected president of the United States, but

William Henry Harrison.

had not been sworn in at that time. Sending the proclamation to world leaders was necessary, but did not guarantee acceptance of the document, for the rulers were "as grass, and all their glory as the flower thereof which soon falleth" (D&C 124:7). Use of the word *grass* was a symbolic reminder that a blade of grass can appear impervious to destruction, yet with the slightest change in nature can vanish like once-proud political leaders.

### D&C 124:27—Who was the architect of the Nauvoo Temple?

Joseph Smith invited architects to submit proposals and drawings of the Nauvoo Temple for his consideration. The rendering of architect William Weeks captured his attention. "You are the man I want!" Joseph exclaimed after examining his drawings. "I wish you to carry out my designs. I have seen in vision the splendid appearance of that building illuminated, and will have it built according to the pattern shown me."[443] The pattern was intricate in design and meticulous in detail. It called for a three-story, gray, limestone structure measuring 128 feet in length and 88 feet in width. It depicted ornamental crescent moonstones, sunstones, and five-pointed star stones carved into the exterior, adorning thirty pilasters. A belfry and a clock tower dome with a gilded weather vane were drawn atop the structure to give height and beauty to the temple. Only after Weeks grew weary with the plans was he allowed to proceed with the building phase.

### D&C 124:31—What descriptive accounts reveal that Latter-day Saints sacrificed their time and talents to build the Nauvoo Temple?

"Let the Saints be diligent in building the Temple," Joseph Smith said.[444] Latter-day Saints responded with enthusiasm, first in the quarries and then at the temple site. As work in limestone quarries commenced, volunteers gave one day in ten cutting and hauling limestone blocks to the temple site. For example, volunteer Byrum Bybee "hitched his team to his wagon and with his son had gone to the quarry to load a large stone into the wagon. . . . their wagon became stuck in a mud hole."[445] Joseph Smith waded in mud halfway to his knees to

Lithograph of the Nauvoo Temple circa 1890.

help the man and his son and to ensure the stone was taken to the temple site. Volunteer Luman Shurtliff wrote of laboring in the quarries: "We labored ten hours a day and got something to take to our families for supper and breakfast. . . . I mention this not to find fault or to complain, but to let my children know how the temple of Nauvoo was built, and how their parents as well as hundreds of others suffered to lay a foundation on which they could build and be accepted of God."[446] Laborers from every state in the union and from nations across the ocean came to help and in so doing left a legacy—an imprint on the temple. Whether carpenter, foreman, joiner, or framer, each knew he was needed and each donated time and talents to build the Nauvoo Temple. Observing their cooperative actions at the temple site, Wandle Mace wrote, "Men were as thick as blackbirds busily engaged upon the various portions."[447]

**D&C 124:45—When was the capstone of the Nauvoo Temple laid?**

At six in the morning on May 24, 1845, Church leaders and laborers watched as the capstone was laid by Brigham Young, who pronounced, "The last stone is now laid upon the temple, and I pray the Almighty, in the name of Jesus, to defend us in this place, and sustain us, until the temple is finished."[448] For Brigham Young, the occasion was "a foretaste of celestial enjoyment and Millennial glory."[449]

**D&C 124:91–96—When did Hyrum Smith learn of his call to the office of patriarch?**

In his final blessing to his son Hyrum Smith, Joseph Smith Sr. pronounced in 1840, "I now give you my dying blessing. You shall have a season of peace, so that you shall have a sufficient rest to accomplish the work which God has given you to do. You shall be as firm as the pillars of heaven unto the end of your days. I now seal upon your head the patriarchal power, and you shall bless the people. This is my dying blessing upon your head in the name of Jesus. Amen."[450] The father's blessing to his son was pronounced months before the January 1841 revelation was given to Joseph Smith. Of Hyrum

Smith, Heber J. Grant said, "No mortal man who ever lived in this Church desired more to do good than did Hyrum Smith, the patriarch. I have it from the lips of my own sainted mother, that of all the men she was acquainted with in her girlhood days in Nauvoo, she admired Hyrum Smith most for his absolute integrity and devotion to God, and his loyalty to the prophet of God."[451]

**D&C 124:95—Did Oliver Cowdery remain second only to Joseph Smith until the appointment of Hyrum Smith to the First Presidency of the Church?**

On January 19, 1841, the name of Oliver Cowdery appeared in a revelation in conjunction with the appointment of Hyrum Smith as a "prophet, and a seer, and a revelator unto my church, as well as my servant Joseph" (D&C 124:94). In the revelation, Hyrum was told, "He may ask and receive, and be crowned with the same blessing, and glory, and honor, and priesthood, and gifts of the priesthood, that once were put upon him that was my servant Oliver Cowdery" (D&C 124:95). Although Oliver had left the Church years earlier, his position as second only to Joseph remained vacant until the appointment of Hyrum Smith in 1841.

**D&C 124:119—What was the Quorum of the Nauvoo House?**

The "Quorum of the Nauvoo House" has reference to the quorum appointed to oversee construction of the Nauvoo House. Members of that quorum were George Miller, Lyman Wight, John Snider, and Peter Haws (see D&C 124:62). Perhaps the word *quorum* was used instead of *committee* to emphasis that the Nauvoo House should be more than a boardinghouse for strangers—it should be a holy house where strangers and travelers alike could "contemplate the glory of Zion" (D&C 124:23, 24, 60). Purchasing stock in the Nauvoo House was limited to those who believed in the Book of Mormon and the revelations of God (see D&C 124:117–118). Those named as worthy to purchase stock in this house were Joseph Smith, Vinson Knight, Hyrum Smith, Isaac Galland, William Marks, Henry Sherwood, and William Law (see D&C 124:56, 74, 77–78, 80–82).

# 7

# Sections 125–Official Declaration 2



## Section 125

**D&C 125:3—Where was the city of Zarahemla located?**

Zarahemla, Lee County, Iowa, was founded in 1839 near Montrose, Iowa, directly across the Mississippi River from Nauvoo. At a Church conference held in Zarahemla on August 7, 1841, approximately 750 members were present. At the time, about 326 Church members lived in Zarahemla.

**D&C 125:4—Why was the success of Nashville as an LDS settlement so short-lived?**

Acreage comprising the village of Nashville, Lee County, Iowa, was purchased by Latter-day Saint leaders as a suitable location for settlement. Although Nashville was a gathering place for the faithful, its success was short-lived. The reason for its brief success was the emphasis placed on gathering to Nauvoo in the early 1840s. To those who had settled in Nashville and considered moving across river to Nauvoo, the Lord revealed to Joseph Smith in March 1841, "Let them gather themselves together unto the places which I shall appoint unto them by my servant Joseph, and build up cities unto my name" (D&C 125:2). Although Nauvoo would remain a gathering place for years, this revelation shows the Lord's intent to strengthen other cities (see D&C 124:2).

# Section 126

## D&C 126: Section Heading—What is Brigham Young's conversion story?

Few men of the nineteenth century match the caliber and dogged determination of Brigham Young. From humble beginnings in an obscure Vermont village, he rose to the applause of thinking men and grew in favor with God. Although some contend that farm labor and unwelcomed poverty dominated his early years, it was his unwavering search for eternal truth that permeated his thoughts. Reading the Book of Mormon, listening to missionaries, and being baptized brought answers to his search for truth: "When I saw a man without eloquence, or talents for public speaking, who could only say, 'I know, by the power of the Holy Ghost, that the Book of Mormon is true, that Joseph Smith is a Prophet of the Lord,' the Holy Ghost proceeding from that individual illuminated my understanding, and light, glory, and immortality were before me."[452] Anxious to learn more about his new religion, Young journeyed

BRIGHAM YOUNG.

to Kirtland to meet the Prophet Joseph Smith. Of their initial meeting, Young said, "Here my joy was full at the privilege of shaking the hand of the Prophet of God, and receiving the sure testimony, by the spirit of prophecy, that he was all that any man could believe him to be as a true Prophet."[453]

## D&C 126:1–2—Why was Brigham Young exempt from missionary service in the 1840s?

While visiting in the Nauvoo home of Brigham Young, Joseph Smith received a revelation that began "Dear and well-beloved brother, Brigham Young" (D&C 126:1). In the unusual directive that followed, the Lord said, "It is no more required at your hand to leave your family as in times past, for your offering is acceptable to me" (D&C 126:1). By revelation Young was directed to remain in Nauvoo and to send others with the word of God to foreign lands (see D&C 126:3).[454]

## Section 127

### D&C 127: Section Heading—Why was Joseph Smith in hiding when he wrote this inspired letter?

During summer and fall of 1842, Joseph Smith was accused of being an accessory with Orrin Porter Rockwell in the attempted assassination of Missouri Governor Lilburn W. Boggs. Joseph viewed the unwarranted accusation as a conspiracy to force him to return to Missouri. Hoping to avoid being arrested and brought to trial in Missouri, Joseph went into hiding. While concealed from his enemies, he wrote two inspired letters (see D&C 127 and 128).[455]

### D&C 127:5—Why are ordinances for the dead necessary?

President Wilford Woodruff served as proxy for temple ordinances for the deceased. Of this privilege, he said, "I remember well the first time I read the revelation given through the Prophet Joseph concerning the redemption of the dead—one of the most glorious principles I had ever become acquainted with on earth. . . . Never did I read a revelation with greater joy than I did that revelation."[456] President Woodruff taught, "For the last eighteen hundred years, the people that have lived and passed away never heard the voice of an inspired man, never heard a Gospel sermon, until they entered the spirit-world. Somebody has got to redeem them, by performing such ordinances for them in the flesh as they cannot attend to themselves in the spirit."[457]

### D&C 127:6—In which river were the first baptisms for the dead performed?

On August 15, 1840, Jane Nyman asked Harvey Olmstead to baptize her in behalf of her deceased son, Cyrus Livingston Nyman. Her request was granted. Elder Olmstead baptized Jane Nyman in the Mississippi River for her deceased son. From that time forward, Latter-day Saints

Looking across the Mississippi River toward Nauvoo.

waded knee-deep into the Mississippi River to be baptized for deceased kindred and friends.

# Section 128

**D&C 128:3—Did the word "ward" have a political connotation in the Nauvoo era?**

In the 1840s the city of Nauvoo was divided into wards for political purposes, much like what was done in other communities in the state of Illinois and elsewhere in the United States. Although bishops had been called as early as 1831, it was not until the Nauvoo era that bishops were associated with a ward or political subdivision.[458]

**D&C 128:11—What is the meaning of the Latin phrase "summum bonum"?**

On September 6, 1842, in an epistle concerning the salvation of the dead, Joseph Smith penned, "The summum bonum of the whole subject that is lying before us" (D&C 128:11). In Latin, the words *summum bonum* mean "the supreme or highest good." When these words are coupled with salvation of the dead, they mean "the supreme good of salvation work for the dead is vested in the powers of the holy priesthood."[459]

### D&C 128:13–14—How did Joseph Smith describe the apostle Paul?

Joseph Smith described the apostle Paul as being "about five feet high; very dark hair; dark complexion; dark skin; large Roman nose; sharp face; small black eyes, penetrating as eternity; round shoulders; a whining voice, except when elevated, and then it almost resembled the roaring of a lion. He was a good orator, active and diligent, always employing himself in doing good to his fellow man."[460]

### D&C 128:20—What is the scriptural reference for a hill in western New York becoming known as the Hill Cumorah?

The only scriptural reference to the word *Cumorah* as being the hill in western New York where Joseph Smith received the plates from the angel Moroni is found in section 128. The hill is not mentioned by name in the Joseph Smith History in the Pearl of Great Price. In that scripture Joseph referred to the hill as "the place where the messenger had told me the plates were deposited" and a "hill of considerable size" (JS–H 1:50–51).

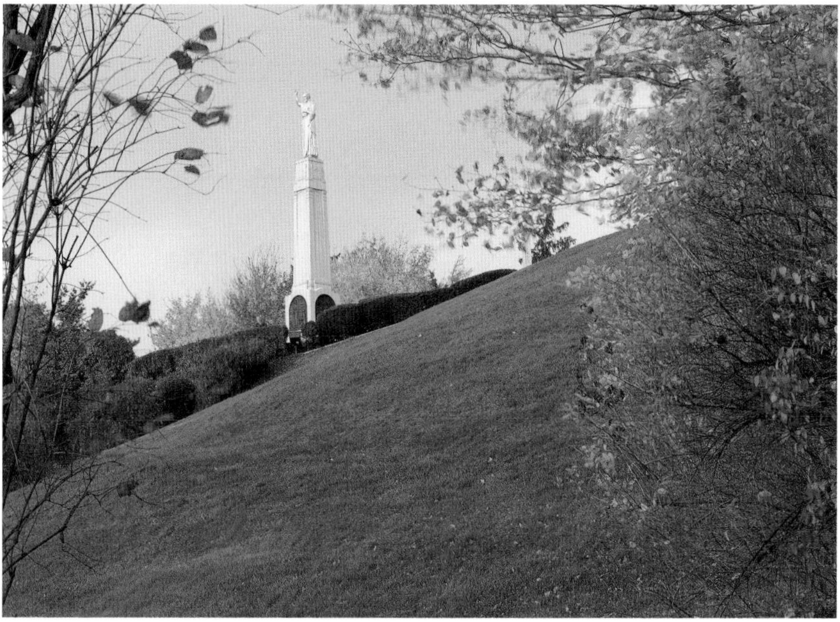

The Hill Cumorah.

### D&C 128:21—Who is the angel Raphael?

The names and mortal identities of only a few angels are known. For example, it is known that Noah is the angel Gabriel. As to the mortal identity of Raphael, it has not been revealed. However, in apocryphal writings the following appears: "I am Raphael, one of the seven holy angels, which present the prayers of the Saints, and which go in and out before the glory of the Holy One."[461]

### D&C 128:23—Is the phrase "the mountains shout for joy" poetic or figurative?

Joseph Smith, in a poetic gesture, invited the mountains to "shout for joy" (D&C 128:23) just as Isaiah in antiquity invited the hills to sing (see Isa. 42:11; 44:23; 55:12; 1 Ne. 21:13). According to scholar Hoyt Brewster, such invitations are "an expression of the rejoicing of nature on occasions when God is praised by his creations or when he is particularly pleased because of the rolling forth of the work of righteousness and redemption."[462]

### D&C 128:24—What is "the refiner's fire" and "the fuller's soap"?

The phrase "for he is like a refiner's fire" is found in the Old Testament (see Mal. 3:2), the Book of Mormon (see 3 Ne. 24:2), and the Doctrine and Covenants (see D&C 128:24). According to scholar Daniel H. Ludlow, "The art of refining precious metals such as gold and silver was known in ancient times. The ores were passed repeatedly through the furnace until their dross was taken away. It is believed that the refiner knew when the process was completed because he could see his image reflected in the purified metal." Interpreting the refining process in a scriptural sense reveals that when the "Savior comes in power and great glory, he will be as a refiner's fire because all the wicked (dross) will be burned, and only those who have been refined (sanctified) will be able to endure his presence" and reflect His image.[463]

In the scriptures, fuller's soap is connected with refiner's fire and the Second Coming of the Savior. A fuller is expected to whiten and cleanse clothing with strong soap "where feet trod out the grime which has been loosened by the lye or soap." The symbolism created by the metaphor is that the fuller's soap, meaning the blood of Jesus Christ, cleans all trace of sin: "When he comes in great glory, he will be like the soap of the fuller, for he will cleanse people from their sins if they will but repent and follow him" (see Mal. 3:2; 3 Ne. 24:2; D&C 128:24).[464]

## Section 129

**D&C 129:1–9—What events preceded Joseph Smith's revelation on the "three grand keys by which the correct nature of ministering angels and spirits may be distinguished"?**

On February 9, 1843, Joseph Smith "spent most of the day in conversation with Parley P. Pratt and others" recently returned from missions in Great Britain. During their conversation, Pratt expressed a desire to discuss the role of angels. Joseph Smith responded by discussing the differences between angels and ministering spirits: "The one a resurrected or translated body, with its spirit ministering to embodied spirits—the other a disembodied spirit, visiting and ministering to disembodied spirits. Jesus Christ became a ministering spirit (while His body was lying in the sepulchre) to the spirits in prison, to fulfill an important part of His mission [1 Peter 3:18–20], without which He could not have perfected His work, or entered into His rest. After His resurrection He appeared as an angel to His disciples." Joseph later added, "Most generally when angels have come, or God has revealed Himself, it has been to individuals in private, in their chamber; in the wilderness or fields, and that generally without noise or tumult. The angel delivered Peter out of prison in the dead of night [Acts 5:19]; came to Paul unobserved by the rest of the crew [Acts 27:23–24]; appeared to Mary and Elizabeth without the knowledge of others [Luke 1:28–30]; spoke to John the Baptist whilst the people around were ignorant of it [John 5:36–38]."[465]

## Section 130

**D&C 130: Section Heading—What sacred events occurred in Ramus, Illinois?**

On March 1, 1843, Brigham Young wrote to Church leaders in Ramus requesting that provisions be sent to provide for the temporal needs of Joseph Smith: "We call on you for immediate relief in this matter, and we invite you to bring our President as many loads of wheat, corn, beef, pork, lard, tallow, eggs, poultry, venison, and everything eatable at your command. . . . The measure you mete shall be measured to you again. If you give liberally to your President in temporal things, God will return to you liberally in spiritual and temporal things too."[466] Two days after the request, Joseph recorded, "Bishop Newel K. Whitney returned from Ramus this evening, with five teams loaded with provisions and grain, as a present to me, which afforded me very seasonable relief. I pray the Lord to bless those who gave it abundantly; and may it be returned upon their heads."[467]

Promised blessings did follow their generosity. Among the blessings received were inspired insights into the Second Coming of Jesus Christ. On Sunday, April 2, 1843, during a morning meeting at Ramus, Orson Hyde told of the Savior appearing "on a white horse as a warrior, and maybe we shall have some of the same spirit. Our God is a warrior. It is our privilege to have the Father and Son dwelling in our hearts, &c." While dining the next day with Hyde, Joseph said, "I was going to offer some corrections to his sermon this morning." Hyde replied that corrections would be "thankfully received." Joseph's doctrinal corrections to Orson Hyde's remarks are contained in verses 1–16 in section 130.[468]

## Section 131

**D&C 131: Section Heading—When were the instructions Joseph Smith gave at Ramus, Illinois, combined to create section 131?**

On May 16, 1843, Joseph Smith, along with William Clayton and others, left Nauvoo with the intention of arriving at Ramus before nightfall. By early evening, the travelers had reached Ramus and were being hosted at the home of Benjamin F. Johnson. Before retiring for the evening, Joseph gave priesthood instructions to Johnson and said

William Clayton.

to William Clayton, "Your life is hid with Christ in God, and so are many others. Nothing but the unpardonable sin can prevent you from inheriting eternal life for you are sealed up by the power of the Priesthood unto eternal life, having taken the step necessary for that purpose."[469] After making a few other observations, Joseph dictated to Clayton instructions found in section 131, verses 1–4. The next morning in a small gathering of faithful friends, Joseph preached from chapter 1 of 2 Peter, showing the correlation between knowledge and power. Verses 5 and 6 were then dictated by Joseph, with Clayton again acting as scribe.[470] That evening, Joseph listened to a lecture by Samuel Prior, a Methodist preacher. After the lecture Joseph corrected the doctrinal misconceptions of the preacher. The corrections are contained in verses 7 and 8.[471] The three instructive insights were combined together to create section 131 and added to the Doctrine and Covenants in 1876.

# Section 132

**D&C 132: Section Heading—Why was the revelation on celestial marriage not published in the Doctrine and Covenants until 1876?**

The revelation on celestial marriage was first recorded on July 12, 1843, although Joseph Smith learned of the doctrine years earlier. The reasons for its late entry in the Doctrine and Covenants may never be known. What is known is that while Joseph was discussing with his brother Hyrum the eternal principle of marriage, Hyrum said, "If you will write the revelation on celestial marriage, I will take it and read it to Emma, and I believe I can convince her of its truth, and you will hereafter have peace."[472] According to the account written by William

Clayton, Joseph remarked, "You do not know Emma as well as I do." To which Hyrum said, "The doctrine is so plain, I can convince any reasonable man or woman of its truth, purity and heavenly origin." Joseph then said, "Well, I will write the revelation and we will see." Clayton wrote as Joseph dictated the revelation. Clayton penned, "I wrote it, sentence by sentence, as he dictated. After the whole was written, Joseph asked me to read it through, slowly and carefully, which I did, and he pronounced it correct. He then remarked that there was much more that he could write on the same subject, but what was written was sufficient for the present."[473]

### D&C 132:19—What is the Lamb's Book of Life?

The "Book of Life" or "Lamb's Book of Life" is a record of the "names of the faithful and an account of their righteous covenants and deeds" (D&C 128:6–7; Ps. 69:28; Rev. 3:5; 21:27). It is a record of those who will inherit eternal life—the greatest gift of God, for they will be sanctified for all eternity (see Dan. 12:1–4; Heb. 12:23).[474]

### D&C 132:19—Inherent promises to the faithful are "thrones, kingdoms, principalities, and powers, dominions, all heights and depths." What are principalities?

A *principality* is a "state, office, or authority of a prince" or the "territory or jurisdiction of a prince." Those who inherit the "fulness of the glory of the Father" will inherit and reign over a principality (D&C 93:16–20).[475]

## Section 133

### D&C 133: Section Heading—Why is this section referred to as "The Appendix" when other sections follow?

On November 3, 1831, near the close of a conference held in Hiram, Ohio, Joseph Smith learned that "there were many things which the Elders desired to know relative to preaching the Gospel to the inhabitants of the earth, and concerning the gathering; and in order to walk by the true light, and be instructed from on high." It was then that Joseph "inquired of the Lord and received the . . .

important revelation, which has since been added to the book of Doctrine and Covenants, and called the Appendix" (D&C 133).[476] This revelation was intended to be an addendum or appendix to the revelations printed in the Book of Commandments.

**D&C 133:49—What physical changes will occur in the heavens and on the earth at the Second Coming of Jesus Christ?**

At his Second Coming, Jesus will come in the fulness of His glory—a glory that will cause the sun to hide, the moon to withhold its light, and the stars to be hurled from their appointed places in the heavens (see D&C 133:46–53). The brightness of His glory will cause mountains to "flow down at His presence" (see D&C 133:40, 44; Micah 1:4) and "waters to boil" (D&C 133:41). Nations will tremble (see D&C 133:42) and the wicked will be consumed (see Mal. 4:1–3; 2 Thess. 2:8).[477]

It is prophesied that the moon will withhold its light.

## Section 134

**D&C 134: Section Heading—Who wrote this section on government and law?**

On August 17, 1835, Oliver Cowdery read to an assembly of Saints an article of his own creation titled, *"Of Governments and Laws in General."* After his reading, those present voted to publish his article in the 1835 Doctrine and Covenants. Of its inclusion in scripture, Joseph Smith penned, "That our belief with regard to earthly governments and laws in general may not be misinterpreted nor misunderstood, we have thought proper to present, at the close of this volume, our opinion concerning the same."[478] The article on government is not a revelation, yet the article "claims the same authority and power as other sections in the Doctrine and Covenants."[479]

**D&C 134:9—What other Church leaders besides Oliver Cowdery have expressed views on the separation of church and state?**

In 1907 the First Presidency of the Church, consisting of Joseph F. Smith, John R. Winder, and Anthon H. Lund, wrote, "The Church of Jesus Christ of Latter-day Saints holds to the doctrine of the separation of church and state; the non-interference of church authority in political matters; and the absolute freedom and independence of the individual in the performance of his political duties. . . . We declare that from principle and policy, we favor: the absolute separation of church and state; no domination of the state by the church; no church interference with the functions of the state; no state interference with the functions of the church, or with the free exercise of religion; the absolute freedom of the individual from the domination of ecclesiastical authority in political affairs; the equality of all churches before the law."[480] Elder N. Eldon Tanner in November 1975 said, "It is the duty of citizens of any country to remember that they have individual responsibilities, and that they must operate within the law of the country in which they have chosen to live."[481]

# Section 135

**D&C 135:1—Did Joseph Smith have a premonition that going to Carthage in June 1844 would end in his death?**

Joseph had a number of premonitions prior to Carthage about his impending death. For Joseph and Hyrum, Carthage was a scene of broken promises, illegal arraignment, and illegal incarceration. Accusations of riot stemming from the *Nauvoo Expositor* incident turned to treason. Rumors once whispered in secret were now shouted. The militant unabashedly declared that the Smith brothers would not leave Carthage: "*There was nothing against these men; the law could not reach them but powder and ball would*, and they should not go out of Carthage alive."[482] A mob loitered outside of the Carthage jail and sang, "Where

Carthage Jail.

now is the Prophet Joseph?" concluding "Safe in Carthage jail!"[483] Even the governor of Illinois, though not a participant in boisterous song, joined the chorus of conspirators, mobbers, and militia in abetting the deaths of Joseph and Hyrum Smith. Joseph's letter to Emma reveals his sorrowful mood as he contemplated death: "I am very much resigned to my lot, knowing I am justified, and have done the best that could be done. Give my love to the children and all my friends. . . . May God bless you all."[484]

**D&C 135:1—Which of the Smith brothers was the first to fall from an assassin's bullet?**

Hyrum Smith was the first to die. A bullet pierced the upper panel of the bedroom door of the jail and struck him on the left side of the nose. As he fell to the floor he exclaimed, *"I am a dead man!"* (D&C 135:1). Bending over the body of his lifeless brother, Joseph sobbed, "Oh dear, brother Hyrum!"[485] As Joseph moved toward the east bedroom window, bullets hit him from the doorway and struck him from the outside. He fell from the second-story window to the ground below and was heard to exclaim, *"O Lord my God!"* (D&C 135:1).

**D&C 135:7—What is the escutcheon and broad seal left upon the State of Illinois?**

In writing of the martyrdom of Joseph and Hyrum Smith, John Taylor penned, "Their *innocent blood* [is] on the escutcheon of the State of Illinois" (D&C 135:7). This is a reference to the state shield on which symbols or memorials are proudly displayed. According to Taylor, the martyrs' blood is a stain upon the once-proud shield of Illinois.[486] The blood of Joseph and Hyrum is further described by Taylor as "a broad seal affixed to Mormonism," meaning the blood of the martyrs is a conspicuous mark on the state shield.[487]

# Section 136

**D&C 136: Section Heading—How soon after Brigham Young received "The Word and Will of the Lord" regarding the Camp of Israel did those encamped in Nebraska and Iowa learn of the revelation?**

On January 14, 1847, at Winter Quarters, Nebraska, Brigham Young and a number of leading brethren discussed ways to organize Latter-day Saint companies for the westward trek. During their discussions Brigham Young received "The Word and Will of the Lord concerning the Camp of Israel in their journeying to the West" (D&C 136:1). Dictation and discussion of this revelation took most of the afternoon and evening of January 14. The following day, January 15, "though the temperatures ranged to below zero, men mounted buckboards and horses, taking copies [of the revelation] to be read to their assigned camps" in Nebraska and Iowa. The revelation was received with gladness by the Latter-day Saints.

**D&C 136:2—What were the Latter-day Saints commanded to do before commencing their journey to the West?**

First and foremost, Latter-day Saints were to make "covenant[s] and promise[s] to keep all the commandments and statutes of the Lord" (D&C 136:2). They were to organize companies under the direction of the Quorum of the

After the martyrdom of Joseph and Hyrum, the Saints were driven from Nauvoo and on to Winter Quarters.

Twelve, "with a president and his two counselors" and with captains of hundreds, fifties, and tens (D&C 136:3). Each company was to "provide themselves with all . . . they can," including food, provisions, and other supplies as prescribed by the Twelve (D&C 136:5). Companies were to "prepare for those who are to tarry" so that all would be blessed (D&C 136:6).

On the journey, the Latter-day Saint pioneers were to follow the "word and will of the Lord" (D&C 136). They were to "keep [themselves] from evil" and to not "take the name of the Lord in vain" (D&C 136:21). They were to "cease to contend one with another; cease to speak evil one of another. . . . Let your words tend to edifying one another" (D&C 136:23–24). They were also to return borrowed or lost items and to "be diligent in preserving what thou hast" (D&C 136:25–27).[488]

# Section 137

**D&C 137: Section Heading—When was the vision Joseph Smith saw of the celestial kingdom first published in the Pearl of Great Price?**

At the April 1976 general conference, Church members agreed to accept Joseph Smith's vision of the celestial kingdom as scripture. An account of that vision was then published in the Pearl of Great Price. In June 1979 the First Presidency of the Church announced that Joseph's vision would become section 137 in the Doctrine and Covenants.[489]

**D&C 137: Section Heading—What historical circumstances led to Joseph Smith's vision of the celestial kingdom?**

On the evening of January 21, 1836, Joseph Smith and other Church leaders were seated in the President's Room located on the third or attic floor of the Kirtland Temple. There Joseph declared, "The power of the Highest rested upon us, the house was filled with the glory of God."[490] It was then that Joseph saw "the celestial kingdom of God, and the glory thereof" and "the blazing throne of God, whereon was seated the Father and the Son" (D&C 137:1, 3). He saw Adam and Abraham and many noble and great, including his deceased brother Alvin.

## Section 138

**D&C 138: Section Heading—What historical events led to President Joseph F. Smith's "Vision of the Redemption of the Dead"?**

At the October general conference of 1918, held six weeks before his death, President Joseph F. Smith said, "As most of you, I suppose, are aware, I have been undergoing a siege of very serious illness for the last five months. . . . I have not lived alone these five months. I have dwelt in the spirit of prayer, of supplication, of faith and of determination; and I have had my communication with the Spirit of the Lord continuously."[491] He then told of pondering the question of how the Savior could have taught the gospel to so many in the spirit world in so short a time, and of seeing a vision of the redemption of the dead. He then said, "The eyes of my understanding were opened, and the Spirit of the Lord rested upon me, and I saw the hosts of the dead, both small and great" (D&C 138:11). He was given to understand that the "Lord went not in person among the wicked and disobedient" (D&C 138:29). The Lord "organized his forces and appointed messengers, clothed with power and authority" to carry His gospel message to the hosts of the dead.[492]

**D&C 138: Section Heading—When did the "Vision of the Redemption of the Dead" become scripture?**

Joseph F. Smith.

On Thursday, October 31, 1918, the "Vision of the Redemption of the Dead" was acknowledged as the word of the Lord by the First Presidency, the Quorum of the Twelve, and the Church Patriarch. At the April 1976 general conference, the vision was "accepted as scripture and approved for publication in the Pearl of Great Price." In June 1979 the First Presidency of the Church announced that the "Vision of the Redemption of the Dead" would become section 138 of the Doctrine and Covenants.

**D&C 138:12–15—Who did the Savior visit in the spirit world?**

The Savior visited the spirits who had been "faithful in the testimony of Jesus while they lived in mortality" (D&C 138:12). They had "offered sacrifice in the similitude of the great sacrifice of the Son of God" and had "suffered tribulation in their Redeemer's name" (D&C 138:13). These spirits had "departed the mortal life, firm in the hope of a glorious resurrection, through the grace of God the Father and his Only Begotten Son, Jesus Christ" and were "filled with joy and gladness, and were rejoicing together because the day of their deliverance was at hand" (D&C 138:14–15).[493]

# Official Declaration 1

**OD 1—When was Official Declaration 1 first printed in the Doctrine and Covenants?**

On September 25, 1890, Wilford Woodruff recorded, "I have arrived at a point in the history of my life as the president of the Church of Jesus Christ of Latter-day Saints where I am under the necessity of acting for

Wilford Woodruff.

the temporal salvation of the church. The United States government has taken a stand and passed laws to destroy the Latter-day Saints on the subject of polygamy, or patriarchal order of marriage; and after praying to the Lord and feeling inspired, I have issued the following proclamation which is sustained by my counselors and the twelve apostles." The Manifesto, now known as Official Declaration 1, followed.[494] On October 6, 1890 Lorenzo Snow, president of the Quorum of the Twelve, presented the Manifesto to those assembled at general conference for a vote of approval. A favorable vote was given. A year later President Woodruff said, "Let me bring your minds to what is termed the manifesto. The Lord has told me by revelation that there are many members of the church throughout Zion who are sorely tried in their hearts because of that manifesto." He then explained, "The Lord showed me by vision and revelation exactly what would take place if we did not stop this practice. . . . all ordinances would be stopped throughout the land of Zion. Confusion would reign throughout Israel, and many men would be made prisoners. . . . But I want to say this: I should have let all the temples go out of our hands; I should have gone to prison myself, and let every other man go there, had not the God of heaven commanded me to do what I did do; and when the hour came that I was commanded to do that, it was all clear to me. I went before the Lord, and I wrote what the Lord told me to write."[495] Following the vote, the Manifesto was first printed in the 1908 Doctrine and Covenants.

# Official Declaration 2

### OD 2—What is the history behind Official Declaration 2?

On June 1, 1978, President Spencer W. Kimball with members of the First Presidency and Quorum of the Twelve Apostles prayed to the Lord for guidance on priesthood matters. "When President Kimball finished his prayer, the Lord gave a revelation by the power of the Holy Ghost. . . . The revelation came to the President of the Church; it also came to each individual present. . . . that the time had now come to extend the gospel and all its blessings and all its obligations, including the priesthood and the blessings of the house of the Lord, to those of every nation, culture, and race."[496] Of this revelation President Kimball said, "We had this special prayer circle, then I knew that the time had come. I had a great deal to fight, of course, myself largely, because I had grown up with this thought that Negroes should not have the priesthood and I was prepared to go all the rest of my life till my death and fight for it and defend it as it was. But this revelation and assurance came to me so clearly that there was no question about it."[497] Elder Bruce R. McConkie added, "It was during this prayer that the revelation came. The Spirit of the Lord rested mightily upon us all; we felt something akin to what happened on the day of Pentecost and at the dedication of the Kirtland Temple. From the midst of eternity, the voice of God, conveyed by the power of the Spirit, spoke to his prophet. . . . And we all heard the same voice, received the same message, and became personal witnesses that the word received was the mind and will and voice of the Lord."[498]

## ENDNOTES


1 Pratt, "Explanation of Substituted Names in the Covenants," in *The Seer* 2 (March 1854):228, as cited in Robinson and Garrett, *A Commentary on the Doctrine and Covenants*, 1:2.

2 Millet and Jackson, *Studies in Scripture*, 1:3–4.

3 Smith, *History of the Church*, 1:259.

4 Robinson and Garrett, *A Commentary on the Doctrine and Covenants*, 1:4.

5 Cannon and Cook, *Far West Record*, 32.

6 "Revelations," *The Evening and the Morning Star* 1, no. 12 (May 1833):89.

7 Letter from John Whitmer and William W. Phelps, July 29, 1833. William W. Phelps to Dear Brethren, July 20, 1833.

8 *JD*, 8:129.

9 Smith, *Teachings of the Prophet Joseph Smith*, 8.

10 Joseph Smith to Church Brethren, June 15, 1835.

11 Millet and Jackson, *Studies in Scripture*, 1:6–7.

12 Ludlow, *A Companion to Your Study*, 1:36.

13 Millet and Jackson, *Studies in Scripture*, 1:10.

14 *Hearken, O Ye People*, 23–24.

15 *Hearken, O Ye People*, 23.

16 Journal History, October 10, 1880.

17 Millet and Jackson, *Studies in Scripture*, 1:17–18.

18 Benson, "The Book of Mormon and the Doctrine and Covenants," *Ensign*, May 1987, 83.

19 Benson, "The Book of Mormon and the Doctrine and Covenants," *Ensign* 11, no. 5 (May 1987):83.

20 Smith, *Doctrines of Salvation*, 3:199.

21 Whitmer, "Address," *Messenger and Advocate* 2, no. 6 (March 1836):287.

22 *Hearken, O Ye People*, 45.

23 Adapted from *Hearken, O Ye People*, 56–57.

24 Smith, *History of the Church*, 2:299.

25 Smith, *History of the Church*, 2:302–303.

26 Smith, *History of the Church*, 2:315.

27 Smith, *History of the Church*, 3:23.

28 Smith, *History of the Church*, 4:112–113, 375–376.

29 Smith, *History of the Church*, 4:503.

30 Smith, *Church History and Modern Revelation*, 1:252.

31 Smith, *Church History and Modern Revelation*, 1:271.

32 Ogden, "Biblical Language and Imagery in the Doctrine and Covenants," in Hartshorn, *A Book of Answers*, 180.

33 Smith, *Church History and Modern Revelation*, 1:254.

34 Romney, *Conference Report*, October 1962, 95.

35 Smith, *History of the Church*, 4:540.

36 Gee, "Book of Mormon Word Usage: 'Seal You His,'" *Insights* 22, no. 1 (2002).

37 Robinson and Garrett, *A Commentary on the Doctrine and Covenants*, 1:21.

38 Smith, *Church History and Modern Revelation*, 1:255.

39 Smith, *Conference Report*, October 1931, 17–18.

40 Smith, *Church History and Modern Revelation*, 1:255.

41 Brewster, *Doctrine & Covenants Encyclopedia*, 261; McConkie, *Mormon Doctrine*, 374.

42 Smith, *History of the Church*, 1:11n; "History of Joseph Smith," *Times and Seasons* 3, no. 12 (April 15, 1842):753; H. Donl Peterson, *Moroni: Ancient Prophet, Modern Messenger* (Springville, UT: Cedar Fort, 2008), 86n1.

43 Lambert, "Moroni," in Largey, *Book of Mormon Reference Companion*, 556 –557.

44 Robinson and Garrett, *A Commentary on the Doctrine and Covenants*, 1:32.

45 DeVries, *World Biblical Commentary: 1 Kings*, 216.

46 McClintock and Strong, *Cyclopaedia of Biblical, Theological, and Ecclesiastical Literature*, 3:150.

47 See Smith, *History of the Church*, 6:59–61; *Utah Genealogical and Historical Magazine* (October 1934):189.

48 Smith, *History of the Church*, 6:253.

49 Smith, *Teachings of the Prophet Joseph Smith*, 337.

50 Smith, *History of the Church*, 1:20; Brown, "Lehi's Personal Record: Quest for a Missing Source," *BYU Studies* 24, no. 1 (Winter 1984):19–42.

51 Clark, *Gleanings by the Way*, 230.

52 Robinson and Garrett, *A Commentary on the Doctrine and Covenants*, 1:70.

53 Brewster, *Doctrine & Covenants Encyclopedia*, 13.

54 Robinson and Garrett, *A Commentary on the Doctrine and Covenants*, 1:37.

55 Smith, *History of the Church*, 1:21.

56 Journal of William Pilkington, 11.

57 Smith, *History of the Church*, 1:21; Anderson, *Lucy's Book*, 410.

58 Brewster, *Doctrine & Covenants Encyclopedia*, 181–182.

59 Smith, *History of the Church*, 1:21.

60 Smith, *Biographical Sketches of Joseph Smith the Prophet*, 143; Smith, *History of the Church*, 1:21.

61 Anderson, *Lucy's Book*, 417–418; Smith, *Biographical Sketches of Joseph Smith the Prophet*, 141.

62 Hardy, "Mormon as Editor," in Sorenson and Thorne, *Rediscovering the Book of Mormon*, 22.

63 Smith, *History of Joseph Smith by His Mother*, 79.

64 Pratt, in *Journal of Discourses*, 15:184.

65 Black, *Who's Who in the Doctrine & Covenants*, 290.

66 *The Doctrine & Covenants Student Manual*, 12.

67 McKay, *Conference Report*, April 1954, 22–23.

68 Smith, *Conference Report*, October 1916, 50–51.

69 Smith, *History of Joseph Smith by His Mother*, 133, 143, 151.

70 Smith, *Church History and Modern Revelation*, 1:40.

71 Smith, *History of Joseph Smith by His Mother*, 152–153.

72 See "Testimony of the Three Witnesses of the Book of Mormon," in the Book of Mormon.

73 Robinson and Garrett, *A Commentary on the Doctrine and Covenants*, 1:47.

74 Robinson and Garrett, *A Commentary on the Doctrine and Covenants*, 1:53.

75 Smith, *Teachings of the Prophet Joseph Smith*, 186.

76 Widtsoe, *Conference Report*, April 1940, 36.

77 Smith, *History of the Church*, 1:35.

78 *Millennial Star* 40 (December 9, 1848): 772.

79 Smith and Sjodahl, *The Doctrine and Covenants Commentary*, 37.

80 Smith, *Church History and Modern Revelation*, 1:119.

81 Smith, *History of Joseph Smith by His Mother*, 141.

82 Smith, *History of the Church*, 1:32–33.

83 Anderson, *Lucy's Book*, 452; Smith, *Biographical Sketches of Joseph Smith the Prophet*, 164.

84 Smith, *History of the Church*, 1:53.

85 Smith, *Biographical Sketches of Joseph Smith the Prophet*, 164; Anderson, *Lucy's Book*, 452.

86 Smith, "History of Joseph Smith," *Times and Seasons* 3, no. 21 (September 1, 1842):897–898.

87 Smith, *History of the Church*, 1:55.

88 See "Testimony of the Eight Witnesses of the Book of Mormon," in the Book of Mormon.

89 Smith, *History of the Church*, 1:35–36.

90 Ludlow, *A Companion to Your Study*, 1:83.

91 Robinson and Garrett, *A Commentary on the Doctrine and Covenants*, 1:58–59.

92 Robinson and Garrett, *A Commentary on the Doctrine and Covenants*, 1:58–59.

93 Smith, *History of the Church*, 1:176.

94 Whitney, *Life of Heber C. Kimball*, 91–92.

95 Snow, *Conference Report*, April 1899, 52.

96 Smith, *History of the Church*, 3:381.

97 Oaks, "Teaching and Learning by the Spirit," *Ensign*, March 1997, 14.

98 Sperry, *Doctrine and Covenants Compendium*, 71.

99 Smith, *Church History and Modern Revelation*, 1:50–51.

100 Ballard, *Conference Report*, April 1931, 37.

101 Packer, *Conference Report*, October 1994, 77.

102 Smith, *History of the Church*, 1:23.

103 Maxwell, "Notwithstanding My Weakness," *Ensign*, November 1976, 12–13.

104 Smith, *History of the Church*, 1:21.

105 Clark, *Gleanings by the Way*, 247–248.

106 Clark, *Gleanings by the Way*, 247.

107 Cook, *Palmyra and Vicinity*, 206.

108 Vogel, *Early Mormon Documents*, 3:479–481.

109 Smith, "Last Testimony of Sister Emma," *Latter Day Saints' Herald* 26, no. 19 (October 1, 1879):290.

110 "O. Cowdery," *Messenger and Advocate* 1, no. 1 (October 1834):14.

111 Bennett, "Mr. Editor:—I occasionally drop into the Prophet's office…," *Nauvoo Neighbor* 1, no. 33 (December 13, 1843):3.

112 Ludlow, *A Companion to Your Study*, 1:105.

113 Smith, *History of the Church*, 1:43, 45.

114 Smith, *Church History and Modern Revelation*, 1:57.

115 Robinson and Garrett, *A Commentary on the Doctrine and Covenants*, 1:83.

116 "To the Patrons of the Times & Seasons," *Times and Seasons* 1, no. 1 (November 1839):23.

117 Smith, *History of the Church*, 1:47–48.

118 Smith, *History of the Church*, 5:124–125.

119 Smith, *History of the Church*, 4:227.

120 Young, in *Journal of Discourses*, 8:53.

121 "O. Cowdery's First Letter to W. W. Phelps," *Millennial Star* 3, no. 8 (December 1842):153.

122 "Oliver Cowdery to William W. Phelps," *Latter Day Saints' Messenger and Advocate* 1, no. 1 (October 1834):15–16.

123 Smith, *History of the Church*, 1:39–40, 42.

124 Robinson and Garrett, *A Commentary on the Doctrine and Covenants*, 1:91.

125 Talmage, *The Articles of Faith*, 205.

126 Smith, *Teachings of the Prophet Joseph Smith*, 172–173.

127 Penrose, "Who and What are the Angels," *Improvement Era*, May 1912, 952.

128 Smith, *Doctrines of Salvation* 3:94.

129 "Mormonism," *Millennial Star* 43, no. 27 (July 4, 1881):421–423.

130 Smith, *History of the Church*, 1:49.

131 Smith, *Doctrines of Salvation*, 2:8.

132 Whitmer, *An Early Latter Day Saint History*, 20.

133 Ludlow, *A Companion to Your Study*, 1:123.

134 Cannon and Cook, *Far West Record*, 21.

135 Oliver Cowdery, "The Closing Year," *Messenger and Advocate* 3, no. 3 (December 1836):426.

136 Reynolds and Sjodahl, *Commentary on the Book of Mormon*, 4:178.

137 "Report of Elders Orson Pratt and Joseph F. Smith," *Deseret Evening News,* November 16, 1878, 1.

138 Millet and Jackson, *Studies in Scripture*, 1:93.

139 "Letter of Addison Everett to Oliver B. Huntington, February 17, 1881," *Young Woman's Journal* 2 (November 1890):76–77.

140 Millet and Jackson, *Studies in Scripture*, 1:93–94.

141 Jessee, "Joseph Knight's Recollection of Early Mormon History," *BYU Studies* 17, no. 1 (Spring 1970):36–37.

142 Tucker, *Origin, Rise, and Progress of Mormonism*, 51.

143 The mortgage agreement between Harris and Grandin is recorded in the Wayne County Mortgages Book, 3:325–326.

144 Manscill, *Sperry Symposium Classics*, 106.

145 Manscill, *Sperry Symposium Classics*, 51.

146 Millet and Jackson, *Studies in Scripture*, 1:113–114.

147 Lee, *Conference Report*, April 1973, 4.

148 Kimball, "Remarks and Dedication of the Fayette, New York, Buildings," *Ensign*, May 1980, 54.

149 Smith, *History of the Church*, 1:336–337.

150 Smith, *History of the Church*, 1:75–76.

151 Black, "Name of the Church," in Ludlow, *Encyclopedia of Mormonism*, 3:979.

152 Brewster, *Doctrine & Covenants Encyclopedia*, 474–475.

153 Smith, *History of the Church*, 1:104–105.

154 Cannon, *Life of Joseph Smith the Prophet*, 82–83.

155 Pratt, in *Journal of Discourses*, 16:293–294.

156 Harper, *Making Sense*, 80.

157 Smith, *History of the Church*, 1:80.

158 Smith, *History of the Church*, 1:44.

159 "William H. Kelley to Editor Herald," *The Saints' Herald* 29 (March 1, 1882):66–69.

160 McLellin, *The Ensign of Liberty of the Church of Christ* 1, no. 7, October 1, 1879, 290.

161 *The Deseret News Weekly*, 38:391.

162 Talmage, *Jesus the Christ*, 321.

163 Smith, *History of the Church*, 4:552–553.

164 Smith, *History of the Church*, 5:107.

165 Smith, *History of Joseph Smith by His Mother*, 190–191.

166 Taylor, "The Order and Duties of the Priesthood, etc.," *Journal of Discourses*, 21:367–368.

167 Smith, *History of the Church*, 2:273.

168 Smith, *History of the Church*, 4:17–18.

169 Millet and Jackson, *Studies in Scripture*, 1:147.

170 Lee, *Conference Report*, April 1970, 103.

171 Smith, *History of the Church*, 1:106.

172 Smith, *History of the Church*, 1:108.

173 Cook, *Revelations of the Prophet*, 127n.

174 Harper, *Making Sense*, 95.

175 Smith, *History of the Church*, 1:109–110.

176 Woodford, *The Historical Development*, 1:404–405.

177 Smith, *History of the Church*, 1:115.

178 "A Warning Voice," *The Improvement Era*, August 1913, 1149.

179 Manscill, *Sperry Symposium Classics*, 56–67.

180 Brewster, *Doctrine & Covenants Encyclopedia*, 5.

181 Smith, in *Journal of Discourses*, 3:283.

182 Kimball, "The Latter-day Kingdom," *Journal of Discourses*, 5:29; *JD*, 5:115, 206–207.

183 Robinson and Garrett, *A Commentary on the Doctrine and Covenants*, 1:191–192.

184 Brewster, *Doctrine & Covenants Encyclopedia*, 630.

185 Autobiography of Ezra Thayre.

186 Smith, in *Journal of Discourses*, 11:4.

187 Pratt, in *Journal of Discourses*, 17:290.

188 Cannon, *Life of Joseph Smith*, 103–104.

189 Smith, *History of Joseph Smith by His Mother*, 192.

190 *The Doctrine & Covenants Student Manual*, 72.

191 "Newel Knight's Journal," *Scraps of Biography, Faith-Promoting Series*, 10:68.

192 Anderson, *Joseph Smith's Kirtland*, 13.

193 Smith, *History of the Church*, 5:423.

194 Smith, *History of the Church*, 3:390.

195 Smith, *History of the Church*, 2:260.

196 *Scraps of Biography, Faith-Promoting Series*, 10:68.

197 Robinson and Garrett, *A Commentary on the Doctrine and Covenants*, 1:256; McConkie, *Mormon Doctrine*, 702–703.

198 *The Doctrine & Covenants Student Manual*, 76.

199 Godfrey, "The Surprising Parables of Jesus," in Van Orden and Top, *The Lord of the Gospels*, 56–57.

200 Harper, *Making Sense*, 132.

201 Smith, *History of the Church*, 1:143.

202 Smith, *Church History and Modern Revelation*, 1:174.

203 Smith, *History of the Church*, 1:145–146.

204 Journal History, 1:50.

205 Smith, *History of the Church*, 1:146–147.

206 Smith, *Church History and Modern Revelation*, 1:184.

207 Smith, *History of the Church*, 2:477.

208 Kimball, *Conference Report*, April 1948, 109.

209 Smith and Sjodahl, *The Doctrine and Covenants Commentary*, 238.

210 Brewster, *Doctrine & Covenants Encyclopedia*, 578.

211 Romney, *Conference Report*, October 1955, 125.

212 Whitmer, *An Early Latter Day Saint History*, 42, 44.

213 Smith, *History of the Church*, 1:175–177.

214 Hinckley, "Message of Inspiration," *LDS Church News*, January 2, 1999, 2.

215 Millet and Jackson, *Studies in Scripture*, 1:134–137.

216 Smith, *History of the Church*, 4:573.

217 Whitmer, *An Early Latter Day Saint History*, 14.

218 Doxey, *Doctrine and Covenants Speaks*, 1:327.

219 Campion, *Ann the Word,* 29.

220 Campion, *Mother Ann Lee, 29,* 30, 41–42.

221 Millet and Jackson, *Studies in Scripture*, 1:213–214.

222 Smith, *History of the Church* 1:167; John Whitmer, Book of John Whitmer, BYU typescript, chapter 6.

223 Flake, "A Shaker View of a Mormon Mission," *BYU Studies* 20, no. 1 (Fall 1979):96–98.

224 Flake, "A Shaker View of a Mormon Mission," *BYU Studies* 20, no. 1 (Fall 1979):96–98.

225 Flake, "A Shaker View of a Mormon Mission," *BYU Studies* 20, no. 1 (Fall 1979):96–98.

226 Pratt, *Autobiography of Parley P. Pratt*, 62.

227 Journal History, 1:55.

228 Pratt, *Autobiography of Parley P. Pratt*, 65.

229 Manscill, *Sperry Symposium Classics*, ix–xx.

230 Cannon, *Life of Joseph Smith*, 116.

231 Smith, "Try the Spirits," *Times and Seasons* 3, no. 11 (April 1, 1842):747.

232 Autobiography of Levi Ward Hancock, 18.

233 Autobiography of Levi Ward Hancock, 18–22.

234 See Bangerter and Black, *My Servant Algernon Sidney Gilbert.*

235 Whitmer, *An Early Latter Day Saint History*, 74.

236 Smith, *History of the Church*, 1:180.

237 Smith, *Teachings of hte Presidents of the Church: Joseph F. Smith*, 56.

238 Alice Phelps to Walter Dean Bowen, as cited in Bowen, "The Versatile W. W. Phelps—Mormon Writer, Educator, and Pioneer," 23.

239 Phelps, "Letter No. 10," *Messenger and Advocate* 1, no. 12 (September 1835):177.

240 Smith, *History of the Church*, 1:184–85.

241 Smith, *History of the Church*, 1:180, 186.

242 Smith, *History of the Church*, 1:189.

243 Smith, *History of the Church*, 2:254.

244 Young, in *Journal of Discourses*, 8:195.

245 Smith, *Doctrines of Salvation*, 3:74.

246 Cannon, *Classic Experiences and Adventures*, 71.

247 Whitmer, *An Early Latter Day Saint History*, 80.

248 Smith, *Church History and Modern Revelation*, 2:85–86; Smith, *History of the Church*, 1:196, 267.

249 Cowan, *Our Modern Scripture*, 95.

250 Ludlow, *A Companion to Your Study*, 1:311.

251 Scott, *Conference Report*, April 1995, 102.

252 Smith, *History of the Church*, 1:198.

253 Smith, *History of the Church*, 1:196.

254 Smith, *History of the Church*, 1:199.

255 Smith, *History of the Church*, 1:199.

256 Brewster, *Doctrine & Covenants Encyclopedia*, 390.

257 Smith, *History of the Church*, 1:203–207.

258 Smith, *History of the Church*, 1:202–203.

259 Roberts, "The Fulfilment of a Prophecy," *The Improvement Era* 6, no. 11 (September 1903):806.

260 Smith, *History of the Church*, 6:254.

261 Smith, *History of the Church*, 1:205.

262 Smith, *History of the Church*, 2:313–314.

263 See Cook, *David Whitmer Interviews.*

264 Young, in *Journal of Discourses*, 10:335.

265 Oaks, "Teaching and Learning by the Spirit," *Ensign*, March 1997, 9.

266 Adapted from Millet and Jackson, *Studies in Scripture*, 1:134–137.

267 Smith, *History of the Church*, 1:215–217.

268 Ludlow, *A Companion to Your Study*, 1:344–345.

269 Smith, *Teachings of the Prophet Joseph Smith*, 366.

270 Kimball, *Conference Report*, April 1976, 10.

271 *LDS Church News*, May 27, 1984, 7.

272 Welch and Shipps, *The Journals of William E. McLellin 1831–1836*, 34.

273 Letter of William E. McLellin to relatives, August 4, 1832, 1–2.

274 McLellin, *Ensign of Liberty of the Church of Christ*, 1:61.

275 Smith, *History of the Church*, 1:226.

276 Lightner, in *Writings of Early Latter-day Saints*, 196.

277 Cannon and Cook, *Far West Record*, 32.

278 Smith, *History of the Church*, 1:217.

279 Smith, *History of the Church*, 1:239.

280 Smith, "History of Joseph Smith," *Millennial Star* 14, no. 3 (April 15, 1852):115.

281 Roberts, *Comprehensive History*, 1:271.

282 Jessee, *Personal Writings of Joseph Smith*, 239.

283 Millet and Jackson, *Studies in Scripture*, 1:133.

284 Smith and Sjodahl, *The Doctrine and Covenants Commentary*, 432.

285 Smith, *History of the Church*, 1:243.

286 Hyde, "History of Brigham Young," *Millennial Star* 26, no. 49 (December 3, 1864):774–775.

287 Smith, *Teachings of the Prophet Joseph Smith*, 304.

288 *Juvenile Instructor* 27, no. 10 (May 15, 1892):303–304.

289 Smith, *History of the Church*, 1:252–253.

290 Young, in *Journal of Discourses*, 6:281.

291 Phelps, "From W. W. to Joseph Smith," *Times and Seasons* 4, no. 6 (February 1, 1843):81–82.

292 Smith, "The Answer," *Times and Seasons* 4, no. 6 (February 1, 1843):82–85.

293 Smith, *Teachings of the Prophet Joseph Smith*, 68.

294 Kimball, *Conference Report*, April 1951, 104–105.

295 Smith, *Conference Report*, October 1945, 172.

296 Penrose, in *Journal of Discourses*, 24:93.

297 Smith, *Teachings of the Prophet Joseph Smith*, 358.

298 Smith, *Church History and Modern Revelation*, 1:291.

299 Smith, *History of the Church*, 5:279.

300 Young, in *Journal of Discourses*, 8:200.

301 Young, "Want of Governing Capacities among Men," *Journal of Discourses*, 7:163.

302 Smith, *Teachings of the Prophet Joseph Smith*, 291.

303 Smith and Sjodahl, *The Doctrine and Covenants Commentary*, 474.

304 Ludlow, *A Companion to Your Study*, 1:397.

305 Pratt, in *Journal of Discourses*, 16:156.

306 Pratt, in *Journal of Discourses*, 2:342.

307 Smith, *Church History and Modern Revelation*, 1:310.

308 Autobiography of Jared Carter, 8.

309 Ostler, "Real Covenants and Real People," in Hartshorn, *A Book of Answers*, 124–125.

310 Ostler, "Real Covenants and Real People," in Hartshorn, *A Book of Answers*, 124.

311 Woodford, "Jesse Gause, Counselor to the Prophet," *BYU Studies* 15, no. 3 (Spring 1975):362–364.

312 Kirtland Revelation Book, 10.

313 Smith, "History of Joseph Smith," *Millennial Star* 14, no. 37 (November 6, 1852):584.

314 Richards, *A Marvelous Work and a Wonder*, 309.

315 Smith, *History of the Church*, 1:266–267.

316 Smith, *History of the Church*, 1:269.

317 Smith, *History of the Church*, 1:286.

318 Smith, *History of the Church*, 3:385–386.

319 Monson, "The Call of Duty," *Ensign*, May 1986, 38.

320 Smith, *Conference Report*, April 1970, 58–59.

321 Smith, *Teachings of the Prophet Joseph Smith*, 347.

322 Smith, *History of the Church*, 1:271.

323 Smith, *History of the Church*, 1:297–298.

324 Smith, *Church History and Modern Revelation*, 1:350.

325 *Deseret News*, November 13, 1905.

326 *Doctrine & Covenants Student Manual*, 188.

327 Smith, *Teachings of the Prophet Joseph Smith*, 101.

328 Pratt, in *Journal of Discourses*, 18:224–225.

329 Smith, *History of the Church*, 1:301.

330 Smith, *History of the Church*, 1:316.

331 Millet and Jackson, *Studies in Scripture*, 1:342.

332 Kimball, *Conference Report*, May 1974, 45.

333 McKay, *Gospel Ideals, Improvement Era*, 1953, 208–213.

334 Taylor, *Conference Report*, October 1974, 17–19; Brewster, *Doctrine & Covenants Encyclopedia*, 175–176.

335 Smith, "Correspondence," *Times and Seasons* 4, no. 8 (March 1, 1843):113.

336 Smith, *History of the Church*, 2:175–176.

337 Young, in *Journal of Discourses*, 12:158.

338 "Minutes Salt Lake School of Prophets," October 13, 1883, 55–56.

339 "General Minutes of Conference," *Millennial Star* 14 (February 1, 1852):35.

340 Smith, *Conference Report*, October 1913, 14

341 Grant, *Conference Report*, October 1942, 7–17.

342 CES, *Doctrine & Covenants Student Manual*, 212.

343 McConkie, *Mormon Doctrine*, 41; Ludlow, *Companion to Your Study*, 1:482..

344 Parkin, "Joseph Smith and the United Firm," *BYU Studies* 46, no. 3 (2007):13.

345 Pratt, in *Journal of Discourses*, 16:58.

346 Kimball, "Give the Lord Your Loyalty," *Ensign*, March 1980, 4.

347 Kimball, "Give the Lord Your Loyalty," *Ensign* 10, no. 3 (March

1980):4; "Section 93—'Truth Is Knowledge of All Things . . .' *Doctrine and Covenants Institute Manual.*

348 Smith, *History of Joseph Smith by his Mother*, 230–233.

349 Cook, *The Revelations of the Prophet Joseph Smith*, 198.

350 Smith and Sjodahl, *The Doctrine and Covenants Commentary*, 603.

351 Young, in *Journal of Discourses*, 2:31.

352 Pratt, *Autobiography of Parley P. Pratt*, 77.

353 Pratt, *Autobiography of Parley P. Pratt*, 75–76.

354 Smith, *Teachings of the Prophet Joseph Smith*, 147.

355 Murdock, *An Abridged Record of the Life of John Murdock*, 26.

356 Journal of John Murdock, 3–5, 8.

357 Cannon, *Life of Joseph Smith*, 160–161.

358 *Gospel Doctrine Teacher's Manual*, 117.

359 Smith, *Teachings of the Prophet Joseph Smith*, 36.

360 Smith, *Church History and Modern Revelation*, 1:469.

361 Smith, *Teachings of the Prophet Joseph Smith*, 31.

362 Smith, *Teachings of the Prophet Joseph Smith*, 35–36.

363 Smith, *History of the Church*, 2:25-26, 31.

364 Kirtland High Council Minute Book, 29–32.

365 Smith and Sjodahl, *Doctrine and Covenants Commentary*, 659–660; Pratt, *Autobiography of Parley P. Pratt*, 88.

366 Backman and Cowan, *Joseph Smith and the Doctrine and Covenants*, 95.

367 Young, "The United Order, etc.," *Journal of Discourses*, 18:355.

368 Young, in *Journal of Discourses*, 11:16.

369 Smith, *History of the Church*, 2:61–65.

370 Smith, *History of the Church*, 2:39.

371 Young, in *Journal of Discourses*, 18:242.

372 Jenson, "Zion's Camp," *Historical Record* 7 (June 1888):585–586.

373 Young, in *Journal of Discourses*, 2:10.

374 Woodruff, in *Journal of Discourses*, 13:158.

375 Smith, *History of the Church*, 2:108–111.

376 Smith, *History of the Church*, 2:42.

377 CES, *Doctrine & Covenants Student Manual*, 261.

378 Smith, *History of the Church*, 2:209–210.

379 Smith, *History of the Church*, 2:210; Millet and Jackson, *Studies in Scripture*, 1:404.

380 Smith, *History of the Church*, 2:345.

381 Cook, "Lyman Sherman—Man of God, Would-Be Apostle," *BYU Studies* 19, no.1 (1979):124.

382 Smith, *History of the Church*, 1:353; Smith, *History of Joseph Smith by His Mother*, 231.

383 Smith, *History of Joseph Smith by His Mother*, 231; *JD*, 10:166.

384 Widtsoe, *Improvement Era*, April 1944, 225.

385 "History of Brigham Young," *Millennial Star* 26, no. 34 (August 20, 1864):535.

386 Smith, *History of Joseph Smith by His Mother*, 231.

387 Smith, *History of the Church*, 2:432–433.

388 Pratt, in *Journal of Discourses*, 18:132; Tullidge, *The Women of Mormondom*, 95.

389 Backman and Cowan, *Joseph Smith and the D&C*, 174–176.

390 Arrington, "Oliver Cowdery's Kirtland, Ohio, 'Sketch Book,'" *BYU Studies* 12, no. 4 (Summer 1972):426.

391 Smith, *History of the Church*, 2:434–435.

392 *Comprehensive History of the Church*, 1:411.

393 Smith, *History of the Church*, 2:464.

394 *Hearken, O Ye People*, 192.

395 Smith, *History of the Church*, 2:487–489.

396 Manscill, *Sperry Symposium Classics*, 283.

397 Young, in *Journal of Discourses*, 7:289–290.

398 Smith, *History of the Church*, 3:9–10.

399 CES, *Doctrine & Covenants Student Manual*, 283.

400 Smith, *History of the Church*, 4:88.

401 Smith, *History of the Church*, 5:421.

402 Smith, *History of the Church*, 4:456.

403 "History of David W. Patten," *Millennial Star* 26, no. 26 (June 25, 1864):406.

404 Wilson, *Life of David W. Patten*, 33.

405 Smith, *History of the Church*, 3:171.

406 Smith, *History of the Church*, 3:8–9.

407 Gunn, *Oliver Cowdery*, 230.

408 Whitmer, *An Address to All Believers in Christ*, 59.

409 Smith, *History of the Church*, 3:225.

410 Smith, *History of the Church*, 3:35.

411 Leland Gentry, "Adam-oni-Ahman: A Brief Historical Survey," *BYU Studies* 13 (1972–1973):553–575.

412 Smith, *History of the Church*, 3:45.

413 Brewster, *Doctrine & Covenants Encyclopedia*, 425–426.

414 *Doctrine and Covenants Student Manual*, 290.

415 McConkie, *Doctrinal New Testament Commentary*, 3:446.

416 CES, *Doctrine & Covenants Student Manual*, 290.

417 Smith, *History of the Church*, 3:174.

418 Smith, *History of the Church*, 3:350.

419 Smith, *History of the Church*, 3:46–47.

420 Smith, *History of the Church*, 3:47.

421 Manscill, *Sperry Symposium Classics*, 293.

422 Woodruff, in *Journal of Discourses*, 13:160.

423 Millet and Jackson, *Studies in Scripture*, 1:450; Watson, *Manuscript History*, 35.

424 Smith, *History of the Church*, 3:44.

425 *Hearken, O Ye People*, 212.

426 Smith, *History of the Church*, 3:44.

427 "Tithing," in Ludlow, *Encyclopedia of Mormonism*, 4:1481.

428 Jessee, *Personal Writings of Joseph Smith*, 389, 408.

429 *Deseret Evening News*, June 27, 1896.

430 Millet and Jackson, *Studies in Scripture*, 1:474.

431 Brewster, *Doctrine & Covenants Encyclopedia*, 416.

432 Smith and Sjodahl, *The Doctrine and Covenants Commentary*, 753.

433 *Oxford English Dictionary*, s.v. "betimes."

434 Grant, *Conference Report*, April 1937, 11–12.

435 Ballard, *Conference Report*, October 1993, 105.

436 Brewster, *Doctrine & Covenants Encyclopedia*, 295.

437 Smith, *History of the Church*, 3:193.

438 Kimball, *Tragedy or Destiny*, 9, 11.

439 Smith and Sjodahl, *The Doctrine and Covenants Commentary*, 763.

440 Brewster, *Doctrine & Covenants Encyclopedia*, 94–95.

441 *Conference Report*, April 1911, 130.

442 Brewster, *Doctrine & Covenants Encyclopedia*, 194.

443 F. M. Weeks to J. Earl Arrington, as cited in Arrington, "William Weeks, Architect of the Nauvoo Temple," *BYU Studies*, 19, no. 3 (Spring 1979):340.

444 Smith, *History of the Church*, 5:2.

445 Lyon, "Recollections of 'Old Nauvooers' Memories from Oral History," *BYU Studies* 18, no. 2 (1978):147.

446 Biographical Sketch of the Life of Luman Andros Shurtliff, in *Writings of Early Latter-day Saints*, 52.

447 Journal of Wandle Mace, in *Writings of Early Latter-day Saints*, 185.

448 *Millennial Star*, 54:365.

449 "Extract from President Young's Letter," *Millennial Star* 6, no. 6 (June 27, 1845):91.

450 Smith and Sjodahl, *The Doctrine and Covenants Commentary*, 786.

451 Grant, in *Conference Report*, October 1920, 84.

452 Young, in *Journal of Discourses*, 1:90.

453 Roberts, *Comprehensive History*, 1:289.

454 Millet and Jackson, *Studies in Scripture*, 1:478.

455 Smith, *Church History and Modern Revelation*, 2:328.

456 Woodruff, "General Conference," *Millennial Star* 53, no. 26 (June 29, 1891):404.

457 Woodruff, in *Journal of Discourses*, 19:228–229.

458 Cowan, *Our Modern Scripture*, 194.

459 Brewster, *Doctrine & Covenants Encyclopedia*, 570.

460 Smith, *Teachings of the Prophet Joseph Smith*, 180.

461 Smith and Sjodahl, *The Doctrine and Covenants Commentary*, 810.

462 Brewster, *Doctrine & Covenants Encyclopedia*, 372–373.

463 Ludlow, *A Companion to Your Study*, 1:643.

464 Ludlow, *A Companion to Your Study*, 643; Black and Black, *Black's Bible Dictionary*, 208.

465 Smith, *History of the Church*, 4:425, 5:31, 267.

466 Smith, "History of Joseph Smith," *Millennial Star* 20, no. 40 (October 2, 1858):629.

467 Smith, *History of the Church*, 5:294–295.

468 Smith, *History of the Church*, 5:323–325.

469 Smith, *History of the Church*, 5:391.

470 Smith, *History of the Church*, 5:392.

471 Smith, *History of the Church*, 5:392–393.

472 Smith, *History of the Church*, 5:xxxii.

473 Smith, *History of the Church*, 5:xxxii–xxxiii.

474 McConkie, *Mormon Doctrine*, 97.

475 Brewster, *Doctrine & Covenants Encyclopedia*, 443.

476 Smith, *History of the Church*, 1:229.

477 CES, *Doctrine & Covenants Student Manual*, 342.

478 Smith, *History of the Church*, 2:243, 247.

479 Millet and Jackson, *Studies in Scripture*, 1:527.

480 *Conference Report*, April 1907, 14.

481 Tanner, "The Laws of God," *Ensign* 5, no. 11 (November 1975):83.

482 Smith, *History of the Church*, 6:566.

483 Roberts, *Comprehensive History*, 2:281.

484 Smith, *History of the Church*, 6:605.

485 Smith, *History of the Church*, 6:618.

486 Brewster, *Doctrine & Covenants Encyclopedia*, 159–160.

487 Brewster, *Doctrine & Covenants Encyclopedia*, 63.

488 *Gospel Doctrine Teacher's Manual*, 197–198.

489 See *LDS Church News*, June 2, 1979, 3.

490 Smith, *History of the Church*, 2:380–381.

491 Smith, *Conference Report*, October 1918, 2.

492 See Derrick, "Moral Values and Rewards," *Ensign*, May 1981, 66–67.

493 *Gospel Doctrine Teacher's Manual*, 230.

494 Clark, *Messages of the First Presidency*, 3:192.

495 *Discourses of Wilford Woodruff*, 214–216.

496 "All are alike unto God," *Symposium on the Book of Mormon*, 2.

497 *LDS Church News*, January 6, 1979, 4.

498 Merrill, *The Heavens Are Open*, 110.

# BIBLIOGRAPHY

**Books**

Anderson, Karl R. *Joseph Smith's Kirtland: Eyewitness Accounts*. Salt Lake City: Deseret Book, 1996.

Anderson, Lavina Fielding. *Lucy's Book: A Critical Edition of Lucy Mack Smith's Family Memoir*. Salt Lake City: Signature Books, 2001.

Backman, Milton Vaughn and Richard O. Cowan. *Joseph Smith and the Doctrine and Covenants*. Salt Lake City: Deseret Book, 1992.

Bangerter, Geraldine Hamblin and Susan Easton Black. *My Servant Algernon Sidney Gilbert: Provide for My Saints (D&C 57:10)*. Provo, Utah: Bangerter Family, 1989.

Black, Adam and Charles Black. *Black's Bible Dictionary*, Second British Edition. London: Adam and Charles Black, 1960.

Black, Susan Easton. *Who's Who in the Doctrine & Covenants*. Salt Lake City: Bookcraft, 1997.

Brewster, Hoyt W. *Doctrine & Covenants Encyclopedia*. Salt Lake City: Bookcraft, 1988.

Campion, Nardi Reeder. *Ann the Word: The Life of Mother Ann Lee, Founder of the Shakers*. Boston: Little, Brown, 1976.

Cannon, Donald Q. and Lyndon W. Cook, ed. *Far West Record: Minutes of The Church of Jesus Christ of Latter-day Saints, 1830–1844*. Salt Lake City: Deseret Book, 1983.

Cannon, George Q. *Classic Experiences and Adventures*. Salt Lake City: Bookcraft, 1969.

Cannon, George Q. *Life of Joseph Smith the Prophet*. Salt Lake City: Deseret Book, 1986.

Church Educational System. *Doctrine and Covenants Student Manual*. Salt Lake City: The Church of Jesus Christ of Latter-day Saints, 1981.

Clark, James R. *Messages of the First Presidency*. 6 vols. Salt Lake City: Deseret Book, 1964–1966.

Clark, John Alonzo. *Gleanings by the Way*. Philadelphia: W. J. & J. K. Simon, 1842.

Collier, Fred C. and William S. Harwell. *Kirtland Council Minute Book*. Salt Lake City: Collier's Publishing, 1996.

Cook, Lyndon W., ed. *David Whitmer Interviews: A Restoration Witness*. Orem, Utah: Grandin Book, 1991.

Cook, Lyndon W. *The Revelations of the Prophet Joseph Smith: A Historical and Biographical Commentary of the Doctrine and Covenants*. Provo, Utah: Seventy's Mission Bookstore, 1981.

Cook, Thomas L. *Palmyra and Vicinity*. Palmyra, New York: Historic Palmyra, Inc., 1980.

Cowan, Richard O. *Doctrine & Covenants: Our Modern Scripture*. Provo, Utah: Young House, Brigham Young University Press, 1978.

DeVries, Simon J. *World Biblical Commentary: 1 Kings*. Waco, Texas: Word Books, 1985.

*Doctrine and Covenants and Church History: Gospel Doctrine Teacher's Manual.* Salt Lake City: The Church of Jesus Christ of Latter-day Saints, 1999.

*Doctrine and Covenants Institute Manual.* Salt Lake City: The Church of Jesus Christ of Latter-day Saints, 2001.

Doxey, Roy W. *The Doctrine and Covenants Speaks.* 2 vols. Salt Lake City: Deseret Book, 1964, 1976.

Graffam, Merle H., ed. *Salt Lake School of Prophets: Minute Book 1883.* Palm Desert, California: ULC Press, 1981.

Gunn, Stanley R. *Oliver Cowdery, Second Elder and Scribe.* Salt Lake City: Bookcraft, 1962.

Harper, Steven Craig. *Making Sense of the Doctrine & Covenants: A Guided Tour through Modern Revelations.* Salt Lake City: Deseret Book, 2008.

Hartshorn, Leon R., Dennis A. Wright, and Craig J. Ostler, ed. *The Doctrine and Covenants: A Book of Answers.* Salt Lake City: Deseret Book, 1996.

*Hearken, O Ye People: Discourses on the Doctrine and Covenants.* Sandy, Utah: Randall Book, 1984.

Jessee, Dean C., ed. *The Personal Writings of Joseph Smith.* Salt Lake City: Deseret Book, 1984.

Kimball, Spencer W. *Tragedy or Destiny.* Provo, Utah: Brigham Young University, 955.

Largey, Dennis L., ed. *Book of Mormon Reference Companion.* Salt Lake City: Deseret Book, 2003.

Ludlow, Daniel H. *A Companion to Your Study of the Doctrine and Covenants.* 2 vols. Salt Lake City: Deseret Book, 1978.

Ludlow, Daniel H., ed. *Encyclopedia of Mormonism.* 4 vols. New York City: Macmillan Publishing, 1992.

Manscill, Craig, ed. *Sperry Symposium Classics: The Doctrine and Covenants.* Salt Lake City: Deseret Book, 2004.

McClintock, John and James Strong. *Cyclopedia of Biblical, Theological, and Ecclesiastical Literature.* New York City: Harper & Brothers, 1867.

McConkie, Bruce R. *Doctrinal New Testament Commentary.* 3 vols. Salt Lake City: Bookcraft, 1965–1973.

McConkie, Bruce R. *Mormon Doctrine.* Salt Lake City: Bookcraft, 1966.

McLellin, William E. *Ensign of Liberty of the Church of Christ.* Kirtland, Ohio, 1847–1849.

Millet, Robert L. and Kent P. Jackson, ed. *Studies in Scripture: The Doctrine and Covenants.* 1 vol. Sandy, Utah: Randall Book, 1984; Salt Lake City: Deseret Book, 1989.

Murdock, John. *An Abridged Record of the Life of John Murdock.*

Nelson, Lee. *Brigham Young: Brigham Young's Own Story in His Own Words.* Provo, Utah: Council Press, 1980.

*Oxford English Dictionary.* Oxford, England: Oxford University Press, 2002.

Peterson, H. Donl. *Moroni: Ancient Prophet, Modern Messenger.* Springville, UT: Cedar Fort, 2008.

Pratt, Parley P. *Autobiography of Parley P. Pratt.* Salt Lake City: Deseret Book, 1874, 1985.

Reynolds, George and Janne M. Sjodahl. *Commentary on the Book of Mormon.* 7 vols. Salt Lake City: Deseret Book, 1955–1976.

Richards, LeGrand. *A Marvelous Work and a Wonder*. Salt Lake City: Deseret Book, 1988.

Roberts, B. H. *A Comprehensive History of the Church of Jesus Christ of Latter-day Saints*. 6 vols. Provo, Utah: Brigham Young University Press, 1965; Salt Lake City: Deseret Book, 1963.

Robison, Stephen E. and H. Dean Garrett, *A Commentary on the Doctrine and Covenants.* 4 vols. Salt Lake City: Deseret Book, 2000–2005.

*Scraps of Biography: Designed for the Instruction and Encouragement of Young Latter-day Saints*. Salt Lake City: Juvenile Instruction Office, 1883.

Shipps, Jan and John W. Welch, ed. *The Journals of William E. McLellin 1831–1836*. Provo, Utah: Corporation of the President, The Church of Jesus Christ of Latter-day Saints, BYU Studies, 1994.

Smith, Hyrum M. and Janne M. Sjodahl. *Doctrine and Covenants Commentary.* Salt Lake City: Deseret Book, 1972.

Smith, Joseph. *History of the Church of Jesus Christ of Latter-day Saints.* 7 vols. Salt Lake City: Deseret Book, 1976.

Smith, Joseph Fielding. *Church History and Modern Revelation.* 4 vols. Salt Lake City: Council of the Twelve Apostles of the Church of Jesus Christ of Latter-day Saints, 1946–1949.

Smith, Joseph Fielding. *Doctrines of Salvation*. 4 vols. Salt Lake City: Bookcraft, 1998.

Smith, Joseph Fielding, ed. *Teachings of the Prophet Joseph Smith.* Salt Lake City: Deseret Book, 1938, 1961.

Smith, Lucy Mack. *Biographical Sketches of Joseph Smith and His Progenitors for Many Generations*. Independence, Missouri: Price Publishing Company, 1998.

Smith, Lucy Mack. *History of Joseph Smith by His Mother*. Salt Lake City: Bookcraft, 1853, 1956.

Smith, William. *The New Smith's Bible Dictionary.* Revel G. Lemmons, ed. Garden City, New York: Doubleday & Company, 1966.

Sorenson, John L. and Melvin J. Thorne, ed. *Rediscovering the Book of Mormon*. Salt Lake City: Deseret Book and Foundation for Ancient Research and Mormon Studies, 1991.

Sperry, Sidney B. *Doctrine and Covenants Compendium*. Salt Lake City: Bookcraft, 1960.

Talmage, James E. *Jesus the Christ.* Salt Lake City: Deseret Book, 1982.

Talmage, James E. *A Study of The Articles of Faith: Being a Consideration of the Principal Doctrines of the Church of Jesus Christ of Latter-day Saints*. Salt Lake City: The Church of Jesus Christ of Latter-day Saints, 1977.

Tucker, Pomeroy. *Origin, Rise, and Progress of Mormonism: Biography of its Founders and History of its Church: Personal Remembrances and Historical Collections hitherto Unwritten.* New York: D. Appleton, 1867.

Tullidge, Edward W. *The Women of Mormondom.* New York, 1877.

Van Orden, Bruce A. and Brent L. Top, ed. *The Lord of the Gospels: The 1990 Sperry Symposium on the New Testament*. Salt Lake City: Deseret Book, 1991.

Vogel, Dan, ed. *Early Mormon Documents*. 5 vols. Salt Lake City: Signature Books, 1996–2003.

Watson, Elden Jay. *Manuscript History of Brigham Young, 1801–1844*. Salt Lake City: Smith Secretarial Service, 1968.

Whitmer, David. *Address to All Believers in Christ*. Part 1 (1886).

Whitmer, John. *An Early Latter Day Saint History: The Book of John Whitmer Kept by Commandment*. Independence, Missouri: Herald Publishing House, 1980.

Whitmer, John. Book of John Whitmer. BYU typescript.

Whitney, Orson F. *Life of Heber C. Kimball*. Salt Lake City: Deseret Book, 2001.

Wilson, Lycurgus A. *Life of David W. Patten: The First Apostolic Martyr*. Salt Lake City: The Deseret News, 1904.

Woodruff, Wilford. *The Discourses of Wilford Woodruff*. Salt Lake City: Bookcraft, 1946.

**Articles / Book Chapters**

Arrington, Joseph Earl. "William Weeks, Architect of the Nauvoo Temple," *BYU Studies* 19, no. 3 (Spring 1979):337–360.

Arrington, Leonard J. "Oliver Cowdery's Kirtland, Ohio, 'Sketch Book,'" *BYU Studies* 12, no. 4 (Summer 1972):410–426.

Benson, Ezra Taft. "The Book of Mormon and the Doctrine and Covenants," *Ensign*, May 1987, 83.

Brown, S. Kent. "Lehi's Personal Record: Quest for a Missing Source," *BYU Studies* 24, no. 1 (Winter 1984):19–42.

Cook, Lyndon W. "Lyman Sherman—Man of God, Would-be Apostle," *BYU Studies* 19, no.1 (Fall 1978):121–124.

Everett, Addison. "Letter of Addison Everett to Oliver B. Huntington, February 17, 1881," *Young Woman's Journal* 2 (November 1890):75–76.

First Presidency. "A Warning Voice," *The Improvement Era*, September 1913, 1148–1149.

Flake, Lawrence R. "A Shaker View of a Mormon Mission," *BYU Studies* 20, no. 1 (Fall 1979):94–98.

Godfrey, Kenneth W. "The Surprising Parables of Jesus," in Van Orden and Top, *The Lord of the Gospels*, 56–60.

Hardy, Grant R. "Mormon as Editor," in Sorenson and Thorne, *Rediscovering the Book of Mormon*, 15–28.

Jenson, Andrew. "Zion's Camp," *Historical Record* 7 (June 1888):585–586.

Jessee, Dean C. "Joseph Knight's Recollection of Early Mormon History," *BYU Studies* 17, no. 1 (Spring 1970):36–37.

Kimball, Heber C. "The Latter-day Kingdom, etc.," *Journal of Discourses*, 5:27–34.

Kimball, Spencer W. "Give the Lord Your Loyalty," *Ensign*, March 1980, 2–4.

Kimball, Spencer W. "Remarks and Dedication of the Fayette, New York, Buildings," *Ensign*, May 1980, 54.

Lambert, Neal Elwood. "Moroni," in Largey, *Book of Mormon Reference Companion*, 556–557.

Lyon, T. Edgar. "Recollections of 'Old Nauvooers': Memories from Oral History," *BYU Studies* 18, no. 2 (Winter 1978):143–150.

Maxwell, Neal A. "Notwithstanding My Weakness," *Ensign*, November 1976, 12–13.

McKay, David O. "On Fasting," *Improvement Era*, March 1963, 156–157.

Monson, Thomas S. "The Call of Duty," *Ensign*, May 1986, 38.

Oaks, Dallin H. "Teaching and Learning by the Spirit," *Ensign*, March 1997, 9–14.

Ogden, D. Kelly. "Biblical Language and Imagery in the Doctrine and Covenants," in Hartshorn, *The Doctrine and Covenants: A Book of Answers*, 169–187.

Ostler, Craig J. "Real Covenants and Real People," in Hartshorn, *The Doctrine and Covenants: A Book of Answers*, 123–135.

Parkin, Max H. "Joseph Smith and the United Firm," *BYU Studies* 46, no. 3 (2007):4–66.

Penrose, Charles W. "The Church of Christ, etc.," *Journal of Discourses*, 24:82–99.

Penrose, Charles W. "Who and What are the Angels," *The Improvement Era* 15, no. 10 (August 1912):949–952.

Pratt, Orson. "Distinguishing Characteristics between the Latter-day Saints and the Various Religious Denominations of Christendom," *Journal of Discourses*, 16:284–300.

Pratt, Orson. "The Holy Spirit and the Godhead," *Journal of Discourses*, 2:334–347.

Pratt, Orson. "Meeting of Adam with His Posterity, etc.," *Journal of Discourses*, 16:47–59.

Pratt, Orson. "On the Dedication of the New Tabernacle," *Journal of Discourses*, 18:131–133.

Pratt, Orson. "The Manifestations of God's Power, etc.,"*Journal of Discourses*, 16:146–159.

Pratt, Orson. "Prophesies of Joseph Smith, etc.,"*Journal of Discourses*, 18:222–229.

Pratt, Orson. "Redemption of Zion, etc.," *Journal of Discourses*, 17:289–306.

Pratt, Orson. "Review of God's Dealings with the Prophet Joseph, etc.," *Journal of Discourses*, 15:178–191.

"Recollections of the Prophet Joseph Smith," *Juvenile Instructor* (May 15, 1892):303–304.

Roberts, B. H. "The Fulfilment of a Prophecy," *The Improvement Era* 6, no. 11 (September 1903):801–809.

Smith, George Albert. "Divine Origin of 'Mormonism,' etc.," *Journal of Discourses*, 7:111–117.

Smith, George Albert. "Historical Discourse," *Journal of Discourses*, 11:1–12.

Smith, George Albert. "The Leaven of the Gospel, etc.," *Journal of Discourses*, 3:280–291.

Swainston, Howard D., "Tithing," in Ludlow, *Encyclopedia of Mormonism*, 4:1481.

Tanner, N. Eldon. "The Laws of God," *Ensign*, November 1975, 82–83.

Taylor, John. "The Order and Duties of the Priesthood, etc.," *Journal of Discourses*, 21:358–372.

Widtsoe, John A. "Are there Guardian Angels?" The Improvement Era 47, no. 4 (April 1944):225.

Woodford, Robert J. "Jesse Gause, Counselor to the Prophet," *BYU Studies* 15, no. 3 (Spring 1975):362–364.

Woodruff, Wilford. "The Holy Ghost, etc.," *Journal of Discourses*, 13:156–169.

Woodruff, Wilford. "Not Ashamed of the Gospel, etc.," *Journal of Discourses*, 19:223–231.

Young, Brigham. "The Gospel, etc.," *Journal of Discourses*, 2:1–10.

Young, Brigham. "Instructions to Missionaries," *Journal of Discourses*, 8:52–56.

Young, Brigham. "Intelligence, etc.," *Journal of Discourses*, 7:282–291.

Young, Brigham. "Joys of Eternity," *Journal of Discourses*, 8:200.

Young, Brigham. "Knowledge in this Life Limited, etc.," *Journal of Discourses*, 11:12–19.

Young, Brigham. "Love for the Things of God, etc.," *Journal of Discourses*, 10:328–338.

Young, Brigham. "March of 'Mormonism,' etc.," *Journal of Discourses*, 1:88–94.

Young, Brigham. "Necessity of Building Temples, etc.," *Journal of Discourses*, 2:29–33.

Young, Brigham. "Persecution—The Kingdom of God, etc.," *Journal of Discourses*, 8:194–200.

Young, Brigham. "The Sacrament, etc.," *Journal of Discourses*, 6:277–283.

Young, Brigham. "School of the Prophets, etc.," *Journal of Discourses*, 12:157–160.

Young, Brigham. "Secret of Happiness, etc.," *Journal of Discourses*, 18:235–249.

Young, Brigham. "The United Order, etc.," *Journal of Discourses*, 18:353–357.

Young, Brigham. "Want of Governing Capacities among Men, etc.,"*Journal of Discourses*, 7:160–166.

**Autobiographies / Journals / Biographies**

Carter, Jared. "Autobiography of Jared Carter." Church History Library, Salt Lake City.

Hancock, Levi Ward. "Levi Hancock, 1803-1882: Autobiography (1803–1836)" [typescript]. L. Tom Perry Special Collections, Harold B. Lee Library, Brigham Young University, Provo, Utah.

Kirtland Revelation Book. Church History Library, Salt Lake City.

Mace, Wandle. "Autobiography of Wandle Mace (1809–1846)" [typescript]. L. Tom Perry Special Collections, Harold B. Lee Library, Brigham Young University, Provo, Utah.

McLellin, William E. "History and Writings of William E. McLellin." Community of Christ Archives, Independence, Missouri.

Murdock, John. "Journal of John Murdock (1792–1864)" [typescript]. L. Tom Perry Special Collections, Harold B. Lee Library, Brigham Young University, Provo, Utah.

Pilkington, William. "Journal of William Pilkington." L. Tom Perry Special Collections, Harold B. Lee Library, Brigham Young University, Provo, Utah.

Shurtliff, Luman Andros. "Autobiography of Luman Andros Shurtliff (1807–1847)" [typescript]. L. Tom Perry Special Collections, Harold B. Lee Library, Brigham Young University, Provo, Utah.

Thayre, Ezra. "Autobiography of Ezra Thayre." Church History Library, Salt Lake City.

Journal History of the Church of Jesus Christ of Latter-day Saints 1830–1972 [microfilm]. J. Willard Marriott Library, University of Utah, Salt Lake City.

**Letters / Unpublished Manuscripts**

John Whitmer and W. W. Phelps to "Dear Brethren," July 20, 1833. Church History Library, Salt Lake City.

Joseph Smith to "Church Brethren," June 15, 1835. Church History Library, Salt Lake City.

William E. McLellin to relatives, August 4, 1832. Church History Library, Salt Lake City.

**Newspapers**

"The Answer," *Times and Seasons* 4, no. 6 (February 1, 1843):82–85.

Bennett, James Arlington. "Mr. Editor:—I occasionally drop into the Prophet's office…," *Nauvoo Neighbor* 1, no. 33 (December 13, 1843):3.

Bullock, Thomas. "Minutes of the General Conference," *Millennial Star* 14, no. 3 (February 1, 1852):33–36.

"Correspondence," *Times and Seasons* 4, no. 8 (March 1, 1843):113.

Cowdery, Oliver. "The Closing Year," *Messenger and Advocate* 3, no. 3 (December 1836):425–428.

Cowdery, Oliver. "O. Cowdery's First Letter to W. W. Phelps," *Millennial Star* 3, no. 9 (January 1843):152–154.

Cowdery, Oliver. "Oliver Cowdery to William W. Phelps," *Messenger and Advocate* 1, no. 1 (October 1834):13–16.

*Deseret Evening News*, June 27, 1896.

First Presidency. "One Mighty and Strong," *Deseret News*, November 11, 1905, 4.

Gee, John. "Book of Mormon Word Usage: 'Seal You His,'" *Insights* 22, no. 1 (2002).

Hinckley, Gordon B. "Message of Inspiration," *LDS Church News*, January 1999, 2.

"History of Joseph Smith," *Millennial Star* 14, no. 8 (April 15, 1852):113–117.

"History of Joseph Smith," *Millennial Star* 14, no. 37 (November 6, 1852):580–584.

"History of Joseph Smith," *Millennial Star* 20, no. 40 (October 2, 1858):628–631.

"History of Joseph Smith," *Times and Seasons* 3, no. 12 (April 15, 1842):753–754.

"History of Joseph Smith," *Times and Seasons* 3, no. 21 (September 1, 1842):897–899.

Hyde, Orson. "History of Brigham Young," *Millennial Star* 26, no. 49 (December 3, 1864):774–776.

*LDS Church News*, January 6, 1979, 4.

*LDS Church News*, May 27, 1984, 7.

*LDS Church News*, June 2, 1979, 3.

"Mormonism," *Millennial Star* 43, no. 27 (July 4, 1881):421–423.

Patten, David W. "History of David W. Patten," *Millennial Star* 26, no. 26 (June 25, 1864):406–408.

Phelps, William W. "From W. W. to Joseph Smith: The Prophet," *Times and Seasons* 4, no. 6 (February 1, 1843):81–82.

Phelps, William W. "Letter No. 10," *Messenger and Advocate* 1, no. 12 (September 1835):177–179.

"Report of Elders Orson Pratt and Joseph F. Smith," *Millennial Star* 40, no. 49 (December 9, 1878):769–774.

"Revelations," *The Evening and the Morning Star* 1, no. 12 (May 1833):89–90.

Smith, Hyrum. "A History, of the Persecution, of the Church of Jesus Christ, of Latter Day Saints in Missouri," *Times and Seasons* 1, no. 2 (December 1839):17–24.

Smith, Joseph III. "Last Testimony of Sister Emma," *Latter Day Saints' Herald* 26, no. 19 (1 October 1879):290.

"Try the Spirits," *Times and Seasons* 3, no. 11 (April 1, 1842):743–748.

Whitmer, John. "Address," *Messenger and Advocate* 2, no. 6 (March 1836):285–288.

"William H. Kelley to 'Editor Herald,'" *The Saints' Herald* 29 (March 1, 1882):66–69.

Woodruff, Wilford. "General Conference," *Millennial Star* 53, no. 26 (June 29, 1891):401–407.

Woodruff, Wilford. "President Wilford Woodruff," *The Deseret Weekly* 38:388–391.

Young, Brigham. "Extract from President Young's Letter," *Millennial Star* 6, no. 6 (September 1, 1845):91–92.

**Dissertations/Theses**

Walter D. Bowen. "The Versatile W. W. Phelps—Mormon Writer, Educator, Pioneer." Master's Thesis, Brigham Young University, 1958.

Woodford, Robert J. "The Historical Development of the Doctrine and Covenants." Ph.D. Dissertation, Brigham Young University, 1974.

**Conference Reports**

Ballard, Melvin J. "Seek Spiritual Guidance," in *Conference Report*, April 1931, 37.

First Presidency, in *Conference Report*, April 1907, 14.

First Presidency, in *Conference Report*, April 1911, 130.

Grant, Heber J. "Message of the First Presidency," in *Conference Report*, October 1942, 7–17.

Grant, Heber J. "Revelation to Hyrum Smith," in *Conference Report*, April 1937, 11–12.

Grant, Heber J. "Tribute to Hyrum Smith," in *Conference Report*, October 1920, 84.

Kimball, Spencer W. "My brothers and sisters, these are momentous days . . . ," in *Conference Report*, April 1951, 104–105.

Kimball, Spencer W. "Objective to Build Faith," in *Conference Report*, April 1948, 109.

Kimball, Spencer W. "The Stone Cut without Hands," in *Conference Report*, April 1976, 10.

Kimball, Spencer W. "What Do We Hear?" in Conference Report, May 1974, 45.

Lee, Harold B. "Anniversary of Church Organization," in *Conference Report*, April 1973, 4.

Lee, Harold B. "President Harold B. Lee," in *Conference Report*, April 1970, 103.

McKay, David O. "The following I take from section 4 . . . ," in *Conference Report*, April 1954, 22–23.

Packer, Boyd K. "Still, Small Voice," in *Conference Report*, October 1994, 76–80.

Romney, Marion G. "My beloved brothers and sisters . . . ," in *Conference Report*, October 1955, 125.

Romney, Marion G. "My beloved brothers and sisters . . . ," in *Conference Report*, October 1962, 95.

Scott, Richard G. "Finding Forgiveness," in *Conference Report*, April 1995, 100–104.

Smith, George Albert. "'Mormonism' the gospel of Jesus Christ," in *Conference Report*, October 1916, 50–51.

Smith, George Albert. "President J. Reuben Clark, of the First Presidency . . . ," in *Conference Report*, October 1945, 172.

Smith, Joseph F. "Continuous Communication with the Spirit of the Lord," in *Conference Report*, October 1918, 2.

Smith, Joseph F. "If I may indulge just a moment . . . ," in *Conference Report*, October 1913, 14

Smith, Joseph F. "Opening Address," in *Conference Report*, October 1909, 8.

Smith, Joseph Fielding. "Magnifying Our Callings in the Priesthood," in *Conference Report*, April 1970, 58–59.

Smith, Joseph Fielding. "Whoso Treasureth Up My Word," in *Conference Report*, October 1931, 17–18.

Snow, Lorenzo. "How to Overcome Temptation—The Holy Spirit an Unerring Guide," in *Conference Report*, April 1899, 52.

Taylor, Henry D. "The Law of the Fast," in *Conference Report*, October 1974, 17–19.

Widtsoe, John A. "Individual Responsibility," in *Conference Report*, April 1940, 36.

## ART CREDITS

Page 1 *1833 Book of Commandments* © Kenneth Mays.

Page 2 *Oliver Cowdery* © Ken Corbett. For more information, visit www.kencorbettart.com.

Page 3 William W. Phelps.

Page 5 *Rescue of the Book of Commandments* by Clark Kelley Price © Intellectual Reserve, Inc.

Page 6 *Joseph Smith* © William Whitaker. For more information, visit www.williamwhitaker.com.

Page 7 *Printing Office in Nauvoo* © Kenneth Mays.

Page 8 Title page from the 1935 edition of the Doctrine and Covenants, © Intellectual Reserve, Inc.

Page 10 *Stereotype Room*, courtesy of Wikimedia, www.wikimedia.org.

Page 12 James E. Talmage.

Page 13 *Setting the Capstone (detail of Washington Monument)*, courtesy of the Library of Congress.

Page 17 *The Evening and the Morning Star,* courtesy of the Church Archives.The Church of Jesus Christ of Latter-day Saints.

Page 18 *Joseph Fielding and Jessie Evans Smith,* courtesy of the Church Archives.The Church of Jesus Christ of Latter-day Saints.

Page 21 *Seal with Ishtar Symbol* © Rama. Courtesy of Wikimedia, www.wikimedia.org.

Page 23 *Petra in Transjordan. Mountains of Edom and the 'Arabah Plain.* Courtesy of the Library of Congress.

Page 24 *Smith, Palmyra, New York, Home* © Kenneth Mays.

Page 26 *Elijah Destroys the Messengers of Ahaziah*, courtesy of Wikimedia, www.wikimedia.org.

Page 27 *Haifa Monastery, 1890.* Courtesy of Wikimedia, www.wikimedia.org.

Page 29 Martin Harris.

Page 32 *Martin Harris, Palmyra New York, Farm Site* © Kenneth Mays.

Page 34 *Emma Sick* © Glen S. Hopkinson. For more information, visit www.glenhopkinson.com.

Page 39 *A Page of the Translated Book of Mormon.* Courtesy of the Church Archives, The Church of Jesus Christ of Latter-day Saints.

Page 40 *Swampy Land at the Back of the Whitmer Farm* © Kenneth Mays.

Page 42 Oliver Cowdery.

Page 44 *Directeur Sword of Siegès* © Rama. Courtesy of Wikimedia, www.wikimedia.org.

Page 48 *The Three Witnesses*, engraved by H. B. Hall & Sons, New York, 1883. Courtesy of the Church Archives, The Church of Jesus Christ of Latter-day Saints.

Page 51 *Saint John the Evangelist's Vision of Jerusalem (detail)* by Alonso Cano. Courtesy of Wikimedia, www.wikimedia.org.

Page 53 *Aaron's Rod that Budded, as in Numbers 17:8*, illustration from the 1890 Holman Bible. Courtesy of Wikimedia, www.wikimedia.org.

Page 55 *Joseph and Emma's small home in Harmony, PA,* courtesy of the Church Archives.The Church of Jesus Christ of Latter-day Saints.

Page 59 *Hyrum Smith* © David Lindsley. For more information visit www.davidlindsley.com.

Page 60 *Joseph Knight Farm* © Kenneth Mays

Page 62 *The Youthful Prophet, Joseph Smith Jr., and Oliver Cowdery, Receiving the Aaronic Priesthood under the hands of John the Baptist*, May 15, 1829. Courtesy of the Library of Congress.

Page 64 *Offering Up a Burnt Sacrifice to God, from the Foster Bible.* Courtesy of Wikimedia, www.wikimedia.org.

Page 66 John Whitmer.

Page 69 *Restoration* © Liz Lemon Swindle. For more information, visit www.foundationarts.com.

Page 71 *Book of Mormon Historic Publication Site* © Kenneth Mays.

Page 73 *April 6th* © Glen S. Hopkinson. For more information, visit www.glenhopkinson.com.

Page 76 *Interior of the Peter Whitmer Home, Fayette, New York* © Kenneth Mays.

Page 79 William E. McLellin.

Page 81 *An Elect Lady* © Liz Lemon Swindle. For more information, visit www.foundationarts.com.

Page 84 *Holy Communion* © MKucova. Courtesy of iStockPhoto.com.

Page 87 *Adam-ondi-Ahman* © Garth Oborn. For more information, visit www.garthoborn.com.

Page 89 *Chief Big Moon.* Courtesy of the Library of Congress.

Page 91 Orson Pratt.

Page 92 *A Farmer Works on His Field* © Jayaseerlourdhuraj. Courtesy of Wikimedia, www.wikimedia.org.

Page 95 *Kirtland Flats* © Kenneth Mays.

Page 96 *The City of Enoch Translated* by Del Parson © Intellectual Reserve, Inc.

Page 101 *Prophet of the Lord* © David Lindsley. For more information, visit www.davidlindsley.com.

Page 103 *Full Moon and Forest Fire* © Jon Beard. Courtesy of iStockPhoto.com.

Page 104 *Translation of the Bible* © Liz Lemon Swindle. For more information, visit www.foundationarts.com.

Page 107 *Shaker Church Family.* Courtesy the Library of Congress.

Page 109 *Shaker Height Houses* © Spencer. Courtesy of Wikimedia, www.wikimedia.org.

Page 112 *Shepherd in Făgăraş Mountains, Romania*. Courtesy of Wikimedia, www.wikimedia.org.

Page 113 Edward Partridge.

Page 115 *Copely Farm Cemetery* © Kenneth Mays.

Page 118-119 *Independence, Mo.* by Frederick J. Bandholtz. Courtesy of the Library of Congress.

Page 120 *Independence Courthouse Missouri, 1855.* Courtesy National Archives and Records Administration. http://arcweb.archives.gov.

Page 123 *Offering Bearers* by Andreas Praefcke. Courtesy of Wikimedia, www.wikimedia.org.

Page 124 *McIlwaine's Bend, Missouri River* © Kenneth Mays.

Page 129 *Prove Me Herewith* © Glen S. Hopkinson. For more information, visit www.glenhopkinson.com.

Page 133 *John Johnson Home in Hiram Township* © Jon Ridinger. Courtesy of Wikimedia, www.wikimedia.org.

Page 135 *Paul Preaching to the Thessalonians* by Gustave Doré, The Doré Bible Illustrations, Dover Publications.

Page 139 Brigham Young.

Page 142 *In His Glory* © Del Parson. For more information, visit www.delparson.com.

Page 146 *Adam-ondi-Ahman* by Ryan Reeder. Courtesy of Wikimedia, www.wikimedia.org.

Page 148 Fredrick G. Williams.

Page 150 *Kirtland Village* © Al Rounds. For more information, visit www.alrounds.com.

Page 154 *Northern views. Gathering tares from wheat at Bethel.* Courtesy of the Library of Congress.

Page 156 *Civil War soldiers in Action* by John Goldin & Co., photographer. Courtesy of the Library of Congress.

Page 159 *School of the Prophets* © Liz Lemon Swindle. For more information, visit www.foundationarts.com.

Page 160 *Rice Gains* © IRRI Images. Courtesy of Wikimedia, www.wikimedia.org.

Page 162 *Whitney Store* © Kenneth Mays.

Page 164 *Kirtland Temple Drawings.* Courtesy of the Library of Congress.

Page 167 Parley P. Pratt.

Page 168 *Constitution of the United States of America.* Courtesy of the National Archives and Records Administration. http://arcweb.archives.gov.

Page 169 John Murdock.

Page 173 *Coulton Map of Missouri 1855.* Courtesy of Wikimedia, www.wikimedia.org.

Page 177 *Railroad Map of Ohio.* Courtesy of the Library of Congress.

Page 179 *Zion's Camp* © Judith Mehr. For more information, visit www.judithmehr.com

Page 184 *Kirtland Temple Interior.* Courtesy of the Library of Congress.

Page 186 *Kirtland Temple Exterior.* Courtesy of the Library of Congress.

Page 187 *Kirtland Temple* by Jon Ridinger. Courtesy of Wikimedia, www.wikimedia.org.

Page 188 *Breastwork.* Courtesy of the Library of Congress.

Page 191 *Ship to Zion* © Glen S. Hopkinson. For more information, visit www.glenhopkinson.com.

Page 195 *Far West Caldwell County Missouri* © Kenneth Mays.

Page 197 *Tower Hill* © Kenneth Mays.

Page 201 *New-York von der Seeseite aus gesehen—Des auswanderers Sehnsucht* by Hesse, Johann Friederick. Courtesy of the Library of Congress.

Page 203 *Cedar City Tithing Office.* Courtesy Utah State Historical Society.

Page 205 *Liberty Jail* © Kenneth Mays.

Page 206 *Joseph in Liberty Jail* © Liz Lemon Swindle. For more information, visit www.foundationarts.com.

Page 209 *William Henry Harrison—Late President of the United States.* Painted by James R. Lambdin Engraved by J. Sartain. Courtesy of the Library of Congress.

Page 210 *Joseph Smith's Original Temple, Nauvoo, Ills.* Courtesy of the Library of Congress.

Page 214 *The City and Valley of the Great Salt Lake, Utah* (detail). Courtesy of Wikimedia, www.wikimedia.org.

Page 216 *Mississippi River at Montrose, Iowa* © Kenneth Mays.

Page 217 *Hill Cumorah* © Paul E. Gilbert. For more information, visit www.paulegilbert.com

Page 221 William Clayton.

Page 223 *The Moon* © Digital Vision. Courtesy of Getty Images.

Page 225 *Carthage Jail, South Wall* © Kenneth Mays.

Page 227 *Waiting to Cross* © Glen S. Hopkinson. For more information, visit www.glenhopkinson.com.

Page 229 *JFS_First_Presidency_1905.* Courtesy of Wikimedia, www.wikimedia.org.

Page 230 *Wilford Woodruff 1889.* Courtesy of Wikimedia, www.wikimedia.org.